S0-ACJ-536

JBoss Tools 3
Developer's Guide

Build functional applications from scratch to server deployment using JBoss Tools

Develop JSF, Struts, Seam, Hibernate, jBPM, ESB, web services, and portal applications faster than ever using JBoss Tools for Eclipse and the JBoss Application Server

Anghel Leonard

BIRMINGHAM - MUMBAI

JBoss Tools 3 Developer's Guide

Build functional applications from scratch to server deployment using JBoss Tools

Copyright © 2009 Packt Publishing

All rights reserved. No part of this book may be reproduced, stored in a retrieval system, or transmitted in any form or by any means, without the prior written permission of the publisher, except in the case of brief quotations embedded in critical articles or reviews.

Every effort has been made in the preparation of this book to ensure the accuracy of the information presented. However, the information contained in this book is sold without warranty, either express or implied. Neither the author, nor Packt Publishing, and its dealers or distributors will be held liable for any damages caused or alleged to be caused directly or indirectly by this book.

Packt Publishing has endeavored to provide trademark information about all of the companies and products mentioned in this book by the appropriate use of capitals. However, Packt Publishing cannot guarantee the accuracy of this information.

First published: April 2009

Production Reference: 1090409

Published by Packt Publishing Ltd.
32 Lincoln Road
Olton
Birmingham, B27 6PA, UK.

ISBN 978-1-847196-14-9

www.packtpub.com

Cover Image by Karl Moore (karl.moore@ukonline.co.uk)

Credits

Author

Anghel Leonard

Reviewers

Joseph Edem Morny

Peter Johnson

Acquisition Editor

Sarah Cullington

Development Editor

Dhiraj Chandiramani

Technical Editor

Abhinav Prasoon

Copy Editor

Ajay Shanker

Indexer

Hemangini Bari

Editorial Team Leader

Abhijeet Deobhakta

Project Team Leader

Lata Basantani

Project Coordinator

Leena Purkait

Proofreader

Laura Booth

Production Coordinator

Aparna Bhagat

Cover Work

Aparna Bhagat

About the Author

Anghel Leonard is a senior Java developer with more than 12 years of experience in Java SE, Java EE, and the related frameworks. He wrote and published more than 20 articles about Java technologies and more than 100 tips and tricks. Also, he wrote two books about XML and Java (one for beginners and one for advanced). In this time, he developed web applications using the latest technologies on the market. In the past two years he has been focused on developing RIA projects for GIS fields. He is interested to bring onto the Web as much desktop as possible, therefore GIS applications represent a real challenge for him.

I want to thank my family, especially my wife.

About the Reviewers

Joseph Edem Morny has been involved in Enterprise Java technologies since he got introduced to Java in 2005, using open source tools and technologies like JBoss AS and JBoss Seam. His favourite web framework is Seam, which he has been using since its pre 1.5 days.

He has been an active promoter of Java EE and Seam, organizing workshops and seminars on university campuses where he worked as a teaching assistant, and on a national scale at Ghana's foremost institution of IT, Kofi Annan Centre for IT Excellence. Edem holds a Bsc Computer Science from KNUST in Ghana. He is also a SCJP, SCWCD and SCBCD.

Edem is a senior developer at the application development center in Accra, Ghana of an international biometric security solutions company, leading thedevelopment of Biocryptic Identity Management Systems for the global market.

Peter Johnson has been working in information technology since 1980, starting with mainframes, then to Solaris, then Windows, and now also on Linux. In the 90s, he developed using C++ and for the last 9 years has been working with Java. He works in a team that evaluates open source software for inclusion in an open source stack that is offered on Unisys and other hardware. In addition, he spends a lot of time on performance tuning and speaks regularly on that topic at various international conferences, such as the Computer Measurement Group Conference, JBoss World and Linux World. Peter is also currently co-authoring a book on JBoss Application Server, and is a JBoss committer and frequent JBoss forum contributor.

Table of Contents

Preface

This book will show you how to develop a set of Java projects using a variety of technologies and scenarios. Everything is described through the "eyes" of JBoss Tools.

After we settle on the project (or scenario) that will be developed, we will configure the proper environment for the current tool (those projects selected will cover between them the main components of a web application in terms of the backstage technology). We continue by exploring the tool for accomplishing our tasks and developing the project's components. A cocktail of images, theoretical aspects, source codes, and step-by-step examples will offer you a thoroughgoing for every tool. At the end, the project will be deployed and tested. In addition, every chapter is "lard" with pure notions about the underlying technology, which will initiate you into, or remind you of, the basic aspects of it.

This book will show you complete and functional applications, and will familiarize you with the main aspects of every tool. By the end you will have been provided with sufficient information to successfully handle your own projects through JBoss Tools.

What this book covers

Chapter 1 is a compressive chapter that will help you discover the features brought by the new JBoss Tools 3.0. The main goal of this chapter is to make an introduction to what will follow in the next chapters and to "wake up" your curiosity. In addition, the reader can see different possibilities of installing JBoss Tools on different platforms and for different goals.

Chapter 2 teaches you how to use Eclipse and JBoss AS in a symbiotic manner. In this chapter you will see how to use the JBoss AS Tools to configure, start, stop and monitor the JBoss AS directly from Eclipse IDE. Also, you can see how to create and deploy new projects.

Chapter 3 is a collection of tag-components from different technologies as Ajax, JSF, RichFaces, Seam, and so on. Because the components are built on the drag-and-drop technique, this tool is very easy to use, especially when you need a fast method for generating tags into JSP pages. This chapter will cover—with description and examples—the most important tags that can be generated through JBoss Palette. Also, the chapter will contain a section about the Palette Options.

Chapter 4 will talk about punctual framework's tools and I will start with JBoss Tools for Java Server Faces. After I present the Faces Config Editor, which is the main visual component for JSF support, I will follow the framework mains characteristics and I will discuss—from the JSF Tools perspective—about managed beans, validators, converters, navigation rules, and so on.

Chapter 5 will give you a complete cover of the graphical Struts editors that are used for generating/managing XML documents (configuration, tiles, validators). Also, you will see how to work with code generation and debug support for Struts projects. Everything will be sustained by images (captures) and examples.

Chapter 6 will show you how to accomplish the most important modules of a Seam project, like Action, Form, Entity, and so on through the Seam Tools filter in the first part. Later, in the second part of the chapter, you will work with the visual editors dedicated to increasing the speed of developing/controlling Seam components.

Chapter 7 will show some advanced skills, like Hibernate and Ant, generation of POJOs, debugging goals and reverse engineering control after a detailed presentation of how to use Hibernate Tools to speed up the configuration and mapping tasks.

Chapter 8 will discuss about the jBPM Tools. You will see how to develop and test a complete jBPM project.

Chapter 9 will detail the main concepts of JBossESB Services, and you will see how to use ESB Tools to develop such a Service.

Chapter 10 will help you create from scratch a WSDL document using WSDL Editor. You will generate a complete web service from a WSDL document and from a Java bean using WS Tools wizards, and you will publish a web service using jUDDI and Web Services Explorer. In addition, you will see how to generate a web service's client, how to test a web service through Web Services Explorer, how to convert WSDL documents to WSIL documents and how to inspect WSDL web services through WSIL and WSE.

Chapter 11 will work with the Portal Tools. You will see how to use the wizards for creating projects with Portlet Facets, creating the Java Portlet wizard and creating the JSF/Seam Portlet wizard.

What you need for this book

As different software products are involved in this book, it is pretty hard to recommend a list of system requirements and operating systems. Nevertheless, we have developed this book using the following specifications (use this configuration as a mark):

- Mobile AMD Sempron (tm)
- Processor 3400+
- 789MHz, 896 MB of RAM
- Physical Address Extension.

Following are the software requirements for this book:

- Microsoft Windows XP Professional Version 2002 Service Pack 2 (or any other supported operating system)
- Java 5 and Java 6 for Windows (or your operating system)

Rest of software, such as Eclipse, JBoss Application Server and so on, will be installed through the book.

Who this book is for

This book is recommended to Java developers that use at least one of the covered technologies (JSF, Struts, Hibernate, Seam and so on). This book is for all Java developers who are looking for a unitary and powerful tool, especially designed for increasing the speed of developing, and for improving the quality of, Java web applications.

No matter how much, or how little, experience you have, developers of all levels will benefit as your use of JBoss Tools is directly proportional to the complexity of your application. Since JBoss Tools covers all level of experience, you may use it at your own level for your own applications, without involving unnecessary features. All you have to be familiar with is Eclipse environment, Java core, and you must have some expertise in the technology for which you want to use the JBoss Tools. Basic expertise for each technology is provided in the book, but for more complete and detailed aspects you should read dedicated specifications, tutorials, and articles.

Conventions

In this book you will find a number of styles of text that distinguish between different kinds of information. Here are some examples of these styles, and an explanation of their meaning.

Code words in text are shown as follows: "We can include other contexts through the use of the `include` directive."

A block of code will be set as follows:

```
<div style="overflow: auto; width: 270px; height:375px; padding:0px;
margin: 0px">
<table cellspacing=0 cellpadding=2>
    <col width=270>
      <tr>
      <td width=270 valign="top" nowrap>
      </td>
      </tr>
</table>
</div>
```

When we wish to draw your attention to a particular part of a code block, the relevant lines or items will be shown in bold:

```
// Global Forwards
public static final String GLOBAL_FORWARD_start = "start";

// Local Forwards
public static final String FORWARD_success = "success";
```

Any command-line input or output is written as follows:

```
eclipse -clean
```

New terms and **important words** are shown in bold. Words that you see on the screen, in menus or dialog boxes for example, appear in our text like this: "clicking the **Next** button moves you to the next screen".

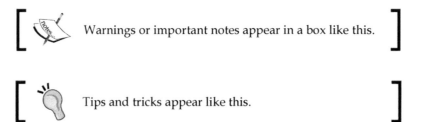

Warnings or important notes appear in a box like this.

Tips and tricks appear like this.

Reader feedback

Feedback from our readers is always welcome. Let us know what you think about this book—what you liked or may have disliked. Reader feedback is important for us to develop titles that you really get the most out of.

To send us general feedback, simply drop an email to feedback@packtpub.com, and mention the book title in the subject of your message.

If there is a book that you need and would like to see us publish, please send us a note via the **SUGGEST A TITLE** form on www.packtpub.com, or send an email to suggest@packtpub.com.

If there is a topic that you have expertise in and you are interested in either writing or contributing to a book on, see our author guide on www.packtpub.com/authors.

Customer support

Now that you are the proud owner of a Packt book, we have a number of things to help you to get the most from your purchase.

Downloading the example code for the book

Visit http://www.packtpub.com/files/code/6149_Code.zip to directly download the example code.

The downloadable files contain instructions on how to use them.

Errata

Although we have taken every care to ensure the accuracy of our contents, mistakes do happen. If you find a mistake in one of our books—maybe a mistake in text or code—we would be grateful if you would report this to us. By doing so, you can save other readers from frustration, and help us to improve the subsequent versions of this book. If you find any errata, please report them by visiting http://www.packtpub.com/support, selecting your book, clicking on the **let us know** link, and entering the details of your errata. Once your errata are verified, your submission will be accepted and the errata added to any list of existing errata. Any existing errata can be viewed by selecting your title from http://www.packtpub.com/support.

Piracy

Piracy of copyright material on the Internet is an ongoing problem across all media. At Packt, we take the protection of our copyright and licenses very seriously. If you come across any illegal copies of our works in any form on the Internet, please provide us with the location address or website name immediately, so that we can pursue a remedy.

Please contact us at copyright@packtpub.com with a link to the suspected pirated material.

We appreciate your help in protecting our authors, and our ability to bring you valuable content.

Questions

You can contact us at questions@packtpub.com if you are having a problem with any aspect of this book, and we will do our best to address it.

An overview of JBoss Tools

As you probably know, JBoss Tools are a set of Eclipse plug-ins that offer support for developing, deploying, and testing applications based on `JBoss.org` (`http://www.jboss.org/`) projects.

If this definition doesn't say much, then let's just say that JBoss Tools is an "all-in-one" product that provides complete support for developing Java SE and Java EE applications. Also, it's important to note that JBoss Tools can sustain the development of each tier of an enterprise/desktop application by providing dedicated components like editors, wizards, syntax-highlighting, import/export skills, code completion, refactoring, etc.

If you are familiar with the JBoss Tools evolution, then it is impossible to skip the fact that the new JBoss Tools 3 Candidate Release 2 (*JBoss Tools 3.0.0 CR2*) version is the "king" of all versions. But, if JBoss Tools is a new challenge for you, then try to be careful; JBoss Tools creates dependency and it seems that the current software market doesn't offer an antidote yet. This compelling superiority is because JBoss Tools provides tools for both standard J2SE/J2EE technologies like EJB3 and JPA as well as open source technologies that have become widely accepted in enterprise Java development, for example, Hibernate, JBPM, Seam, etc. It brings everything that you'll ever need—together!

Looking inside the 3.0.0 CR2 bundle, we see the following tools (this is just a brief overview meant to reveal the JBoss Tools covered technologies):

- **JBoss AS Tools**: To manage application servers (especially for JBoss AS)
- **JBoss JSF Tools**: Tools dedicated to supporting JSF/JSF-related technologies
- **JBoss Struts Tools**: Tools dedicated to the Struts framework
- **JBoss Seam Tools**: Tools dedicated to Seam projects
- **JBoss Hibernate Tools**: Tools dedicated to the Hibernate framework

- **JBoss jBPM Tools**: Tools to design and deploy jBPM business processes
- **JBossWS Tools**: WTP Tooling for JBoss Web Services
- **Portlet Tools**: Tooling for Portlets
- **JBoss ESB Tools**: Tools to develop ESB components
- **JBoss XDoclet Tools**: Tools to integrate XDoclet in Eclipse
- **JBoss Freemarker IDE**: Syntax-highlighting editor for Freemarker files
- **JBoss RichFaces VPE**: Visual Page editor for Richfaces, JSF, HTML, and CSS
- **BIRT Tools**: Reporting Tooling for JBoss J2EE Servers (not presented in this book)
- **JBoss Smooks**: Tooling Tools for Smooks (not presented in this book)

Next, in this chapter, you will see a brief listing of the features of JBoss Tools and after that we will proceed to install and configure the 3.0.0 CR2 release.

Further, in the following chapters, we will discuss the main tools and see that JBoss Tools can be a complete solution for Java developers.

What's new in JBoss Tools 3?

To amaze its fans and win new ones, JBoss Tools comes with a long list of bug fixes and very important add-ons, like Seam 2, JBossWS, and Mac OS X support. Based on new features and the finest interactivity, JBoss Tools give us a strong feeling of control and robustness.

Here is a short list of the JBoss Tools features. These are the "checkpoints" in JBoss Tools evolution from its first release until version 3.0.0 CR2:

- Seam Tools:
  - Change Seam parent project
  - Easier view-id selection
  - Seam pages editor preferences
  - Seam Ear project validator
  - Seam project settings validator
  - Seam components/EL
  - Sub classes/inner classes

- Hibernate Tools:
    - ○ Console configuration created for JPA project
    - ○ Export diagram
    - ○ Query editor
    - ○ Code completion for Hibernate configuration properties
    - ○ `hbm.xml` and `cfg.xml` editor

- JBoss AS Tools:
    - ○ Drag-and-drop to JBoss Server View
    - ○ "Explore" shortcut in Server View
    - ○ More strict server launches
    - ○ JBoss AS 5 support
    - ○ JMX Console

- JBoss ESB Tools:
    - ○ XSD
    - ○ `jboss-esb.xml` editor

- VPE:
    - ○ Richfaces 3.3
    - ○ Restore Default for Palette
    - ○ Tabbed Page Design Option dialog
    - ○ New CSS Dialog performance
    - ○ Folding in source editor
    - ○ Memory tuning
    - ○ TLD Version support
    - ○ XUL Runner

 For a complete list of the JBoss Tools features, please check the `http://docs.jboss.org/tools/whatsnew/ features` page.

"Pretty impressive!" you may say! Well, the above list was just a brief overview of the JBoss Tools features. It is only when put under a microscope that every individual JBoss tool reveals its real power. So, what are we waiting for? Let's install it!

Installing JBoss Tools

Installing JBoss Tools is a straightforward process that can be accomplished in multiple ways. Next, you will see two of the most secure and used methods for installing JBoss Tools on the supported platforms.

Installing Eclipse version 3.4.x (Eclipse Ganymede)

It is obvious that before installing JBoss Tools, you will need to download and install the Eclipse IDE. For getting the best results in a short time, it is recommended to use Eclipse version 3.4.x (we downloaded the Eclipse 3.4.1 – component of Eclipse Ganymede Packages) and the embedded WTP version. The quickest way to get this is to download the **Eclipse IDE for Java EE Developers**, which is available at `http://www.eclipse.org/downloads/` for three platforms: Windows, Linux, and Mac OS X. Notice that for all the platforms, the Eclipse IDE for Java EE Developers requires at least Java 5.

 In this book, we have used the Eclipse IDE version 3.4.1 and the embedded WTP, which was the latest stable release when this book was written. In addition to this, the examples were developed and tested on Windows XP operating system.

Uaually Eclipse is provided as a ZIP/RAR archive that should be unzipped in your favorite location. Afterwards, the Eclipse can be launched through `eclipse.exe` executable file. Anyway, for troubleshooting, you have a detailed documentation of Eclipse at `http://help.eclipse.org/ganymede/index.jsp`.

Installing JBoss Tools through Eclipse software updates

The quickest and simplest way to install the JBoss Tools consists of using a great facility of Eclipse, named **Software Updates**. This is a graphical wizard that will guide you through the search/install process of the latest plug-ins/add-ons for Eclipse. For installing JBoss Tools, you can use this wizard as follows:

1. Launch the Eclipse IDE.
2. From the **Help** menu, select **Software Updates**.
3. Switch to the **Available Software** tab.
4. Click on the **Manage Sites** button.

5. Click on the the **Add** button and type `http://download.jboss.org/` `jbosstools/updates/development` in the **Add Site** window — if it is already listed, make sure it is enabled (checked).

> **The JBoss Tools update sites are:**
> - **Stable Updates**: `download.jboss.org/jbosstools/` `updates/stable`.
> - **Development Updates**: `download.jboss.org/jbosstools/` `updates/development`.
> - **Nightly Updates**: `download.jboss.org/jbosstools/` `updates/nightly/trunk`.

6. Return to the previous wizard and expand the newly added node (left-panel) — this is the checkbox especially created for `http://download.` `jboss.org/jbosstools/updates/development` resource. Wait for Eclipse to pending this resource. When the pending ends, you should see a list of checkboxes (one for each JBoss Tools component) under the resource node.

7. For this book, it is recommended to download and install the entire package of tools by selecting all the corresponding checkboxes. Note that in case you want to install only a subset of tools, you have to keep in mind the *dependencies between standalone plug-ins* (a diagram of dependencies between the most used plug-ins is in the first figure). After you decide what tools to install, just click on the **Install** button and follow the wizard instructions.

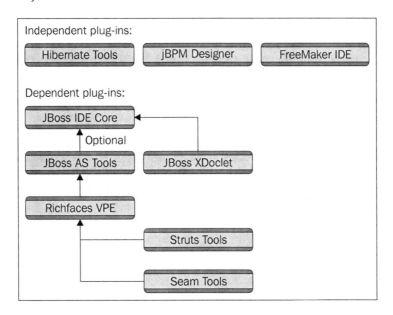

Any error/warning/info that occurs while download/install is in progress will be reported in the **Problems** view or in installation wizard pages. This Problems view will appear automatically when the download process begins and in the best case, it will remain empty during the download/install process (as shown in the following screenshot).

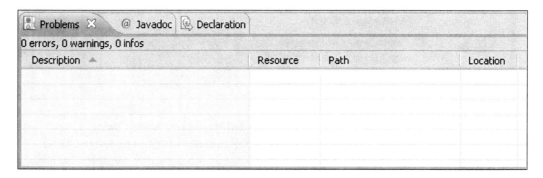

A common error while installing JBoss Tools 3 under Eclipse 3.4, appears in the installation wizard after we click on the **Install** button. These errors are about invalid jars or missing dependencies. To be precise, the message error is something like this: **Unable to satisfy dependency from org.eclipse.birt.report.viewer....** Fixing this error can be done by the following steps:

1. Cancel current operation, close and reopen the **Software Updates** wizard.

2. Use the **Manage Site** button to add two more sites, as follows (if they already exist, then just check them): `http://download.eclipse.org/birt/update-site/2.3/` and `http://download.eclipse.org/releases/ganymede/`. Check these two entries in the **Available Software Sites** wizard, and click the **OK** button.

3. Returning to the main wizard page, make sure that all checkboxes are deselected and click on the **Refresh** button.

4. Wait until the refresh is accomplished, then mark as selected the checkbox corresponding to `http://download.jboss.org/jbosstools/updates/development`. After pending ends, select all under-checkboxes and click on the **Install** button. This time you should not get any errors.

Manual installation of JBoss Tools

If you want to get more involved in the installation process, then you can choose to "manually" download and install JBoss Tools. This is a three-step process as follows:

1. To start, you have to download the JBoss Tools according to your platform (Windows/x86, Linux/GTK/x86, Linux/GTK/x86_64, Mac OS X Carbon/ Universal) from the `http://www.jboss.org/tools/download/index. html` address (or this link: `http://sourceforge.net/project/showfiles. php?group_id=22866&package_id=242269`).

 You can download a bundle of all the JBoss Tools plug-ins (recommended for this book) or you can download a subset of tools. In case of downloading a subset of tools, you have to keep in mind the *dependencies between standalone plug-ins* (shown in the previous figure).

2. Next, unzip the files into your eclipse `plugins/features` directory, and restart Eclipse with the **-clean** option, like this:

```
eclipse -clean
```

3. When Eclipse restarts, the new features will be ready to serve you! To check if something was installed, try the **New | Other** option in the **File** menu. In the projects type list, you should see new entries like **Hibernate**, **Web Services**, **ESB** and so on. These appear because you just successfully installed JBoss Tools.

Summary

In this chapter, we learnt some basic notions about the JBoss Tools package. Also, we saw how to download and install JBoss Tools as a bundle or as a sub-set.

Being an introduction to JBoss Tools, we focused on covering the main questions about JBoss Tools, like "What is it good for?", "What exactly is contained in the JBoss Tools package?", "What is the latest stable version?", "Can I see some features?", "Can I install it on my machine?", and so on.

2
JBoss AS Tools

In this chapter, we will discuss the main steps that will offer us a functional environment for developing, running, and testing J2EE applications by using the Eclipse IDE, JBoss Tools, and a J2EE Application Server. The first and one of the most important things is to understand how to connect a J2EE Application Server with the Eclipse IDE, through the JBoss AS plug-in. After you successfully accomplish this task, we will see a brief description of creating and deploying J2EE applications on the chosen server.

 In this book, we recommend that you to use the JBoss AS (version 4.2), which is a free J2EE Application Server that can be downloaded from http://www.jboss.org/jbossas/downloads/ (complete documentation can be downloaded from http://www.jboss.org/jbossas/docs/).

JBoss AS plug-in and the Eclipse Web Tools Platform

JBoss AS plug-in can be treated as an elegant method of connecting a J2EE Application Server to the Eclipse IDE. It's important to know that JBoss AS plug-in does this by using the WTP support, which is a project included by default in the Eclipse IDE. WTP is a major project that extends the Eclipse platform with a strong support for Web and J2EE applications. In this case, WTP will sustain important operations, like starting the server in run/debug mode, stopping the server, and delegating WTP projects to their runtimes. For now, keep in mind that Eclipse supports a set of WTP servers and for every WTP server you may have one WTP runtime.

Now, we will see how to install and configure the JBoss 4.2.2 runtime and server.

Adding a WTP Runtime in Eclipse

In case of JBoss Tools, the main scope of **Server Runtimes** is to point to a server installation somewhere on your machine. By runtimes, we can use different configurations of the same server installed in different physical locations. Now, we will create a **JBoss AS Runtime** (you can extrapolate the steps shown below for any supported server):

1. From the **Window** menu, select **Preferences**.

2. In the **Preferences** window, expand the **Server** node and select the **Runtime Environments** child-node. On the right side of the window, you can see a list of currently installed runtimes, as shown in the following screenshot, where you can see that an Apache Tomcat runtime is reported (this is just an example, the Apache Tomcat runtime is not a default one).

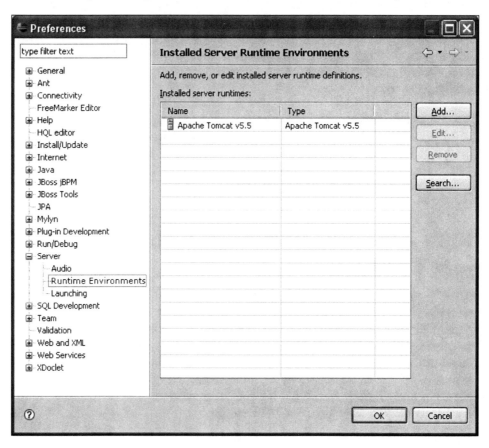

3. Now, if you want to install a new runtime, you should click the **Add** button from the top-right corner. This will bring in front the **New Server Runtime Environment** window as you can see in the following screenshot. Because we want to add a JBoss 4.2.2 runtime, we will select the **JBoss 4.2 Runtime** option (for other adapters proceed accordingly). After that, click **Next** for setting the runtime parameters.

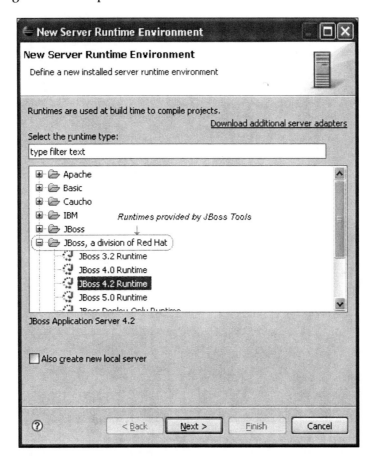

In the runtimes list, we have runtimes provided by WTP and runtimes provided by JBoss Tools (see the section marked in red on the previous screenshot). Because this book is about JBoss Tools, we will further discuss only the runtimes from this category. Here, we have five types of runtimes with the mention that the **JBoss Deploy-Only Runtime** type is for developers who start/stop/debug applications outside Eclipse.

4. In this step, you will configure the JBoss runtime by indicating the runtime's name (in the **Name** field), the runtime's home directory (in the **Home Directory** field), the Java Runtime Environment associated with this runtime (in the **JRE** field), and the configuration type (in the **Configuration** field). In the following screenshot, we have done all these settings for our **JBoss 4.2 Runtime**.

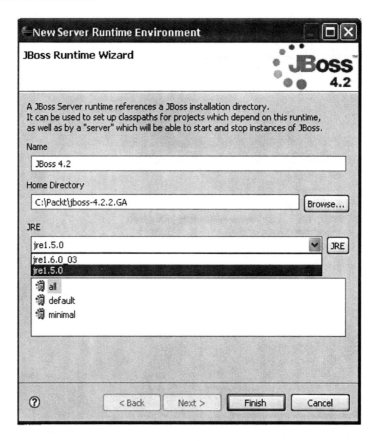

The official documentation of JBoss AS 4.2.2 recommends using JDK version 5. If you don't have this version in the **JRE** list, you can add it like this:

4.1 Display the **Preferences** window by clicking the **JRE** button. In this window, click the **Add** button to display the **Add JRE** window. Continue by selecting the **Standard VM** option and click on the **Next** button. On the next page, use the **Browse** button to navigate to the JRE 5 home directory.

4.2 Click on the **Finish** button and you should see a new entry in the **Installed JREs** field of the **Preferences** window (as shown in the following screenshot). Just check the checkbox of this new entry and click **OK**. Now, JRE 5 should be available in the **JRE** list of the **New Server Runtime Environment** window.

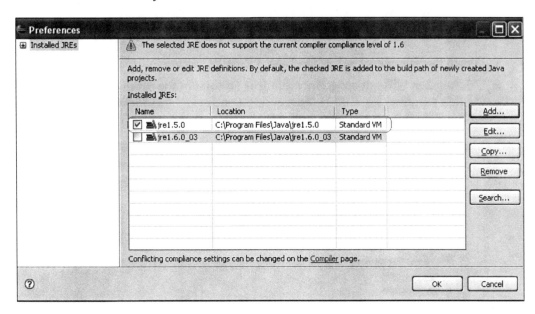

5. After this, just click on the **Finish** button and the new runtime will be added, as shown in the following screenshot:

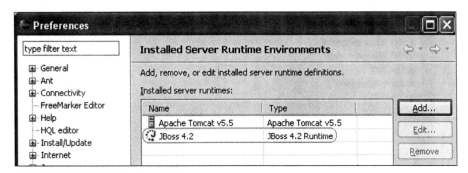

 From this window, you can also edit or remove a runtime by using the **Edit** and **Remove** buttons. These are automatically activated when you select a runtime from the list.

6. As a final step, it is recommended to restart the Eclipse IDE.

Adding a WTP server in Eclipse

By a WTP server, we mean an Eclipse-mechanism that is able to control the main operations of a real server (start/stop/debug/deploy/un-deploy operations). In other words, a WTP server is an Eclipse representation of a backing server installation.

For installing a new server, we can follow these steps:

1. From the **File** menu, select the **New | Other...** option.

2. This option will open the **New** window (shown in the following screenshot). In this window, expand the **Server** node and select the **Server** child-node. After that click on the **Next** button.

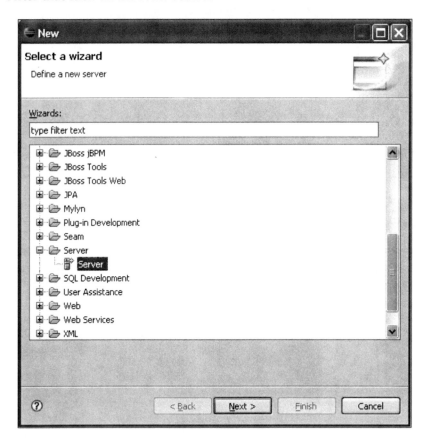

3. In the **New Server** window, you have to configure the new server settings by selecting the server's host name (in **Server's host name** list), the server type (in the **Select the server type** panel), and the associated runtime (from the **Server runtime environment** list). In case you don't have any runtime or you want to create a new runtime, just click on the **Add** link to open the **New Server Runtime Environment** window (this wizard was presented in the previous section). In addition to this, if you want to configure an existing runtime, then follow the **Configure runtime environments** link. In our example, you can choose the **localhost** host, the **JBoss AS 4.2** server type, and the **JBoss 4.2** runtime that was created in the previous section of this chapter (as shown in the following screenshot). After that click on the **Next** button.

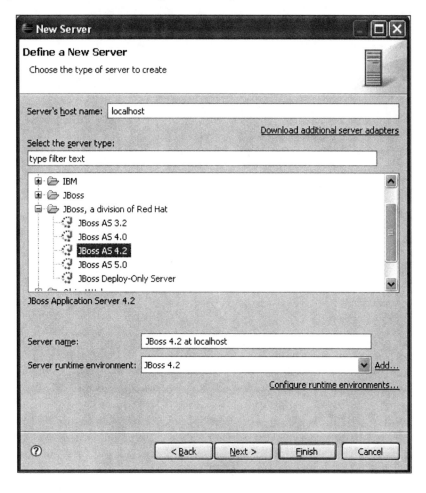

4. In this step, you can specify a name for your server (in the **Name** field, type **JBoss 4.2 Server**) and the login credentials for the JMX console (in the **Login Credentials** field). This window also offers a brief overview of the settings made in the previous steps and a good chance to adjust them before the last step of this process (as shown in the following screenshot). When you are ready, click on the **Next** button.

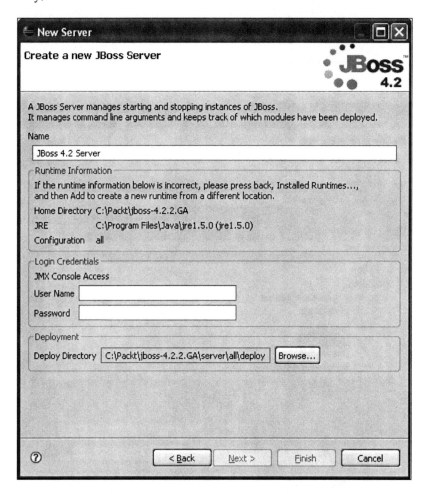

5. This step will allow you to add/remove your currently available projects to/from this new server. For adding a project, you select that project from the left panel and press the **Add** button and for removing a project, you select it from the right panel and press the **Remove** button. When you are done, just click on the **Finish** button. By default, no projects are provided, so the list is empty (as shown in the following screenshot).

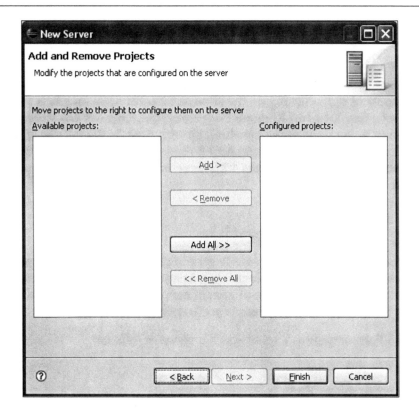

The new server was added! Just restart the Eclipse IDE.

Creating our first web project—a dynamic web project stub

Now that we have installed and configured a JBoss AS 4.2 server instance, it is time to create our first web project. To be honest with you, this is less of a useful project and more of an "instrument" used to reveal as much as possible the facilities of JBoss AS Tools.

So, we decide to use a **Dynamic Web Project** stub, created straightforward from the **New menu | Other | Web node | Dynamic Web Project** leaf (Eclipse helps you organize your web applications using a type of project called a **Dynamic Web Project**). In the creation wizard, just type the *test* name as the project name and click the **Finish** button (note that the target runtime was automatically detected as **JBoss 4.2**, while the rest of fields were filled-up with the default values). Without a web project, many of the JBoss Tools AS facilities will be disabled.

Deploying the test project on JBoss 4.2 Server

Deploying a project is a task that can be accomplished in many ways. The quickest solution consists of right-clicking on the **JBoss 4.2 Server** node (in **JBoss Server View**) and selecting **Add and Remove Projects** option. This will open the wizard (the one shown in the previous screenshot), but this time, in the left panel, you can see the test project. Select it, click the **Add** button, and close the wizard by clicking on the **Finish** button. When the **JBoss 4.2 Server** will be started, the new project will be deployed.

JBoss AS Perspective

As you know, Eclipse offers an ingenious system of perspectives that helps us to switch between different technologies and to keep the main-screen as clean as possible. Every perspective is made of a set of components that can be added/removed by the user. These components are known as **views**.

The JBoss AS Perspective has a set of specific views as follows:

- **JBoss Server View**
- **Project Archives View**
- **Console View**
- **Properties View**

For launching the **JBoss AS** Perspective (or any other perspective), follow these two simple steps:

1. From the **Window** menu, select **Open Perspective | Other** article.
2. In the **Open Perspective** window, select the **JBoss AS** option and click on **OK** button (as shown in the following screenshot).

3. If everything works fine, you should see the **JBoss AS** perspective as shown in the following screenshot:

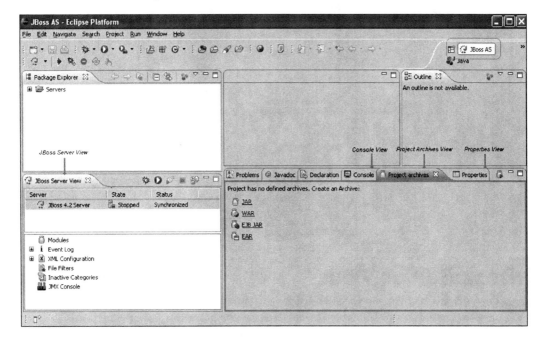

4. If any of these views is not available by default in your **JBoss AS** perspective, then you can add it manually by selecting from the **Window** menu the **Show View | Other** option. In the **Show View** window (shown in the following screenshot), you just select the desired view and click on the **OK** button.

JBoss Server View

This view contains a simple toolbar known as **JBoss Server View Toolbar** and two panels that separate the list of servers (top part) from the list of additional information about the selected server (bottom part). Note that the quantity of additional information is directly related to the server type.

Top part of JBoss Server View

In the top part of the **JBoss Server View**, we can see a list of our servers, their states, and if they are running or if they have stopped.

Starting the JBoss AS

The simplest ways to start our JBoss AS server are:

- Select the **JBoss 4.2 Server** from the server list and click the **Start the server** button from the **JBoss Server View Toolbar** (as shown in the following screenshot).

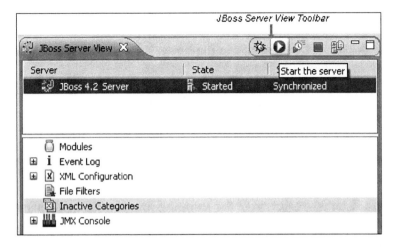

- Select the **JBoss 4.2 Server** from the server list and right-click on it. From the context menu, select the **Start** option (as shown in the following screenshot).

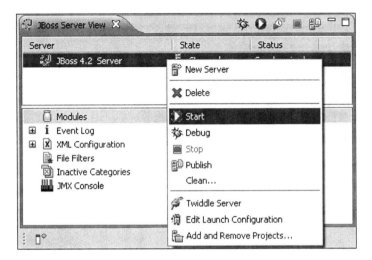

In both cases, a detailed evolution of the startup process will be displayed in the **Console View**, as you can see in the following screenshot.

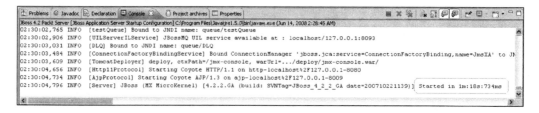

Stopping the JBoss AS

The simplest ways to stop JBoss AS server are:

- Select the **JBoss 4.2 Server** from the server list and click the **Stop the server** button from the **JBoss Server View Toolbar**.

- Select the **JBoss 4.2 Server** from the server list and right-click on it. From the context menu, select the **Stop** option.

In both cases, a detailed evolution of the stopping process will be displayed in the **Console View**, as you can see in the following screenshot.

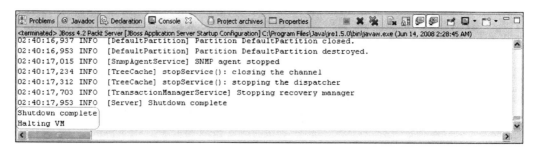

Additional operations on JBoss AS

Beside **Start** and **Stop** operations, **JBoss Server View** allows us to:

- Add a new server (the **New Server** option from the contextual menu)
- Remove an existing server (the **Delete** option from the contextual menu)
- Start the server in debug mode (first button on the **JBoss Server View Toolbar**)

- Start the server in profiling mode (third button on the **JBoss Server View Toolbar**)

- Publish to the server or synching the publish information between the server and the workspace (the **Publish** option from the contextual menu or the last button on the **JBoss Server View Toolbar**)

- Discard all publish state and republish from scratch (the **Clean** option from the contextual menu)

- Twiddle server (the **Twiddle Server** option from the contextual menu)

- Edit launch configuration (the **Edit Launch Configuration** option from the contextual menu as shown in the following screenshot)

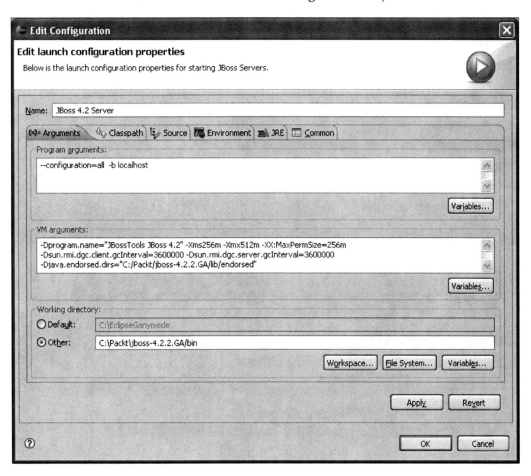

- Add/remove projects (the **Add** and **Remove Projects** option from the contextual menu)

- Double-click the server name and modify parts of that server in the **Server Editor**—if you have a username and a password to start the server, then you can specify those credentials here (as shown in the following screenshot).

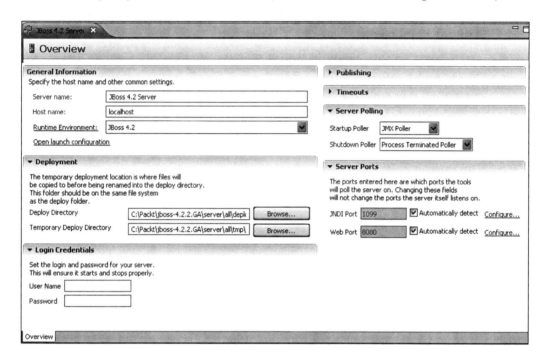

 Twiddle is a JMX library that comes with JBoss, and it is used to access (any) variables that are exposed via the JBoss JMX interfaces.

Server publish status

A server may have one of the following statuses:

- **Synchronized**: Allows you to see if changes are sync (as shown in the following screenshot)

- **Publishing**: Allows you to see if changes are being updated

- **Republish**: Allows you to see if changes are waiting

Bottom part of JBoss Server View

The bottom part of **JBoss Server View** offers a set of additional information structured in six categories. By default, all categories are visible, but you can add or remove a category like this:

1. Select the **Preferences** window from the **Window** main menu.

2. In the **Preferences** window, expand the **Server** node, and select the **JBoss Server View** leaf (as shown in the following screenshot).

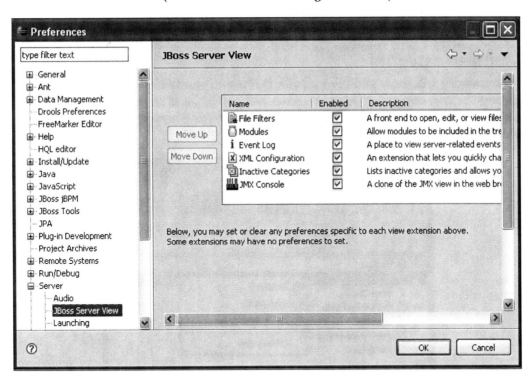

3. After you select all the categories (or a sub-set of categories), click on the **Apply** and **OK** buttons. Note that the selected categories appear in the **JBoss Server View** (as shown in the following screenshot).

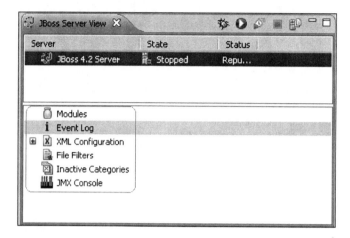

Modules category

This category will show you the modules that are currently deployed on the server through Eclipse support. You can remove, full publish, and incremental publish a module by the contextual menu's options that appear when you right-click on a module (as shown in the following screenshot).

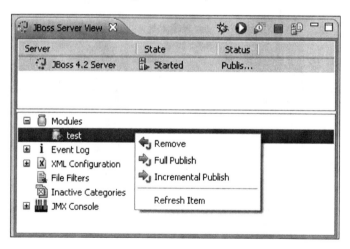

Event Log category

As the name suggests, this category is an events log reporter. You will get information about important events like start/stop of the server and publishing tasks. Detailed information will appear in the **Properties** view every time you select a subcategory of **Event Log**. At any moment, you can clear the **Event Log** reports by selecting the **Clear Event Log** option from the contextual menu that appears when you right-click on this category (as shown in the following screenshot).

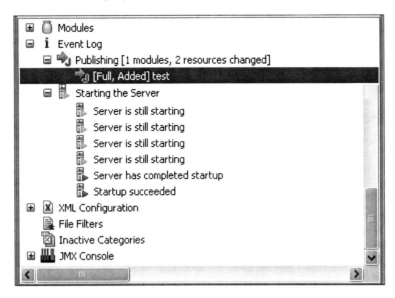

Notice that in the above screenshot we have selected a task related to the **Publishing** operation. The following output is displayed in the **Properties View**:

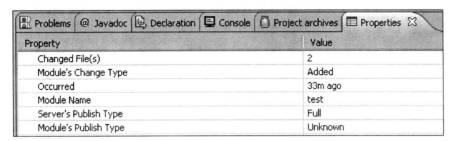

Property	Value
Changed File(s)	2
Module's Change Type	Added
Occurred	33m ago
Module Name	test
Server's Publish Type	Full
Module's Publish Type	Unknown

XML configuration category

This category is focused on working with XML descriptors files. It has a default **Ports** subcategory that fills up the **Properties** view with a series of nodes (sections) that contain paths indicating locations of XML descriptors. Also, we can see a list of values that are associated with XML components (elements, attributes) that belong to those XML descriptors. As you can see, by default, these values are the most used ports of our JBoss AS (as shown in the following screenshot).

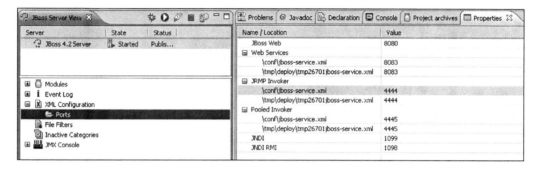

These paths and values are extracted by using XPath expressions dedicated to filter XML elements and attributes. In the following screenshot, you can see the XPath expression that corresponds to the **Web Services** field. Note that for displaying an XPath expression, you can select the section from the **Properties** view, right-click on it, and select the **Edit XPath** option. You may also create a new XPath under that section (using the **New XPath** option) or delete an existing XPath (using the **Delete XPath** option).

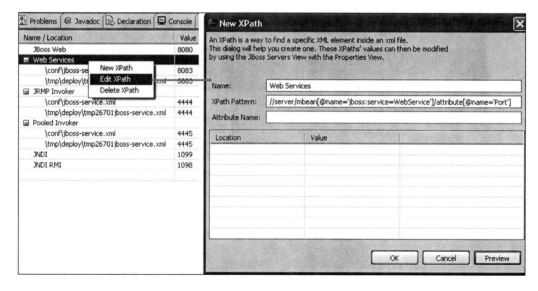

If you are not familiar with XPath vocabulary, then you should consult a specialized tutorial.

If you want to create a new subcategory in the **XML Configuration** category, right-click on it and select the **New Category** option from the contextual menu. You will be prompted for the subcategory's name and after that it will be added under **XML Configuration** category. As per our example, in the following screenshot, we have created a subcategory named **MyPorts**.

Going further, you can create a new XPath expression by right-clicking on a subcategory name and selecting the **New XPath** option. This will display the **New XPath** window where you can set the new XPath's characteristics. Note that you will be sustained by the auto-completion facility for obtaining the desirable XPath expression. Next, we'll see three examples of new XPath expressions:

- The following screenshot shows you how to create an XPath expression named **testPorts_1**, which will be a shortcut for changing the text of all elements named `attribute` that contain an **Attribute Name** with the value **BaseDir**. Note that the location and value are extracted after you click on the **Preview** button. If what you see in the preview panel is what you want, then click on the **OK** button and the new XPath will be added in the `MyPorts` subcategory. It will also be visible in the **Properties** view.

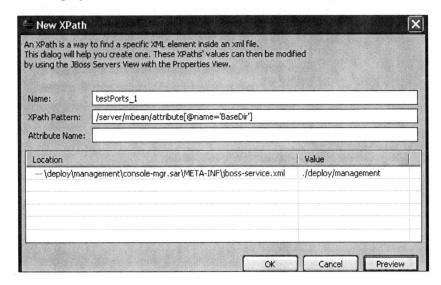

- If we want to create an XPath expression named **testPorts_2**, which will be a shortcut for changing the text of all elements named `attribute` that contain an **Attribute Name** with any value, the following screenshot shows how to do it.

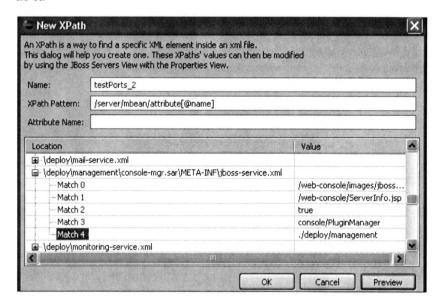

- If we want to create an XPath expression named **testPorts_3**, which will be a shortcut for changing the values of all attributes' `name` that belong to elements named **attribute**, the following screenshot shows you how to do it:

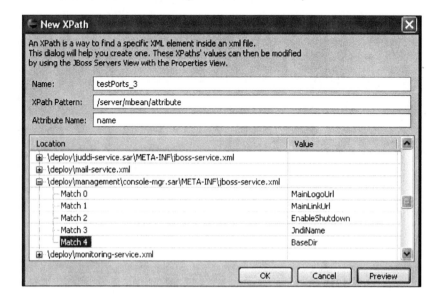

If you look in the **Properties** view, you should see the following XPaths (as shown in the following screenshot):

Now, for changing an element's/attribute's value, just double-click inside the **Properties** view on the right XML file and modify the associated value.

JMX Console category

The **JMX Console** is a special category that offers access to the JMX beans on the server. What follows is a screenshot of the **JMX Console**:

Project archives view

As a Java developer, you should be familiar with notions like JAR, WAR, and EAR archives, and I'm sure that you know what they are good for and how to create such archives by using different tools. Packaging Java applications in these kind of archives is one of the main goals of the **Project archives** view. For this, you should start by using the **Project archives** view, which is able to create and set up each **packaging configuration**. Note that by packaging configuration, we understand an XML file named .packages that is stored in every project's root folder.

For creating an archive, you have two options:

- If the project has no .packages file, then in the **Project archives** view you will see something like what is shown in the following screenshot. Here, just click on the desirable archive type:

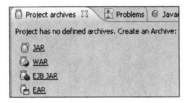

- If the project has a `.packages` file, then you should move the mouse cursor inside the **Project archives** view and right-click here (shown in the following screenshot) for displaying the context menu.

As you can see, there are four types of archives available. All of them have a common wizard-page used to configure the archive name, destination (anywhere on your computer), and type (exploded or packaged). The following screenshot is a wizard-page form displayed for JAR archives, but it belongs to WAR, EJB JAR, and EAR archives as well.

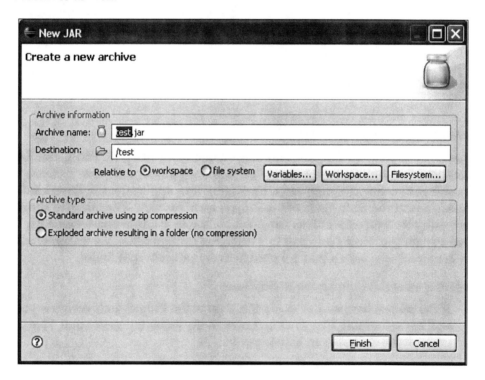

In case of a WAR, EJB JAR, and EAR archive, we also have a second wizard-page that presents a preview of the archive's stub. The following screenshot is a preview of the archive's stub of a WAR archive:

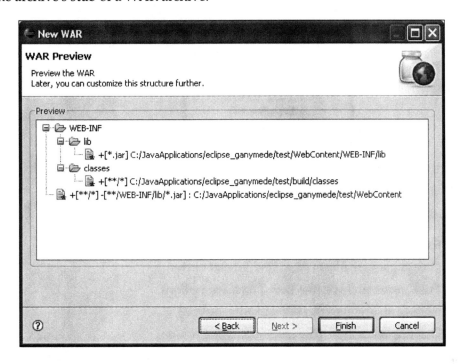

After the archive is created (when you clicked on the **Finish** button), it will appear in the **Project archives** view as you can see in the following screenshot where we have created a WAR archive, named **test.war**.

Now, a new set of operations become available. For seeing these operations, just right-click on the archive name (or on a nested archive or on a folder within an archive), as shown in the following screenshot:

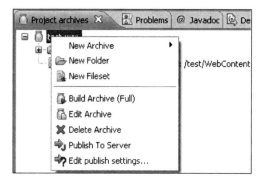

As you can see, here there are options for:

- Creating a new folder (the **New Folder** option)
- Creating a new fileset (the **New Fileset** option)
- Building an archive (the **Build Archive** option)
- Editing an archive (the **Edit Archive** option)
- Deleting an archive (the **Delete Archive** option)
- Publishing to server (the **Publish To Server** option as shown in the following screenshot)

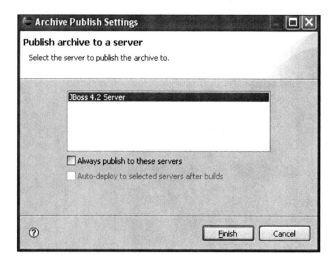

- Editing publish settings (the **Edit publish settings ...** option)

Creating and deploying projects

An important category of projects that can be developed/deployed through Eclipse and JBoss Tools are **faceted projects**. Usually, these projects start from an empty **Dynamic Web Project** and are decorated with different facets. In this category, we have projects like:

- Struts projects
- Seam projects
- JSF projects
- J2EE projects

Adding facets to a project can be done in two ways:

- Include facets in an existing project
- Include facets when a project is created

To include facets in an existing project, you have to follow these steps (we are showing you for the `test` project, but they are available for any other project):

1. In **Package Explorer** view, right-click on the **test** node and select the **Properties** option from the contextual menu.
2. In the **Properties** window, select the **Project Facets** node (as shown in the following screenshot).

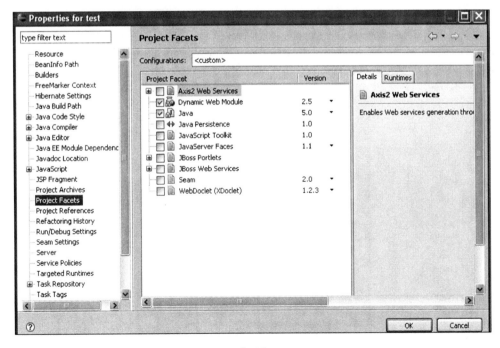

3. In this wizard, middle panel, you can select/deselect facets. In addition to this, you can select a target runtime from the right-panel, by switching to **Runtimes** tab and selecting/deselecting the desired runtimes. Finally, click on the **Apply** and **OK** buttons.

Depending on the selected facets, we have to provide additional configuration or meet dependency criteria. As per our example, if we select the **JavaServer Faces** facet, then a red bullet and a link will indicate that further configurations are required (as shown in the following screenshot). Later in this book, you will see what those configurations are and how they should be provided.

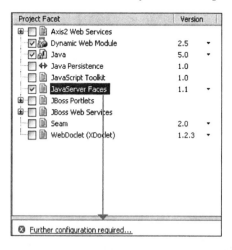

Facet dependencies are also reported as shown in the following screenshot, where we have selected the **JBoss Seam Portlet** facet. The warning messages will disappear when all the selected facets respect their dependencies.

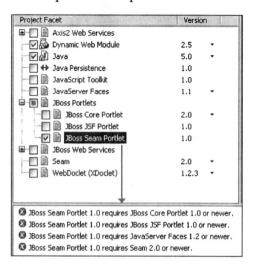

Now, speaking about the deployment process, you have to know that this can be accomplished in different ways from different contexts through WTP and JBoss Tools support. For example, the most used deployment schemas are:

- Deploy from **JBoss Server View**
- Deploy from the **Package Explorer**

From the **JBoss Server View,** you can use the **Add and Remove Projects** option from the contextual menu that appears when you right-click on the server name in the top part of this view. This wizard was presented earlier in *Adding a WTP Server in Eclipse* section and it allows you to add or remove a project by two simple and intuitive panels.

In the bottom part of the same view, you can expand the **Modules** section and right-click on a module for selecting the **Full Publish/Incremental Publish** options from the contextual menu. Notice that by **incremental publish,** we understand that the only parts to be published will be those where changes have been made.

Now, if you want to deploy your projects from the **Package Explorer** view then you should select the **Run As | Run on Server** option from the contextual menu that is displayed when you right-click on a project name (as shown in the following screenshot).

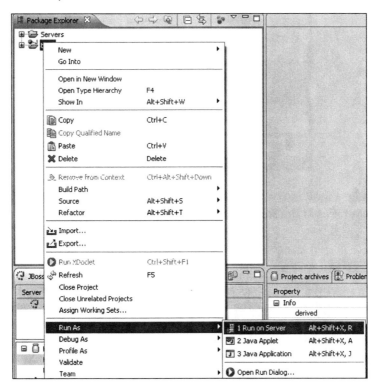

This option will display a wizard for selecting the server that will host the project. Clicking on the **Next** button will display the wizard that was presented earlier in *Adding a WTP Server in Eclipse* section. After you add/remove the projects, you should click on the **Finish** button and wait until the deployment/un-deployment is successfully done!

If you want to deploy single files/projects that are non-WTP then right-click on them, and from the contextual menu, select the **Deploy to Server** option (as shown in the following screenshot).

Now, if you take a look in the **Modules** section from the **JBoss Server View**, you will see the deployed files at the same level as other projects.

Summary

This chapter is essential for a good and easy understanding of what you will read in the following chapters. You have learnt how to configure the JBoss AS server and runtime in Eclipse, how to use the JBoss AS Tools to start/stop your server, how to manage the server's statuses, and how to deploy/un-deploy/manage your projects. All these operations are required to be able to start developing projects through JBoss Tools support.

3
JBoss Tools Palette

In this chapter, we will discuss the JBoss Tools Palette, which is a very useful tool designed especially for speeding up the development of JSP, JSF, HTML, XHTML or any other text file that contains tags. In principle, JBoss Tools Palette is a collection of common tags, exposed through a flexible and easy-to-use interface.

By default, JBoss Tools Palette is available in the **Web Development** perspective that can be displayed from the **Window** menu by selecting the **Open Perspective | Other** option. In the following screenshot, you can see the default look of this palette:

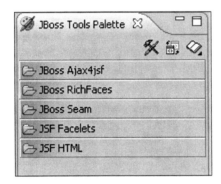

Let's dissect this palette to see how it makes our life easier!

JBoss Tools Palette Toolbar

Note that on the top right corner of the palette, we have a toolbar made of three buttons (as shown in the following screenshot). They are (from left to right):

- **Palette Editor**
- **Show/Hide**
- **Import**

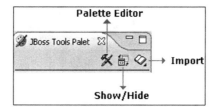

Each of these buttons accomplishes different tasks for offering a high level of flexibility and customizability. Next, we will focus our attention on each one of these buttons.

Palette Editor

Clicking on the **Palette Editor** icon will display the **Palette Editor** window (as shown in the following screenshot), which contains groups and subgroups of tags that are currently supported. Also, from this window you can create new groups, subgroups, icons, and of course, tags—as you will see in a few moments.

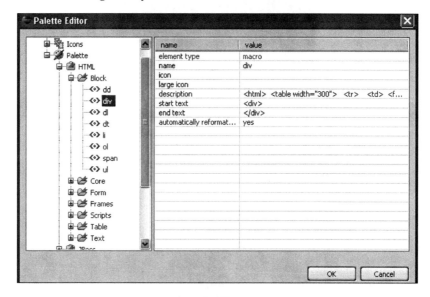

As you can see, this window contains two panels: one for listing groups of tag libraries (left side) and another that displays details about the selected tag and allows us to modify the default values (extreme right). Modifying a tag is a very simple operation that can be done like this:

1. Select from the left panel the tag that you want to modify (for example, the **<div>** tag from the **HTML | Block** subgroup, as shown in the previous screenshot).

2. In the right panel, click on the row from the **value** column that corresponds to the property that you want to modify (the **name** column).

3. Make the desirable modification(s) and click the **OK** button for confirming it (them).

Creating a set of icons

The **Icons** node from the left panel allows you to create sets of icons and import new icons for your tags. To start, you have to right-click on this node and select the **Create | Create Set** option from the contextual menu (as shown in the following screenshot).

This action will open the **Add Icon Set** window where you have to specify a name for this new set. Once you're done with the naming, click on the **Finish** button (as shown in the following screenshot). For example, we have created a set named **eHTMLi**:

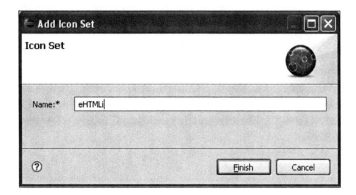

Importing an icon

You can import a new icon in any set of icons by right-clicking on the corresponding set and selecting the **Create | Import Icon** option from the contextual menu (as shown in the following screenshot):

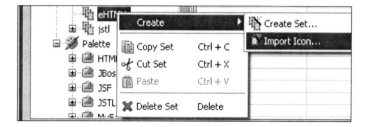

This action will open the **Add Icon** window, where you have to specify a name and a path for your icon, and then click on the **Finish** button (as shown in the following screenshot). Note that the image of the icon should be in GIF format.

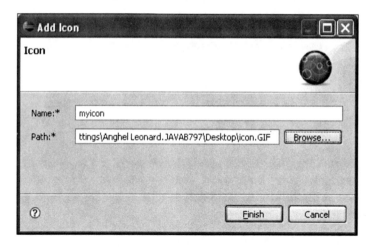

Creating a group of tag libraries

As you can see, the JBoss Tools Palette has a consistent default set of groups of tag libraries, like HTML, JSF, JSTL, Struts, XHTML, etc. If these groups are insufficient, then you can create new ones by right-clicking on the **Palette** node and selecting the **Create | Create Group** option from the contextual menu (as shown in the following screenshot).

This action will open the **Create Group** window, where you have to specify a name for the new group, and then click on **Finish**. For example, we have created a group named **mygroup**:

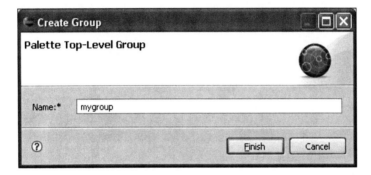

Note that you can delete (only groups created by the user) or edit groups (any group) by selecting the **Delete** or **Edit** options from the contextual menu that appears when you right-click on the chosen group.

Creating a tag library

Now that we have created a group, it's time to create a library (or a subgroup). To do this, you have to right-click on the new group and select the **Create Group** option from the contextual menu (as shown in the following screenshot).

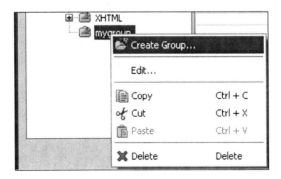

This action will open the **Add Palette Group** window, where you have to specify a name and an icon for this library, and then click on the **Finish** button (as shown in the following screenshot). As an example, we have created a library named **eHTML** with an icon that we had imported in the *Importing an icon* section discussed earlier in this chapter:

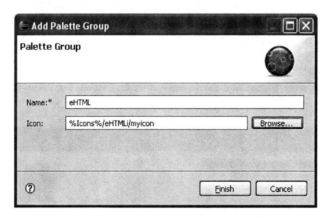

Note that you can delete a tag library (only tag libraries created by the user) by selecting the **Delete** option from the contextual menu that appears when you right-click on the chosen library.

Creating a new tag

After you have created a tag library, it is time to place your first tag in it. To do this, you have to right-click on the tag library and select the **Create | Create Macro** option from the contextual menu (as shown in the following screenshot).

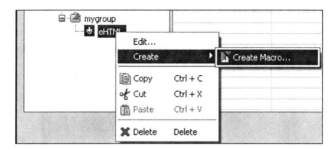

This action will open the **Add Palette Macro** window, where you can configure the new tag. In this window, you have to specify:

- The tag **Name** (mandatory)—it is displayed in Tools Palette
- An **Icon** (optional)
- **Start Text** of the tag (optional)
- **End Text** of the tag (optional)
- **Automatically Reformat Tag Body** (mandatory).

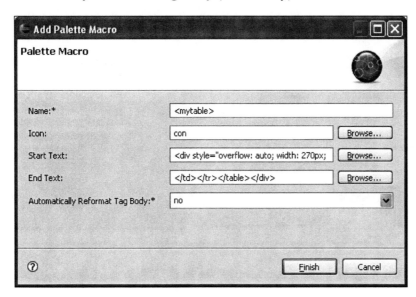

For example, let's create a tag for representing the following HTML code, which is a scrollable HTML table with a single column. We have named the tag `<mytable>`:

```
<div style="overflow: auto; width: 270px; height:375px; padding:0px;
margin: 0px">
<table cellspacing=0 cellpadding=2>
    <col width=270>
      <tr>
       <td width=270 valign="top" nowrap>
       </td>
      </tr>
</table>
</div>
```

For this, we fill up the **Add Palette Macro** as seen in the previous screenshot.

Note that you can delete a tag (only tags created by the user) by selecting the **Delete** option from the contextual menu that appears when you right-click on the chosen tag.

As you can see in the previous screenshot, there is no section for describing your tag definition, syntax, attributes, etc. For that you can click on the tag name and modify the description row from the right panel of the **Palette Editor** or you can right-click on the tag name and select the **Edit** option from the contextual menu. This will open the **Edit** window that contains a **Description** section as you can see in the following screenshot:

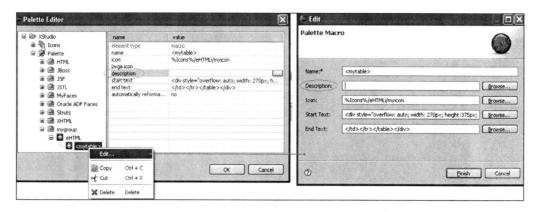

In this section, we can write a tag description in HTML format. For example, for the <mytable> tag, we have created the following description:

```html
<html>
  <table width="300">
   <tr>
    <td>
     <font color="OLIVE">
      <b>Name:</b>
     </font>
     <code>
      <br>Scrollable table
     </code><br>
     <font color="OLIVE">
      <b>Syntax:</b>
     </font>
     <code><br>&lt;div...&gt;&lt;table...&gt;<br>
     &lt;/table&gt;&lt;/div&gt;</code><br>
     <font color="OLIVE"><b>Atributes:</b></font>
     <br><code>CSS and table specific attributes</code>
```

```
        </td>
      </tr>
    </table>
  </html>
```

Now, closing the **Palette Editor** by clicking the **OK** button will automatically add the new group, the tag library, and the tag into the JBoss Tools Palette as shown in the following figure (note the description that appears on mouse over).

Show/Hide

As the name suggests, this feature allows us to customize the number of groups displayed in the palette. By default, the palette shows only five groups, but we can add or remove groups by clicking on this button, which displays the window as shown in the following screenshot.

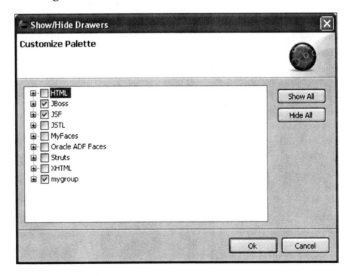

In this window, select the groups and/or tag libraries that you want to see in the palette and deselect the ones that you want to remove from the palette.

Importing third-party tag libraries

A great facility of JBoss Tools Palette is the ability to import third party tag libraries. This can be done using the **Import** button, which opens the **Import Tags from TLD file** window as shown in the following screenshot.

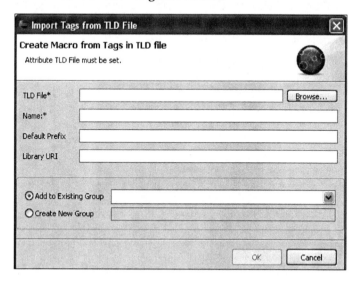

Now, it is mandatory to set the TLD file, and a name for the new tag library. Optionally, we can specify a default prefix, a library URI, and a group that will host the tag library (this can be an existing group or a new one). For example, in the following screenshot you can see how we have imported the sql.tld library into a JSF project (for now, all you can do is imagine this case, but keeping this in mind will help you in the following chapters, where we will create real projects):

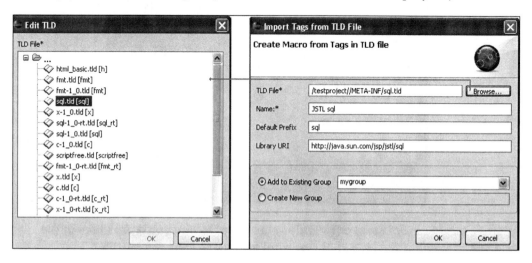

Using tags in text files

In this section, we will discuss inserting tags from the Palette into our text files. This is a very simple task that consists of the following steps:

1. Navigate through the Palette until you see the tag that will be inserted.

2. Click on this tag as you click on any button.

3. If the tag has attributes, then you will see the **Insert Tag** window that allows you to customize the values of these attributes (the following screenshot represents the **Insert Tag** window for the **<table>** tag that can be found in **HTML** group, **Table** tag library). Note that if the selected tag doesn't have any attributes to be set, then this step will be skipped and the tag will be inserted into your page.

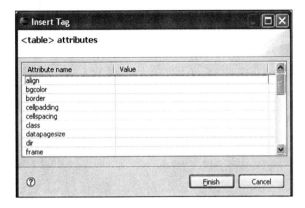

4. After you have set the values of the attributes, simply click the **Finish** button. This action will automatically insert the chosen tag into your page. For example, in the following screenshot you can see the effect of inserting the <mytable> tag, created in the **Create a new tag** section, into an empty HTML page.

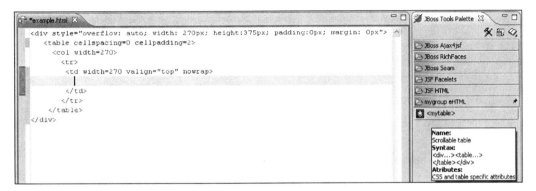

If you followed Chapter 2, then now you should have an empty project named `test`. Expand the **test | WebContent** node, right-click on it, and select **New | Other** option. In the **New** window, expand **Web** node and select **HTML** leaf. Type *example* (without the `.html` extension) in the **File name** field and click on the **Finish** button. Now, you have the shown `example.html` page and you can try to add our tag to it. Also, you can play with other tags to get used to them! In the following chapters this will be no more a task, it will simply be routine.

Summary

In this chapter, you have learnt how to use and customize the JBoss Tools Palette for speeding up the development process of different kinds of pages, like JSP, HTML, XHTML, etc. This will be an important skill to possess in the following chapters when we will develop projects that contain many such pages.

4
JSF Tools

JSF Tools is a set of tools designed for improving the development process of JSF projects. In this chapter, we will see that these tools offer amazing skills for creating different kinds of JSF projects and JSF components, such as converters, validators, managed beans, referenced beans, and so on. Also, we will talk about integrating JSF and the Facelets framework, and how to add/remove JSF support for an existing project.

Throughout this chapter, we will follow the "learning by example" technique, and we will develop a completely functional JSF application that will represent a JSF registration form as you can see in the following screenshot. These kinds of forms can be seen on many sites, so it will be very useful to know how to develop them with JSF Tools.

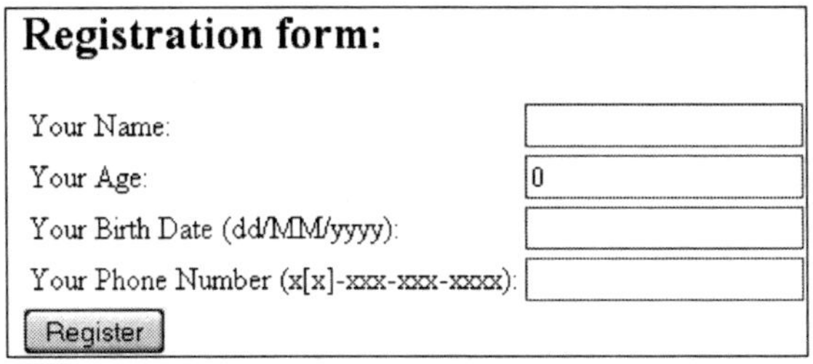

The example consists of a simple JSP page, named `register.jsp`, containing a JSF form with four fields (these fields will be mapped into a managed bean), as follows:

- `personName` – this is a text field for the user's name
- `personAge` – this is a text field for the user's age
- `personPhone` – this is a text field for the user's phone number
- `personBirthDate` – this is a text field for the user's birth date

The information provided by the user will be properly converted and validated using JSF capabilities. Afterwards, the information will be displayed on a second JSP page, named `success.jsp`.

Overview of JSF

Java Server Faces (JSF) is a popular framework used to develop **User Interfaces (UI)** for server-based applications (it is also known as JSR 127 and is a part of J2EE 1.5). It contains a set of UI components totally managed through JSF support, like handling events, validation, navigation rules, internationalization, accessibility, customizability, and so on. In addition, it contains a tag library for expressing UI components within a JSP page. Among JSF features, we mention the ones that JSF provides:

- A set of base UI components
- Extension of the base UI components to create additional UI component libraries
- Custom UI components
- Reusable UI components
- Read/write application date to and from UI components
- Managing UI state across server requests
- Wiring client-generated events to server-side application code
- Multiple rendering capabilities that enable JSF UI components to render themselves differently depending on the client type
- JSF is tool friendly
- JSF is implementation agnostic
- Abstract away from HTTP, HTML, and JSP

Speaking of JSF life cycle, you should know that every JSF request that renders a JSP involves a JSF component tree, also called a **view**. Each request is made up of phases. By standard, we have the following phases (shown in the following figure):

- The restore view is built
- Request values are applied
- Validations are processed
- Model values are updated
- The applications is invoked
- A response is rendered
- During the above phases, the events are notified to event listeners

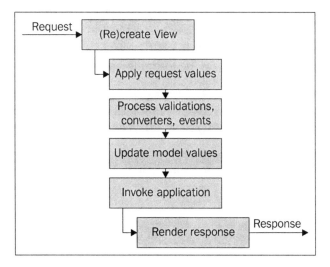

We end this overview with a few bullets regarding JSF UI components:

- A UI component can be anything from a simple to a complex user interface (for example, from a simple text field to an entire page)
- A UI component can be associated to model data objects through value binding
- A UI component can use helper objects, like converters and validators
- A UI component can be rendered in different ways, based on invocation
- A UI component can be invoked directly or from JSP pages using JSF tag libraries

Note that these are the theoretical aspects of the JSF framework meant to get you familiar with the model and components of the JSF engine. For practical examples and a complete tutorial, you can access resources like `http://java.sun.com/ javaee/javaserverfaces/reference/docs/`.

If you have never worked with JSF or have less experience in doing so, then it is absolutely mandatory to access a more detailed documentation before going further.

Creating a JSF project stub

In this section you will see how to create a JSF project stub with JSF Tools. This is a straightforward task that is based on the following steps:

1. From the **File** menu, select **New | Project** option. In the **New Project** window, expand the **JBoss Tools Web** node and select the **JSF Project** option (as shown in the following screenshot). After that, click the **Next** button.

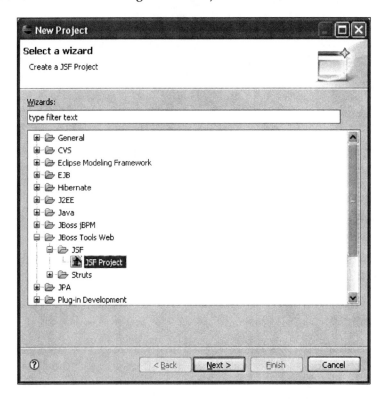

2. In the next window, it is mandatory to specify a name for the new project (**Project Name** field), a location (**Location** field—only if you don't use the default path), a JSF implementation (**JSF Environment** field), and a template (**Template** field). As you can see, JSF Tools offers a set of predefined templates as follows:

- ° **JSFBlankWithLibs**—this is a blank JSF project with complete JSF support.
- ° **JSFKickStartWithLibs**—this is a demo JSF project with complete JSF support.
- ° **JSFKickStartWithoutLibs**—this is a demo JSF project without JSF support. In this case, the JSF libraries are missing for avoiding the potential conflicts with the servers that already offer JSF support.
- ° **JSFBlankWithoutLibs**—this is a blank JSF project without JSF support. In this case, the JSF libraries are missing for avoiding the potential conflicts with the servers that already offer JSF support (for example, JBoss AS includes JSF support).

The next screenshot is an example of how to configure our JSF project at this step. At the end, just click the **Next** button:

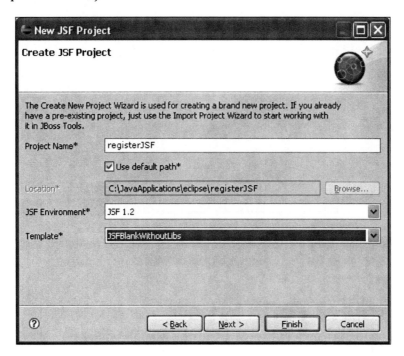

This step allows you to set the servlet version (**Servlet Version** field), the runtime (**Runtime** field) used for building and compiling the application, and the server where the application will be deployed (**Target Server** field). Note that this server is in direct relationship with the selected runtime. The following screenshot shows an example of how to complete this step (click on the **Finish** button):

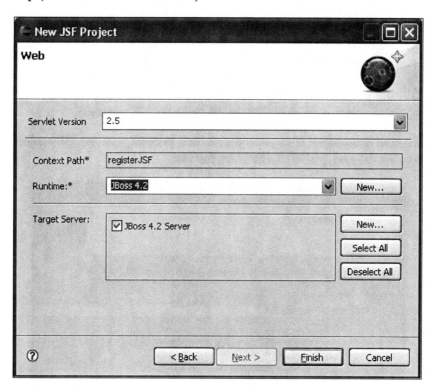

After a few seconds, the new JSF project stub is created and ready to take shape! You can see the new project in the **Package Explorer** view.

JSF Project Verification

Before starting to develop a JSF application, you can take advantage of an important facility of JSF Tools that is, ability to verify and report any dysfunction that may affect the application flow. This facility, known as the *JSF Project Verification*, will verify the application when it is saved and help you to easily identify errors. For this, you can follow these steps:

1. From the **Window** main menu, select the **Preferences** option.

2. In the **Preferences** window, expand the **JBoss Tools | Web | Verification** node from the left panel.

3. Select the desired checkboxes and click on **Apply** and **OK** (it is recommended to select all of them).

JSF application configuration file

A very useful facility of JSF Tools consists of an editor especially designed for managing everything that is related to the JSF main configuration file (`faces-config.xml`). You can start this editor like this:

1. Place the cursor in the **Package Explorer** view on your project node.

2. Expand your JSF project node: **registerJSF| WebContent|WEB-INF**.

3. Double-click on the **faces-config.xml** file.

When the editor is available, it will appear as in the screenshot shown below:

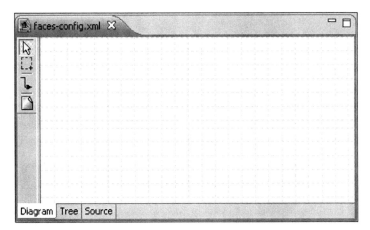

The Diagram view

From this view, you can easily manage pages and transitions between the application's pages (navigation rules). You can create, modify, or delete a page/transition in just a few seconds, and you will always have a clear image of the application flow, thanks to the graphical representation mode.

Creating pages

As an example, let's create two pages named `register.jsp` and `success.jsp`. Usually, you would have had to edit these files by hand to describe the pages flow, but using **Diagram** view features, we can do it visually. For this, you have to apply the following steps:

1. Right-click inside the **Diagram** view and select the **New View...** option from the contextual menu:

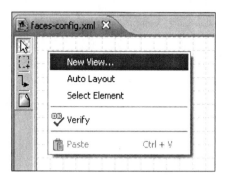

   Another way to create a new page is selecting the **View Template** icon (fourth from the top) from the toolbar placed in the top-left corner of the **Diagram** view and, following that, clicking inside the **Diagram** view surface.

2. The above step will open the **New View** window (as shown in the following screenshot). In the **From-View-ID** field, enter the relative path and name of the new page. For example, you can type **pages/register** (without the `.jsp` extension). Leave everything else unchanged and click on the **Finish** button.

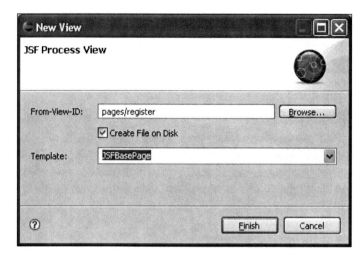

3. Repeat step 2, but this time type **pages/success** in the **From-View-ID** field. Note that both pages are represented on the **Diagram** view surface as you can see in the following screenshot. Also, they are present under the **registerJSF/WebContent/pages** directory in the **Package Explorer** view.

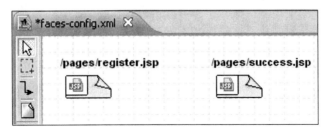

Adding navigation rules

Now, it is time to connect the two pages by creating a transition (navigation rule) from register.jsp to success.jsp. To do this, follow these steps:

1. Select the **Create New Connection** icon (third from the top) from the toolbar placed in the top-left corner of the **Diagram** view. This will change the cursor into an arrow cursor with a two-pronged plug at the arrow's bottom.

2. Click on register.jsp and after that click on success.jsp. You should see something resembling that shown in the following screenshot:

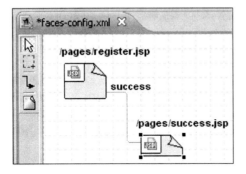

3. Save the changes by selecting **Save** option from the main **File** menu.

The Tree view

Maybe the most important view of this editor is the **Tree** view, which is made of a set of nodes that put the configuration file in a graphical and easy-to-use manner. Just with a few clicks, we can create and modify the properties of the JSF components by skipping the annoying process of manually editing the configuration file. In this section you will see how to exploit this view for managing the most important components of a JSF application, such as managed beans, converters, and validators. The **Tree** view can be seen as shown in the following screenshot:

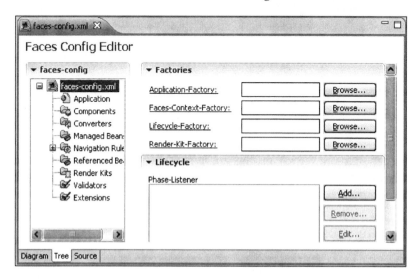

Working with Managed Beans

A very powerful facility of the **Tree** view is the support for managed beans. Now, we can create, modify, and delete managed beans without touching the source code. Next, you will see how to create beans properties, how to create getter and setter methods, and how to obtain the generated source code in just a few steps.

As you have seen in the introduction of this chapter, we want to develop a registration form (`register.jsp`) with four fields representing name (`java.lang.String`), age (`int`), birth date (`java.util.Date`), and phone number (`register.PhoneNumber`) of the user. Each of these fields can be encapsulated as a property of a managed bean that can be developed by following these steps:

1. Select the **Managed Beans** node from the left panel inside the **Tree** view.

2. From the right panel (which is displaying the current managed beans status), click on the **Add** button. This will open the **New Managed Bean** window (as shown in the following screenshot):

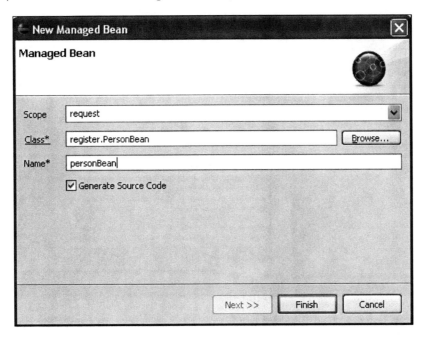

3. In this window you have to specify the scope where the managed bean is active (in our case, the **request** scope), the class that represents the managed bean (for example, type **register.PersonBean**), and a bean's alias name used as a shortcut name (for example, type **personBean**). Because we want to allow JSF Tools to generate the managed bean source code, we mark as selected the **Generate Source Code** checkbox. Note that if you click on the **Class** link, you can configure internal aspects of the bean class (in our example, we will use the default settings).

4. Clicking the **Finish** button of the **New Managed Bean** window will generate the managed bean, and it will display as shown in the following screenshot:

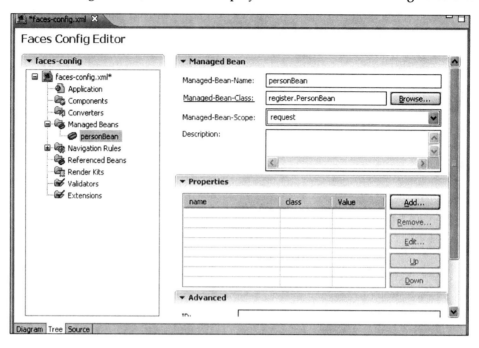

Now that we have created the managed bean stub, it is time to create the bean's properties. For doing this, you can follow these steps:

1. Click on the **Add** button in **Properties** panel. This will open the **Add Property** window (as shown in the following screenshot):

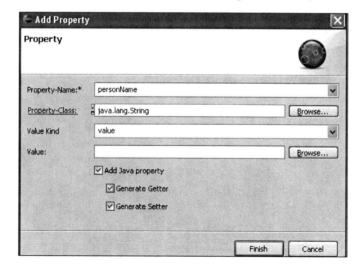

2. In this window, you have to specify the new property name (for example, for mapping the username—**Your Name** field of our registration form—type in the **Property-Name** field, **personName**), the property type (in our example, the username is a string), the value kind, and default value (fill up the **Value** field only if you want to use a different default value). Note that we have marked as selected the three checkboxes for adding the new property to our bean and to generate the corresponding getter/setter methods. At the end, click on the **Finish** button for generating the new property. The following screenshot will appear:

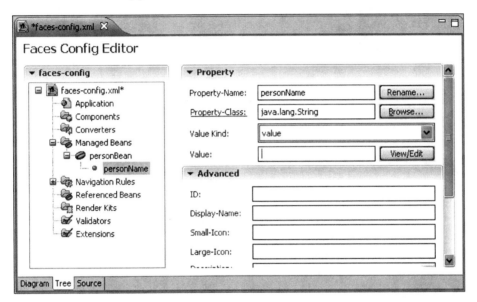

 For primitive types (including strings), the value kind is recommended to be set as **value**. For objects, it is recommended to set it as **null-value**. **List-entries** and **map-entries** values are also supported.

3. Now, if you repeat the above two steps you can map the user age (Your Age field), user birth date (Your Birth Date field), and user phone number (Your Phone Number field) in the same way. The following three screenshots represent the settings that should be made in the **Add Property** window for mapping these fields to bean properties:

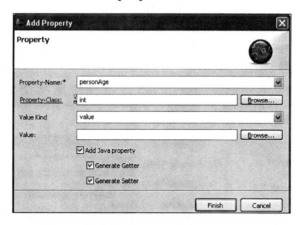

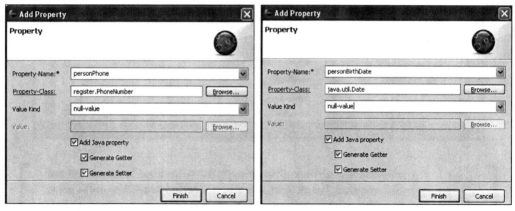

An interesting aspect is represented by the Your Phone Number field, because this field is mapped to another managed bean named register.PhoneNumber. This managed bean has three properties used for extracting from the inserted phone number, the country code (countryCode property), area code (areaCode property), prefix number (prefixNumber property), and a property for keeping the entire phone number (allNumber property). These four properties are all strings (java. lang.String). Now, use what you have learnt so far to create this managed bean with JSF Tools (for alias name, use the phoneNumber text).

In the end, you should have the two managed beans as shown in the following three screenshots:

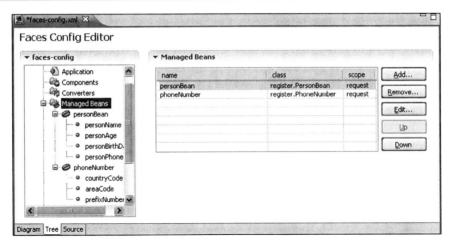

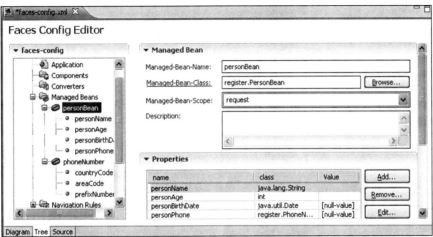

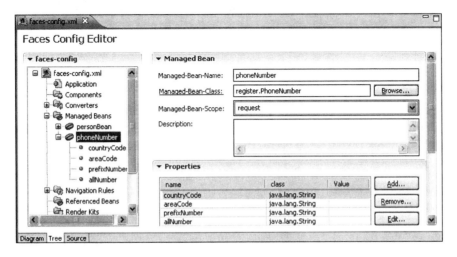

Finally, save the project state by selecting the **Save** option from the **File** main menu.

If you want to see the generated code source for our beans, you can double-click the **Managed-Bean-Class** link that appears in the right panel of the **Tree** view when you select a bean from the left panel of the same view (as shown in the following screenshot).

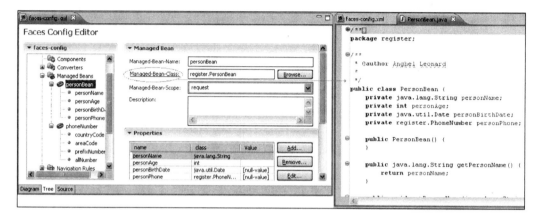

You can also open a bean from the **Package Explorer** view by expanding the project node and double-clicking on the bean's name.

 In addition, JSF Tools allows us to add existing Java Beans to the configuration file. This is a very useful facility because it allows us to import existing Java Beans so that we don't have to recreate them from the start. For this, we select the **Managed Beans** node (in **Tree** view) and click the **Add** button in the right panel. In the **New Managed Bean** wizard, we browse to the existing Java Bean, click the **Next** button (adding an exiting bean will deactivate the **Generate Source Code** checkbox and activate the **Next** button), select the properties to be imported (from the **Managed Properties** wizard), and click on the **Finish** button.

Working with custom converters

Creating and registering a custom converter is a very elegant method for accomplishing conversion issues that can't be resolved by JSF default converters. For example, in our registration form, we need the following conversions:

- The username (`personName` bean property) doesn't need a conversion as the name is a `String`.

- The user age (`personAge` bean property) needs to be converted from a `String` to an `Integer`. We will use a default JSF converter.

- The user birth date (`personBirthDate` bean property) needs to be converted from a `String` to a `java.util.Date` instance. This conversion can be accomplished by the JSF `f:convertDateTime` default converter.

- The user phone number (`personPhone` bean property) needs to be converted from a `String` to a `register.PhoneNumber` instance. This task can be accomplished only by a custom converter because no default converter can help us obtain this conversion.

Now, creating a custom converter can be done like this:

1. Click on the **Converters** node inside the left panel of **Tree** view.

2. From the right panel of **Tree** view, click on the **Add** button for opening the **Add Converter** window (as shown in the following screenshot).

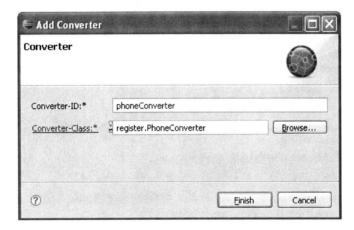

3. Fill in the **Converter-ID** field with the converter name and the **Converter-Class** field with the converter class name. If you want to customize the converter class, click on the **Converter-Class** link (in our example, we will use the default settings).

4. In the **Add Converter** window, click on the **Finish** button for generating the new converter.

Edit the converter-generated source code by clicking on the **Converter-Class** link that appears in the right panel of the **Tree** view (as shown in the following screenshot):

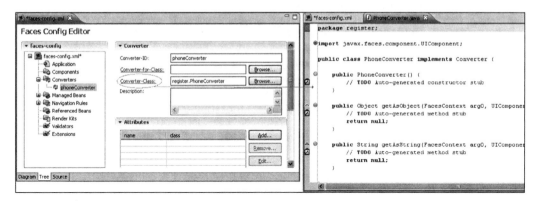

Note that you have to manually insert the behavior of the `getAsObject` and `getAsString` methods. For example, we convert the inserted phone number into a `register.PhoneNumber` object by adding the following code to these methods:

```
import java.util.StringTokenizer;
...
   public Object getAsObject(FacesContext arg0, UIComponent arg1,
String arg2) {
      // TODO Auto-generated method stub
      System.out.println("//getAsObject method//");

      StringTokenizer st = new StringTokenizer(arg2,"-");
      PhoneNumber pn = new PhoneNumber();
      try{
         pn.setAllNumber(arg2);
         pn.setCountryCode(st.nextToken());
         pn.setAreaCode(st.nextToken());
         pn.setPrefixNumber(st.nextToken());
         }catch (Exception e){ return pn; }

      return pn;
   }

   public String getAsString(FacesContext arg0, UIComponent arg1,
Object arg2) {
      // TODO Auto-generated method stub
      System.out.println("//getAsString method//");
      if(arg2 != null)
        {
```

```
    String value = ((PhoneNumber)arg2).getAllNumber();
    return value;
    }

  return "";
}
```

Finally, save the project state by selecting the **Save** option from the **File** main menu.

Working with custom validators

When JSF default validators don't satisfy your application's needs, it is time to implement a custom validator. For example, for our registration form, we have the following situation:

- The username (`personName` bean property)—doesn't need validation.
- The user age (`personAge` bean property)—needs to be a valid age. This can be accomplished with the JSF `f:validateLongRange` default validator.
- The user birth date (`personBirthDate` bean property)—doesn't need validation.
- The user phone number (`personPhone` bean property)—needs to be validated as a string that respects the next pattern: x[x]-xxx-xxx-xxxx. This task can be accomplished only by a custom validator because no default validator can help us.

Now, creating a custom validator can be done like this:

1. Click on the **Validators** node inside the left panel of **Tree** view.
2. From the right panel of **Tree** view, click on the **Add** button for opening the **Add Validator** window.

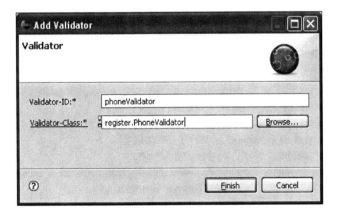

3. Fill in the **Validator-ID** field with the validator name and the **Validator-Class** with the validator class name. If you want to customize the validator class, click on the **Validator-Class** link. (In our example, we will use the default settings.)

4. In the **Add Validator** window, click on the **Finish** button for generating the new validator.

Edit the validator-generated source code by clicking on the **Validator-Class** link that appears in the right panel of the **Tree** view as shown in the following screenshot:

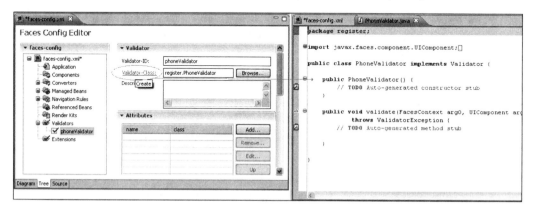

Notice that you have to manually insert the behavior of the `validate` method. For example, we validate the inserted phone number by adding the following code to this method:

```java
import javax.faces.application.FacesMessage;
import java.util.regex.Matcher;
import java.util.regex.Pattern;
...
public void validate(FacesContext arg0, UIComponent arg1, Object arg2)
        throws ValidatorException {
    // TODO Auto-generated method stub
    System.out.println("//validate method//");

    String value = ((PhoneNumber)arg2).getAllNumber();
    String countryCode = "^[0-9]{1,2}";
    String areaCode = "( |-|\\(){1}[0-9]{3}( |-|\\)){1}";
    String prefixNumber = "( |-)?[0-9]{3}";
    String number = "( |-)[0-9]{4}$";
    Pattern mask =  Pattern.compile(countryCode + areaCode +
                    prefixNumber + number);

    Matcher matcher = mask.matcher(value);
```

```
      if (!matcher.find()){
        FacesMessage message = new FacesMessage();
        message.setDetail("Your phone number is not valid!");
        message.setSummary("Your phone number is not valid!");
        message.setSeverity(FacesMessage.SEVERITY_ERROR);
        throw new ValidatorException(message);
      }
   }
```

Finally, save the project state by selecting the **Save** option from the **File** main menu.

In addition to this, JSF Tools allows us to create custom referenced beans (note that referenced beans are used very rarely and they basically are Java Beans available in a JSF scope—the application must create an instance of the referenced bean and place it in the desired scope). For this, select the **Referenced Beans** node (**Tree** view) and click the **Add** button from the right panel. In the **Add Referenced Bean** wizard, fill up the **Referenced-Bean-Name** with a name for your referenced bean and the **Referenced-Bean-Class** with the full name of the referenced bean class. Optionally, click on the **Referenced-Bean-Class** link if you want to customize the referenced bean stub class. Click **Finish**.

The Source view

In the **Source** view, you can see the source of the `faces-config.xml` document. This source is synchronized with the other two views, so you will always see the reflection of your modifications. This view allows you to modify the configuration file manually or by using the **Outline** view that displays a tree view of it.

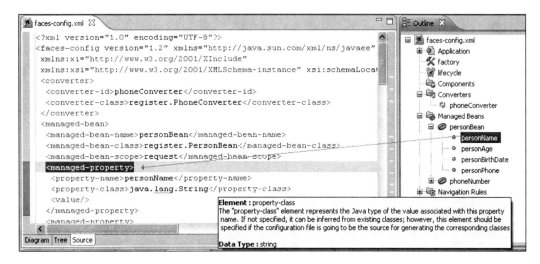

Editing pages code sources

In this section, we will generate the source code of the register.jsp and success.jsp pages. You will also see how to develop a start page for the application.

Editing the register.jsp page

For editing the source code of a page that appears in the **Diagram** view, just double-click on it. For example, double-click on the **register.jsp** icon to open the page source in the **Visual Page Editor** as you can see in the following screenshot:

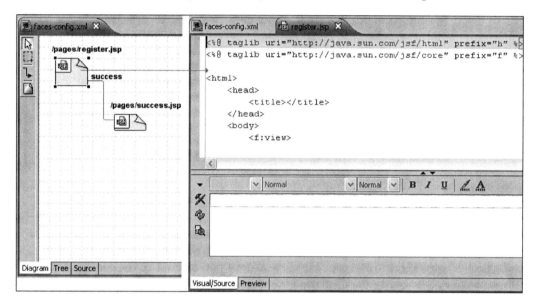

The **Visual Page Editor** is made of two parts: source code along the top and a WYSIWIG view along the bottom.

Now, we can use the JBoss Tools Palette (for details see Chapter 3) for editing the page source code in an easy manner. For example, for editing the register.jsp source code, follow these steps:

1. Place the cursor in source code, right after the f:view tag.

2. Type here the following code and place the cursor after it:

   ```
   <h2>Registration form:</h2>
   ```

3. Expand the **JSF HTML** section of the JBoss Tools Palette.

4. Click on the **form** tag and wait until the **Insert Tag** window appears.

5. Type **success** in the **Value** column, next to the **id** row, and click on **Finish**.

6. Place the cursor inside the h:form tag, and click on the **panelGrid** tag from the JBoss Tools Palette. Wait until the **Insert Tag** window appears.

7. Type **3** in the **Value** column, next to the **columns** row, and click on **Finish**.

8. Place the cursor inside the h:panelGrid tag.

9. Click on the **outputLabel** tag from the JBoss Tools Palette.

10. In the **Insert Tag** window, type **#{personBean.personName}** in the **Value** column next to the **for** row. You can fill this field by manually typing or by browsing to the personName property (as shown in the following screenshot).

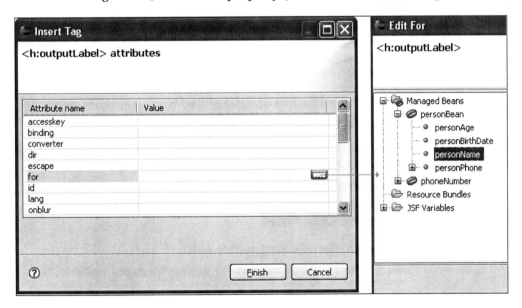

11. Switch to **Advanced** tab. Type **personNameLabel** in the **Value** column, next to the **id** row and click on **Finish**.

12. Place the cursor inside the h:outputLabel tag and click on the **outputText** tag from the JBoss Tools Palette.

13. In the **Insert Tag** window, type **Your Name:** in the **Value** column, next to the **value** row, and then click on **Finish**.

Steps 9—13 will generate the following source code:

```
<h:outputLabel for="#{personBean.personName}"
id="personNameLabel">
    <h:outputText value="Your Name:"/>
</h:outputLabel>
```

14. Now, place the cursor after the `h:outputLabel` and repeat steps 9–13 for inserting a label with text for every property of the `PersonBean` managed bean (`personAge`, `personBirthDate`, `personPhone`). The generated source code should look like this:

```
<h:outputLabel for="#{personBean.personAge}" id="personAgeLabel">
    <h:outputText value="Your Age:"/>
</h:outputLabel>

<h:outputLabel for="#{personBean.personBirthDate}" id="personBirth
DateLabel">
    <h:outputText value="Your Birth Date (dd/MM/yyyy):"/>
</h:outputLabel>

<h:outputLabel for="#{personBean.personPhone}"
id="personPhoneLabel">
    <h:outputText value="Your Phone Number (x[x]-xxx-xxx-xxxx):"/>
</h:outputLabel>
```

15. Place the cursor between the first and the second `h:outputLabel` tags.

16. Click on the **inputText** tag from the JBoss Tools Palette.

17. In the **Insert Tag** window, switch to **Advanced** tab. Type **personName** in the **Value** column, next to the **id** row.

18. Also, type **#{personBean.personName}** in the **Value** column, next to the **value** row. You can fill in this field manually or by browsing to the `personName` property. Click **Finish**.

    Steps 15–17 generate the following source code:

```
<h:inputText id="personName" value="#{personBean.personName}"/>
```

Now, place the cursor after each `h:outputLabel` tag and repeat steps 15–17 for inserting a text field for each property of the `PersonBean` managed bean (`personAge`, `personBirthDate`, `personPhone`). The generated source code should look like this:

```
<h:inputText id="personAge" value="#{personBean.personAge}"/>
<h:inputText id="personBirthDate" value="#{personBean.
personBirthDate}"/>
<h:inputText id="personPhone" value="#{personBean.personPhone}"/>
```

19. Place the cursor after the first `h:inputText` tag.

20. Click on the **message** tag from the JBoss Tools Palette.

21. In the **Insert Tag** window, switch to **Advanced** tab. Type **personName** in the **Value** column, next to the **for** row.

22. Type **color: red; text-decoration: overline** in the **Value** column, next to the **style** row.

23. Type **personNameError** in the **Value** column, next to the **id** row. Click **Finish**.

Steps 19−22 generate the following source code:

```
<h:message for="personName" id="personNameError"

          style="color: red; text-decoration: overline"/>
```

Now, place the cursor after each **h:inputText** tag and repeat steps 19−22 for inserting a **h:message** tag for each property of the PersonBean managed bean (personAge, personBirthDate, personPhone). The generated source code should look like this:

```
<h:message for="personAge" id="personAgeError"
          style="color: red; text-decoration: overline"/>
<h:message for="personBirthDate" id="personBirthDateError"
          style="color: red; text-decoration: overline"/>
<h:message for="personPhone" id="personPhoneError"
          style="color: red; text-decoration: overline"/>
```

24. Place the cursor after the h:panelGrid tag.

25. Click on the **commandButton** tag from the JBoss Tools Palette.

26. In the **Insert Tag** window, type **success** in the **Value** column, next to the **action** row.

27. Type **Register** in the **Value** column, next to the **value** row. Click on **Finish**.

28. Place the cursor inside the h:inputText tag that corresponds to the personAge property. Place here the following default converter and validator:

```
<h:inputText id="personAge" value="#{personBean.personAge}">
   <f:converter converterId="javax.faces.Integer"/>
   <f:validateLongRange maximum="150" minimum="0"/>
</h:inputText>
```

29. Place the cursor inside the h:inputText tag that corresponds to the personBirthDate property. Place here the following default converter:

```
<h:inputText id="personBirthDate" value="#{personBean.
personBirthDate}">
   <f:convertDateTime pattern="dd/MM/yyyy"/>
</h:inputText>
```

30. Place the cursor inside the `h:inputText` tag that corresponds to the `personPhone` property. Place here the following custom converter:

```
<f:converter converterId="phoneConverter" />
```

31. Place the cursor inside the `h:inputText` tag that corresponds to the `personPhone` property. Place here the following custom validator:

```
<f:validator validatorId="phoneValidator" />
```

The complete source code of `register.jsp` is:

```
<%@ taglib uri="http://java.sun.com/jsf/html" prefix="h" %>
<%@ taglib uri="http://java.sun.com/jsf/core" prefix="f" %>
<html>
 <head>
  <title></title>
 </head>
 <body>
 <f:view>
  <h2>Registration form:</h2>
  <h:form id="success">
  <h:panelGrid columns="3">

  <h:outputLabel for="#{personBean.personName}"
            id="personNameLabel">
   <h:outputText value="Your Name:"/>
  </h:outputLabel>
  <h:inputText id="personName"
            value="#{personBean.personName}"/>
   <h:message for="personName" id="personNameError"
                    style="color: red; text-decoration: overline"/>
   <h:outputLabel for="#{personBean.personAge}" id="personAgeLabel">
    <h:outputText value="Your Age:"/>
   </h:outputLabel>
   <h:inputText id="personAge" value="#{personBean.personAge}">
    <f:converter converterId="javax.faces.Integer"/>
    <f:validateLongRange maximum="150" minimum="0"/>
   </h:inputText>
   <h:message for="personAge" id="personAgeError"
                    style="color: red; text-decoration: overline"/>

   <h:outputLabel for="#{personBean.personBirthDate}"
                    id="personBirthDateLabel">
     <h:outputText value="Your Birth Date (dd/MM/yyyy):"/>
       </h:outputLabel>
   <h:inputText id="personBirthDate"
                value="#{personBean.personBirthDate}">
        <f:convertDateTime pattern="dd/MM/yyyy"/>
   </h:inputText>
   <h:message for="personBirthDate" id="personBirthDateError"
```

```
                          style="color: red; text-decoration: overline"/>
        <h:outputLabel for="#{personBean.personPhone}"
                       id="personPhoneLabel">
         <h:outputText value="Your Phone Number (x[x]-xxx-xxx-xxxx):"/>
              </h:outputLabel>
         <h:inputText id="personPhone" value="#{personBean.personPhone}">
          <f:converter converterId="phoneConverter" />
          <f:validator validatorId="phoneValidator" />
         </h:inputText>
         <h:message for="personPhone" id="personPhoneError"
                       style="color: red; text-decoration: overline"/>

        </h:panelGrid>
       <h:commandButton action="success" value="Register"/>
      </h:form>
    </f:view>
   </body>
   </html>
```

Editing the success.jsp page

Using the JBoss Tools Palette and the experience from the above section, you can easily develop a success.jsp page that looks like this (here, we just display on screen the submitted information using a set of h:outputText tags):

```
<%@ taglib uri="http://java.sun.com/jsf/html" prefix="h" %>
<%@ taglib uri="http://java.sun.com/jsf/core" prefix="f" %>

<html>
 <head>
  <title></title>
 </head>
 <body>
  <f:view>
   <h2>Registration successfully done!</h2>
    <h:panelGrid columns="2">
     <h:outputText value="Inserted Name:"/>
     <h:outputText value="#{personBean.personName}"/>
     <h:outputText value="Inserted Age:"/>
     <h:outputText value="#{personBean.personAge}"/>
     <h:outputText value="Inserted Birth Date:"/>
     <h:outputText value="#{personBean.personBirthDate}"/>
     <h:outputText value="Inserted Phone Number:"/>
     <h:outputText value="#{personBean.personPhone.allNumber}"/>
     <h:outputText value="Inserted Phone Number Country Code:"/>
     <h:outputText value="#{personBean.personPhone.countryCode}"/>
     <h:outputText value="Inserted Phone Number Area Code:"/>
```

```
      <h:outputText value="#{personBean.personPhone.areaCode}"/>
      <h:outputText value="Inserted Phone Number Prefix:"/>
      <h:outputText value="#{personBean.personPhone.prefixNumber}"/>
    </h:panelGrid>
  </f:view>
 </body>
</html>
```

Editing a start page for the registerJSF project

Now, it is time to create a start page for the application. This can be done by following these steps:

1. In the **Package Explorer** view navigate to your **WebContent** directory (**registerJSF | WebContent**).

2. Right-click on the **WebContent** directory and select the **New | JSP File** from the contextual menu.

3. In the **New JSP File** window, type **index** in the **Name** field and select **JSPRedirect** option from the **Template** field. Click on **Finish** (if you click on the **Next** button, you will be able to add tag libraries to your JSP—here it is not the case).

4. A JSP editor will open the source code of the index.jsp. Type **/pages/register.jsf** between the quotes of the page attribute.

The start page will look like this:

```
<!doctype html public "-//w3c//dtd html 4.0 transitional//en">
<html>
<head></head>
 <body>
  <jsp:forward page="/pages/register.jsf" />
 </body>
</html>
```

Save the project status by selecting the **Save** option from the **File** main menu.

Testing the registerJSF project

Finally, it is time to test our registerJSF project to see how it works. For this, start the *JBoss 4.2 Server* server (do this from **JBoss AS** view) and deploy the application on this server (do this by , and then on the project name in **Package Explorer** view and select **Run As | Run On Server** option).

The application will start in **Eclipse Internal Web Browser**, but you may also open it in your own web browser by accessing the http://localhost:8080/registerJSF/ URL. Following are some screenshots of the application:

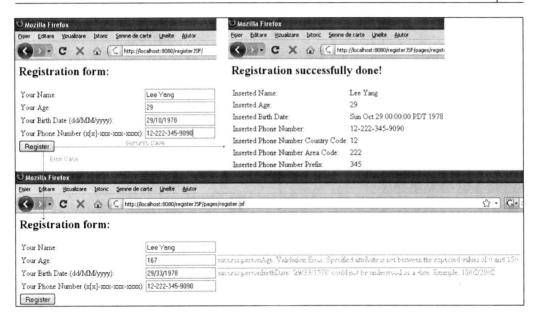

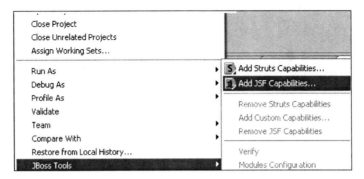

Adding/Removing JSF capabilities for an existing project

For almost any existing project, you can add JSF capabilities by right-clicking on the project name in the **Package Explorer** view and selecting the **JBoss Tools | Add JSF Capabilities** option from the contextual menu (as shown in the following screenshot). For example, try to do this for the empty `test` project developed in Chapter 2:

Below the **Add JSF Capabilities** option, you have the **Remove JSF Capabilities** that allows you to remove JSF capabilities from a project that has these capabilities.

After you select the **Add JSF Capabilities** option, you have to indicate the project name and the location of the web.xml configuration file. After that, just click the **Next** button.

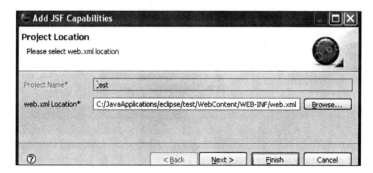

In the last step of adding JSF capabilities, you have to indicate a set of project folders, a servlet version, a runtime, and a target server (as shown in the following screenshot). In principle, you have to make the same configurations as you have seen in the *Creating a JSF Project Stub* section. At the end, just click on the **Finish** button, and if everything was okay, then , and then ready for JSF support.

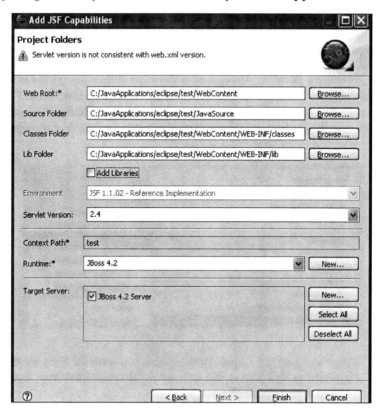

Facelets support

Facelets is a templating language for JSF that enables the rendering of JSF components on XHTML files, serving as an alternative rendering medium for JSF components other than standard JSPs. As you know, Facelets is an extension of JSF especially created to simplify the design of presentation pages for JSF. To add Facelets support to your JSF projects, you start by creating a JSF project exactly as you have seen in the *Creating a JSF Project Stub* section. The main difference is that in the **New JSF Project** window (as seen in the following screenshot), you have to select **JSF 1.2 with Facelets**.

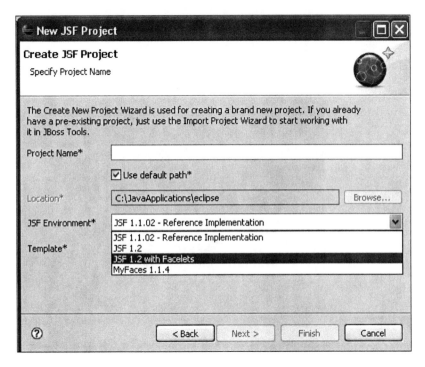

After you have selected the **JSF Environment** as **JSF 1.2 with Facelets,** you have to select a **Template** from the following list:

- **FaceletsBlankWithoutLibs** — this is a blank JSF project without JSF support. In this case, the JSF libraries are missing for avoiding the potential conflicts with the servers that already offer JSF support.

- **FaceletsKickStartWithRILibs** — this is a demo JSF/Facelets project with complete JSF/Facelets support.

- **FaceletsKickStartWithoutLibs** — this is a demo JSF/Facelets project without JSF/Facelets support.

Once the project stub has been created, it is important to know that the Facelets components can be taken from the JBoss Tools Palette, **JSF Facelets** section (as shown in the following screenshot). For more details about how to work with JBoss Tools Palette, please see Chapter 3.

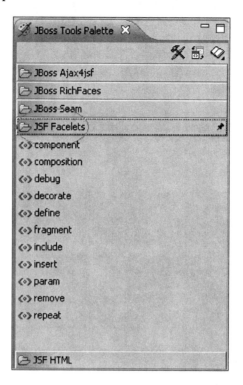

Summary

In this chapter, you have seen how to use JSF Tools for modeling the most important components of a traditional JSF project. You have developed a complete functional JSF project by using the most important skills of JSF Tools (managed beans, converters, validators), but you also have learnt about some of the "hidden goodies", like validation JSF projects, adding Facelets support, and creating referenced beans.

5
Struts Tools

Struts Tools is a complex and complete solution for developing web applications using the Struts framework. Based on views, editors, and wizards, Struts Tools provides powerful support for developing and managing Struts configuration files, validator files, tiles files, and other Struts components. In this chapter we will see how to exploit these features of Struts Tools to develop a Struts application faster and easier than you have ever done before.

Speaking of Struts applications, in the following sections we will develop a classic Struts application that will take advantage of the most used Struts capabilities, such as Struts tags, validation, and tiles. The example consists of a simple JSP page containing a Struts form with three fields, as follows:

- `name` — this is a text field that will allow the user to insert his name
- `zip` — this is a text field that will allow to the user to provide a zip code
- `email` — this is a text field for the user's email address

The information provided by the user will be client-side validated, submitted (using a Struts `</html:submit>` button), server-side validated, and displayed again in a new JSP page. As a particularity, both JSPs will have the same header and footer, which will be represented by a small and simple HTML code.

Tasks such as building the form, preserving information between pages, transitions between JSPs, copying header and footer in both JSPs, validating information, and so on, will be accomplished based on Struts capabilities and respecting Struts architecture. Obviously, because we want to do this fast and easy, we will use Struts Tools.

The following diagram presents our application in Struts style and using Struts terminology (to understand it, think in Struts!). This may look a little complicated at the moment, so you may want to come back to it after you have read a little further and things start becoming clearer.

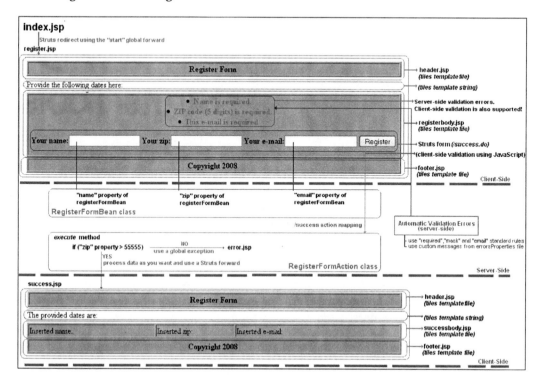

Overview of Struts

Struts is one of the most popular open source frameworks for developing web applications based on Java programming language. Developed by Apache, under Jakarta project, Struts encourage the **MVC (Model-View-Controller)** design paradigm and it is based on standard technologies such as Java Beans, Java Servlets, Resource Bundle, XML, and so on. Using a few bullets, we can resume the Struts implementation of MVC as follows:

- There is a servlet controller that manages the flow between JSP pages
- There are a set of special classes dealing with data access
- Action forwards and action mappings translate the decisional flow control out of the presentation layer
- JSP pages can refer to logical destinations

- Controller component provides actual URIs at runtime
- Special tag library for JSP pages can be used to employ the framework in a productive way

Basically, Struts is made up of a set of components that interact with each other to sustain the MVC architecture. From the Struts components, we mention the following:

Model (M) components:

- `ActionForm` beans
  - Each application input form has an `ActionForm` bean
  - It defines a property for each form's field and the corresponding `getXXX` and `setXXX` methods
  - It places the bean instance on form and uses the nested property references

View (V) components:

- Tag libraries
  - JSP tag extension for HTML forms (`struts-html.tld`)
  - JSP tag extension for Java Beans (`struts-bean.tld`)
  - JSP tag extension for testing the values of properties (`struts-logic.tld`)
- Input field types
  - Checkboxes, radio buttons, text input fields, select lists, options, hidden fields, and so on
- Presentation tags
  - `<iterate>` – repeat its tag body for each element of a `Collection`. This is a logic tag
  - `<present>` – checks the current request for a particular attribute, and evaluates its body only if the tested attribute is present. This is a logic tag.
  - `<notPresent>` – opposite of `<present>` tag. This is a logic tag.
  - `<parameter>` – Retrieves the value of the specified parameter and defines the result as a page scope attribute. This is a bean tag.
  - `<img>` – dynamically generates an HTML `<img>` element. This is an HTML tag.
  - `<link>` – dynamically generates an HTML `<a>` element. This is an HTML tag.

Controller (C) components:

- `ActionServlet` class
    - ° This is the controller servlet responsible for mapping requests URIs to `Action` classes.

- `Action` class
    - ° An extension of `Action` class that deals with a logical request

- `struts-config.xml`
    - ° The Struts main configuration file. Among many other things, it contains the action mapping used to configure the controller servlet.

- `validation.xml`
    - ° Contains entries directly related to data validation issues

- `web.xml`
    - ° Contains the necessary Struts components

Note that these are the theoretical aspects of the Struts framework meant to get you familiar with the model and components of the Struts engine. For practical examples and a complete tutorial, you can access resources such as `http://www.roseindia.net/struts/` or `http://www.strutstutorial.com/`. If you never worked with Struts, or you have minimum experience, then it is absolutely mandatory to access a more detailed documentation before going further.

Struts project verification

Before starting to develop a Struts application, you can take advantage of an important facility, that is, the ability to verify and report any dysfunctions that may affect the application flow (activating this facility is optional, but strongly recommended). This facility, known as the **Struts Project Verification**, will verify the application and will help you to easily identify and solve a variety of common errors. For this, you can follow these steps:

1. From the **Window** main menu, select the **Preferences** option.

2. In the **Preferences** window, left panel, expand the **JBoss Tools | Web | Verification** node. In the following screenshot, you can see the verification section reserved to the Struts framework:

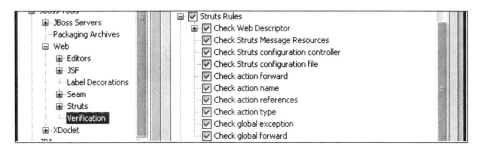

3. Select the desired checkboxes and click on the **Apply** and **OK** buttons.

Creating a Struts project stub

Before we build a house, we need a foundation. Likewise, before we build a Struts project, we need to build a Struts project stub. Using the right tools, the house is built in days. Using Struts Tools and the following four simple steps, the Struts project stub can be made ready in seconds:

1. From the **File** menu, select the **New | Project** option. In the **New Project** window, expand the **JBoss Tools Web** node and select the **Struts Project** leaf. After that, click the **Next** button.

2. In the next window, it is mandatory to specify a name for the new project (**Project Name** field), a location (**Location** field—only if you don't use the default path), a Struts implementation (**Struts Environment** field), and a template (**Template** field). As you can see, Struts Tools offers two predefined templates as follows:

   ° **Blank**—this will create an empty Struts project
   ° **KickStart**—this will create a demo Struts project

The following screenshot is an example of how to configure a Struts project at this step (just click the **Next** button):

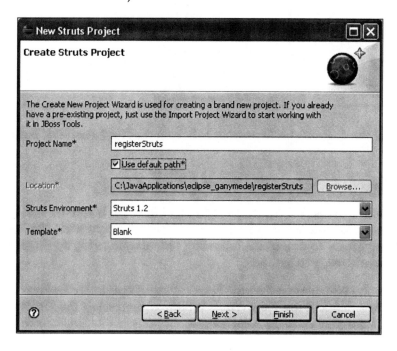

3. This step allows you to set the servlet version (**Servlet Version** field), the runtime (**Runtime** field) used for building and compiling the application, and the server where the application will be deployed (**Target Server** field). Note that this server is in direct relationship with the selected runtime. The following screenshot is an example of how to deal with this step (click on the **Next** button):

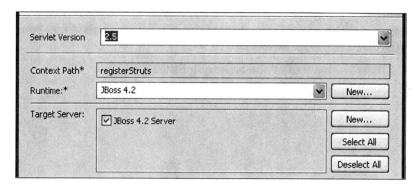

4. The next window allows you to select the desired Tag Library Descriptors (TLDs) that will be included in the project (as shown in the following screenshot). Besides the default selected TLDs, we need to add the `struts-tiles.tld`, which is used for having access to Struts tiles tags. After selection, click on the **Finish** button.

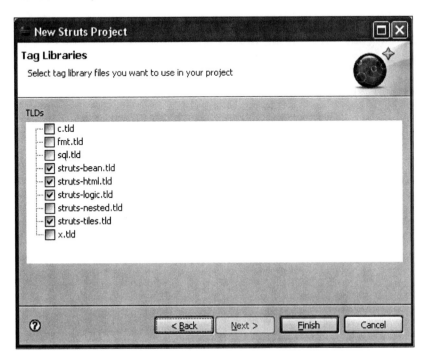

After a few seconds, the new Struts project stub is created and ready to take shape! You can see the new project in the **Package Explorer** view.

Struts editors

As you know, Struts encourages developers to place as much code as possible in configuration files, and to keep the application's source code focused on business logic. Following this pattern, Struts Tools have a set of editors designed for offering a visual and interactive medium that allows us to obtain configuration files without "touching" the source code of these files. In this section we will be discussing these editors and you will see how to develop the `registerStruts` application started in the above sections.

Graphical editor for struts-config.xml

A very useful facility of Struts tools consists of an editor especially designed to manage everything that is related to the Struts main configuration file (`struts-config.xml`). You can start this editor like this:

1. Place the cursor in the **Package Explorer** view on your project node.

2. Expand your Struts project node: **registerStruts | WebContent | WEB-INF**.

3. Double-click on the **struts-config.xml** leaf.

When the editor is available, you will see it as shown in the following screenshot:

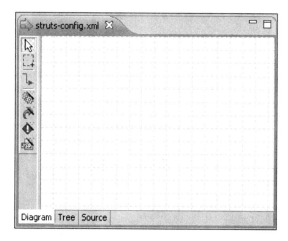

Diagram view

From this view, you can easily manage your application's **pages**, **actions**, **global forwards/exceptions**, and **transitions**; in other words, all the "ingredients" of a Struts application. You can create, modify, or delete these kinds of components in just a few seconds, and you will always have a clear image of the application flow thanks to the graphical representation mode.

Creating JSP pages

Conforming to our scenario, we will need two JSPs; one that will contain the user form and another one that displays the submitted information. We can create these two JSPs pages using the following steps (let's name these empty JSPs `registerbody.jsp` and `success.jsp`).

1. Right-click inside the **Diagram** view surface and select **Add | Page** from the contextual menu (as shown in the following screenshot).

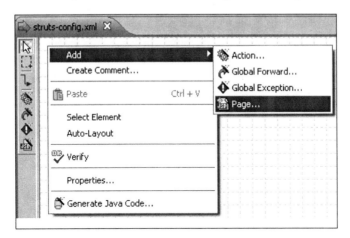

Another possible way to create a new page is to select the **Add Page** icon (last from the bottom) from the toolbar placed in the top-left corner of the **Diagram** view and after that click inside the **Diagram** view surface.

2. The above step will open the **Add Page** window (as shown in the following screenshot). In the **Name** field, enter the relative path and name of the new JSP page. For example, you may type **/WEB-INF/registerbody** (without the .jsp extension). Mark the **Create File** checkbox as selected (allow Struts Tools to create the file stub) and select **Blank** from the **Template** drop-down list. Click on the **Finish** button.

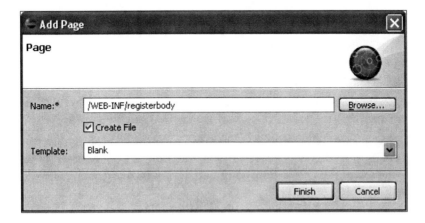

3. Repeat steps 1 and 2, but this time type **/pages/success** in the **Name** field. Note that both pages are represented on the **Diagram** view surface as you can see in the following screenshot. Also, they are present under the **registerStruts/WebContent/pages** (`success.jsp` page) and **registerStruts/ WebContent/WEB-INF** (`registerbody.jsp` page) directories in the **Package Explorer** view.

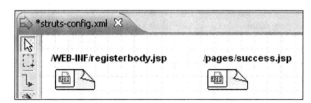

At this point, we have two empty JSPs that are waiting for us to add some Struts functionality in them. We start by creating an action mapping.

Creating an action mapping

As you know, a Struts **action** is an instance of a subclass of an `Action` class. Its responsibility is to implement a fragment of a web application and whose `perform` or `execute` method returns a forward. In our example, this action will be named `RegisterFormAction`, and it will be responsible for processing the information provided through the Struts form. Associating an action name with an action is accomplished by an entry in `struts-config.xml`, named **action mapping**. Optionally, an action mapping can refer a form bean for that action, and can define a list of action's local forwards.

Our application (`registerStruts`) will have a Struts action that can be created by performing the following steps:

1. Right-click inside the **Diagram** view surface and select **Add | Action** from the contextual menu.

   Another way of creating a new Struts action is to select the **Add Action** icon (fourth from above) from the toolbar placed in the top-left corner of the **Diagram** view and, after that, clicking inside the **Diagram** view surface.

2. The above step will open the **Add Action** window (as shown in the following screenshot). In this window you have to configure the action's parameters (see the examples in the following list) and, following that, click on the **Finish** button:

   ° In the **Path** field, enter the relative path of the Struts action (for example, type `/success`).

   ° In the **Name** field, enter the name for the form bean (for example, type `registerFormBean`). This bean will be created later.

- ° In the **Scope** field, enter the scope where this action exists (for example, select the **request** option for request scope).

- ° In the **Type** field, enter the fully qualified name of the Struts action class (for example, type `register.RegisterFormAction`).

- ° Leave the **Validate** field as default and click on the **Finish** button.

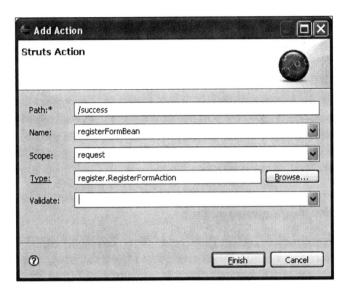

Note that the new action is graphically visible in the **Diagram** view as shown in the following screenshot:

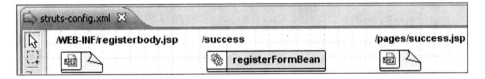

Connecting a JSP page with action mappings

For creating a connection (**link**) between a JSP page and its corresponding Struts action, follow the steps shown below (these steps are an example for creating a link from `registerbody.jsp` to the `/success` action (`register.RegisterFormAction`), but you can follow them for your own links as well with just the obvious modifications):

1. In the **Diagram** view, select the **Create New Connection** icon from the toolbar placed in the top-left corner (third from the top). The cursor will change into an arrow cursor with a two-pronged plug at the arrow's bottom.

2. Click on the **registerbody.jsp** icon and after that click on the **/success** action icon. An arrow will mark the new link, as you can see in the following screenshot:

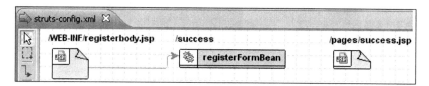

Creating a forward

Conforming to Struts documentation, a Struts **forward** is an object returned by a Struts action. It is characterized by a name and a path that indicates the next stop for the request. A forward can be **local** (for a particular action) or **global** (for any action). The next forward is local, and it is returned by the `RegisterFormAction` action to forward the request to the `success.jsp` page.

Creating a Struts forward can be done like this (in the following steps, we will create a Struts forward for the `/success` action):

1. In the **Diagram** view, select the **Create New Connection** icon from the toolbar placed in the top-left corner (third from the top). The cursor will change into an arrow cursor with a two-pronged plug at the arrow's bottom.

2. Click on the **/success** action and after that click on the **success.jsp** icon. An arrow will mark the new Struts forward, as you can see in the following screenshot:

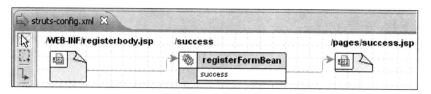

 By default, the Struts forwards name will be automatically set based on the name of the target JSP filename. If you want, you can modify this name from the **Tree** view, **action-mappings** node.

Creating a global forward

For experience purposes, a Struts **global forward** can be very useful for creating a starting page for our application (index.jsp is the application's start page). Of course, as you know from the Struts documentation, global forwards can be used in many issues of Struts applications, but the steps are exactly the same as the ones below:

1. Right-click inside the **Diagram** view surface and select **Add | Global Forward** from the contextual menu.

    Another way to create a new Struts global forward is to select the **Add Global Forward** icon (third from the bottom) from the toolbar placed in the top-left corner of the **Diagram** view and, following that, clicking inside the **Diagram** view surface.

2. In the **Add Forward** window (shown in the following screenshot), it is mandatory to specify a name for the Struts global forward (**Name** field) and a path indicating the global forward's destination (**Path** field). For example, type **start** for global forward's name and type **/pages/register.jsp** for path (setting path can be done by typing by hand or by using the **Browse** button, which will open the **Edit Path** window that contains the application's pages in the **Pages** tab). Optionally, you may set redirection (**Redirect** field) and indicate if your application needs a context relativity for this global forward (**ContextRelative** field). At the end, just click on the **Finish** button.

Now, your diagram should look like this:

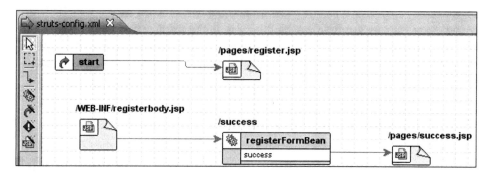

Creating a global exception

Global exceptions are important components in Struts applications because they offer us an elegant method for dealing with issues. For example, in our application, we know that one of the Struts form fields is the field corresponding to the zip code. Assuming that we want to allow only zips smaller than 55555 integer value, we can use a global exception to display a proper error message for every zip bigger than this value. The comparison between the provided zips and the 55555 constant is done in the action class by the `execute` method. When a zip is bigger than 55555, a `java.lang.Exception` is thrown, and, conforming to our global exception, the flow goes directly to the `error.jsp` page. Creating a global exception is a simple task as you will see next:

1. Right-click inside the **Diagram** view surface and select **Add | Global Exception** from the contextual menu.

   Another way of creating a new Struts global exception is to select the **Add Global Exception** icon (second from bottom) from the toolbar placed in the top-left corner of the **Diagram** view and, following that, clicking inside the **Diagram** view surface.

2. In the **Add Exception** window, it is mandatory to specify the exception's key (**Key** field) and the exception's type (**Type** field). Optionally, you may indicate the exception's path (**Path** field) and the exception's scope (**Scope** field). In our example, the key is **exception.key**, the exception's type is **java.lang.Exception**, and the path is **/WEB-INF/error.jsp**. Note that the JSP page indicated by the exception's path will be automatically created as a blank JSP page. At the end, just click on the **Finish** button.

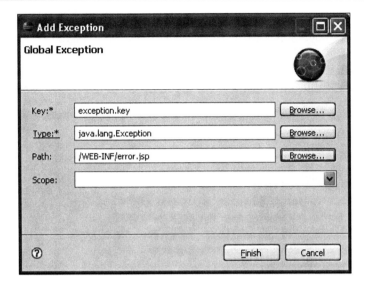

If you prefer to fill them up without hand typing, then use the **Browse** button next to the **Key**, **Type**, and **Path** sections, but keep in mind that in case of **Key**, you should have created it separately in a properties file and in case of **Path**, the JSP page should exist before this moment.

Now, your diagram should look like this:

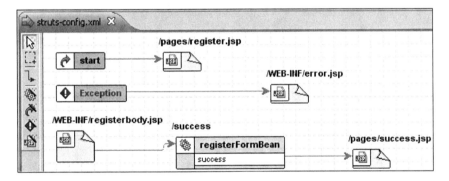

Let's add some code inside JSPs

At this point, our JSPs are just some empty files. Regarding our application scope, the below implementations should be pretty intuitive. Therefore, edit one by one the following JSPs pages and add the corresponding code.

The source code for `registerbody.jsp` is listed below. As you can see, it is a very simple code, even for a Struts beginner, therefore no dissection is needed.

Note that you can manually insert this code, but we recommend that you generate it through the JBoss Tools Palette (see Chapter 3, *JBoss Tools Palette*). We consider that you now have sufficient experience to edit the source code of a file using this tool, so we can skip the steps of this process. Anyway, as a clue, you will need the Struts Common, HTML Table, and Struts Form tag libraries of the JBoss Tools Palette.

```
<%@ taglib uri="/WEB-INF/struts-html.tld" prefix="html" %>

<table bgcolor="#c0c0c0" border="1" width="100%">
   <tr>
      <th>
      <html:form action="/success.do" >
         Your name:<html:text property="name"/>
         Your zip:<html:text property="zip"/>
         Your e-mail:<html:text property="email"/>
         <html:submit value="Register">
        </html:submit>
      </html:form>
      </th>
   </tr>
</table>
```

The source code for `success.jsp` is listed below. For this source code, you will need the Struts Common and Struts Tiles tag libraries of the JBoss Tools Palette.

```
<%@ taglib uri="/WEB-INF/struts-tiles.tld" prefix="tiles" %>
<tiles:insert definition="tiles.success"></tiles:insert>
```

The `register.jsp` source code is listed below (using the Struts Common and Struts Tiles tag libraries of the JBoss Tools Palette):

```
<%@ taglib uri="/WEB-INF/struts-tiles.tld" prefix="tiles" %>
<tiles:insert definition="tiles.register"></tiles:insert>
```

Don't bother too much at this point about understanding the `<tiles>` tags from `success.jsp` and `register.jsp` pages; everything will become clear after you read the section dedicated to Struts tiles. Nevertheless, a quick look on the first figure, page number 5 and a little bit of intuition may make things clear right away.

The `error.jsp` source code is listed as follows. (Use HTML Core and HTML Table tag libraries of the JBoss Tools Palette.)

```
<html>
 <head>
  <title>Error Page</title>
 </head>
```

```
<body>
  <table bgcolor="#cc0000" border="1" width="100%">
   <tr>
      <th>
         Exception: The ZIP code can't be bigger that 55555 !
      </th>
   </tr>
  </table>
 </body>
</html>
```

Generate source code

Struts Tools can generate Java class stubs (like actions and form bean classes) for all the components from the **Diagram** view. For this, right-click inside the **Diagram** view and select the **Generate Java Code** option from the contextual menu. This will open a multi-step wizard that allows you to select/deselect the components types and modify the base classes for these components.

Once you click on the **Generate** button, you will see a brief log that will show you how many classes will be generated and what their types are. Just click on the **Finish** button.

In our example, at this moment we are only obtaining one class that corresponds to our /success action. If you navigate through the project from the **Package Explorer** view, then the stub class source can be found in **registerStruts | Java Source | register | RegisterFormAction.java** leaf.

Now, you have to customize the generated source code. More precisely, we have to implement the execute method. Basically, we query a RegisterFormBean instance (this is the form bean of our action mapping) and we extract the name, zip, and email field's values. After that, we check to see if the provided zip code is smaller than 55555 arbitrary constant. If it is, then we follow our local forward, otherwise we throw a java.lang.Exception. At the end, the source code for RegisterFormAction.java should look like the following:

```
package register;

import javax.servlet.http.HttpServletRequest;
import javax.servlet.http.HttpServletResponse;

import org.apache.struts.action.ActionForm;
import org.apache.struts.action.ActionForward;
import org.apache.struts.action.ActionMapping;

public class RegisterFormAction extends org.apache.struts.action.
Action {
```

```
    // Global Forwards
    public static final String GLOBAL_FORWARD_start = "start";
    // Local Forwards
    public static final String FORWARD_success = "success";

    public RegisterFormAction() {
    }
    public ActionForward execute(ActionMapping mapping, ActionForm
form, HttpServletRequest request, HttpServletResponse response) throws
Exception {
        RegisterFormBean registerData = (RegisterFormBean)(form);
        int zip = Integer.valueOf(registerData.getZip());
        String name = registerData.getName();
        String email = registerData.getEmail();
        if(zip > 55555) { throw new Exception(); }
        else {
            // process the inserted data
            }
        return mapping.findForward(FORWARD_success);
    }
}
```

Because the `RegisterFormBean` isn't created yet, you will see an obvious error. In the next section, we will fix this error by creating the needed form bean.

Tree view

Since **Diagram** view can't help us to create a form bean, we need to focus next on the **Tree** view. Before jumping to our task, let's say that this view is a tree representation of the `struts-config.xml` file. From this view, you can create and/or modify the base components of a Struts application. As you can see, you have access to components like Struts actions, global exceptions, global forwards, form beans, etc.

Creating Struts components from the **Tree** view can be accomplished by right-clicking on the desired components category (node) and selecting the first option of the contextual menu (left panel of the **Tree** view). This will open a corresponding wizard that will guide you through the creation process (in the above sections you saw a part of these wizards). Modifying the characteristics of a component can be very easily accomplished from the right panel of the **Tree** view by typing the desired value in the corresponding field. Modifications will take place when the project is saved.

 In this section, we will skip the Struts components presented in the Diagram View section. Notice that everything that we have created in that section is reflected in the `struts-config.xml` tree representation. The reverse is also true!

Creating a form bean

As you probably know, a **form bean** is a Struts component that extends the
`ActionForm` class. Its main scope is to store data that comes from submitted HTML
forms or input data that comes from a Struts action link clicked by the user. In our
case, we need a form bean to store the `name`, `zip`, and `email` fields of our Struts form.
To create such a form bean, follow these steps:

1. In the left panel of the **Tree** view, right-click on the **form-beans** node and
   select the **Create Form Bean** option from the contextual menu.

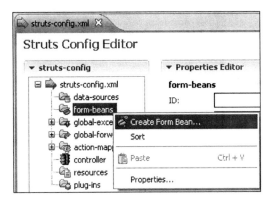

2. The above step will open the **Add Form Bean** window, where it is
   mandatory to specify the form bean name (**Name** field) and type (**Type**
   field). For example, use `registerFormBean` for name and `register.`
   `RegisterFormBean` for type. After that just click on the **Finish** button.

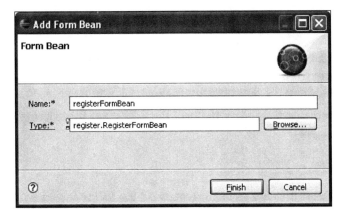

Note that the new Struts form bean has been added in the **Tree** view under the
form-beans node. Save the current state of the application.

Now you can generate the stub class for this form bean by right-clicking on the **registerFormBean** node and selecting the **Generate Java Code** option. When the corresponding wizard appears, just click on the **Finish** button. If everything went according to our plan, you should see a new Java source in the **Package Explorer** view, under the **registerStruts | Java Source | register** directory, that is named `RegisterFormBean.java`. The following screenshot reveals the entire process of generating form bean source code:

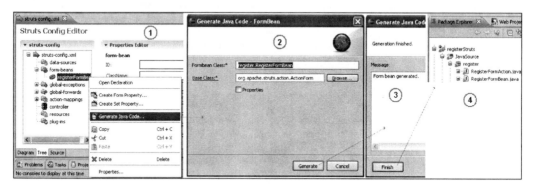

 If the form bean exists, then you can also generate its stub classes from the **Diagram** view, as you saw in the section *Generate Source Code*.

Next you need to customize the generated source code.

1. First, insert the following three lines right after the class definition:
    ```
    private String name="";
    private String zip="";
    private String email="";
    ```

2. Right-click inside the editor surface and select **Source | Generate Getters and Setters** from the context menu. This will generate getters/setters methods for our three properties (`name`, `zip`, and `email`).

3. Now, insert into the `reset` method the following three lines:
    ```
    this.name="";
    this.zip="";
    this.email="";
    ```

4. Finally, insert into the `validate` method the following lines (don't forget to import the `org.apache.struts.action.ActionErrors` class):
    ```
    ActionErrors errors = new ActionErrors();
    return errors;
    ```

At the end, the source code for `RegisterFormBean.java` should look like this:

```java
package register;
import javax.servlet.http.HttpServletRequest;
import org.apache.struts.action.ActionErrors;
import org.apache.struts.action.ActionMapping;
public class RegisterFormBean extends org.apache.struts.action.
ActionForm {
    private String name="";
    private String zip="";
    private String email="";
     public RegisterFormBean () {
     }
     public String getName() {
       return name;
     }
    public void setName(String name) {
       this.name = name;
    }
    public String getZip() {
       return zip;
    }
    public void setZip(String zip) {
       this.zip = zip;
    }
    public String getEmail() {
       return email;
    }
    public void setEmail(String email) {
       this.email = email;
    }
    public void reset(ActionMapping actionMapping, HttpServletRequest
request) {
         this.name="";
         this.zip="";
         this.email="";
    }
     public ActionErrors validate(ActionMapping actionMapping,
HttpServletRequest request) {
       ActionErrors errors = new ActionErrors();
       return errors;
    }
}
```

At this moment, the error from `RegisterFormAction.java` should disappear.

Source view

At any moment, you can check the source code of `struts-config.xml` by selecting the **Source** view.

Graphical editor for tiles files

Struts **tiles** is a templating system that can be used to create reusable view components. Based on this, tiles offers many advantages for avoiding redundant code in pages with a similar look and feel, but it can be a little annoying to develop their architecture and flow. Struts solves this problem by providing a dedicated editor that allows us to create complex tiles patterns even if we are not senior Struts developers. Our application has the following tiles structure:

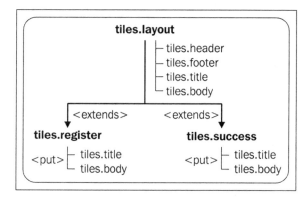

Before going further, we create the JSP pages that are behind these tiles. So, create the following JSPs blanks in their corresponding directories:

- `registerStruts/WebContent/WEB-INF/layout.jsp`
- `registerStruts/WebContent/WEB-INF/header.jsp`
- `registerStruts/WebContent/WEB-INF/footer.jsp`
- `registerStruts/WebContent/WEB-INF/successbody.jsp`

Creating a new tiles file

Right-click any folder of the `registerStruts` project and select **New | Tiles File** from the contextual menu. Alternatively, you can try the **File** menu, and the **| New | Other | JBoss Tools Web | Struts | Tiles File** path.

In the **New Tiles File** window, it is mandatory to specify a name for the new tiles file (for example, type **register-tiles** here). Also, if the **Folder** field wasn't automatically filled, then type **/registerStruts/WebContent/META-INF** here (by default, this is the place where the tiles files should be stored). Click on the **Finish** button.

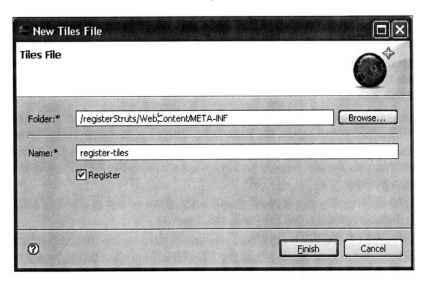

When you click on the **Finish** button, a new tiles file named `register-tiles.xml` will be created and the **Tiles Editor** will be launched.

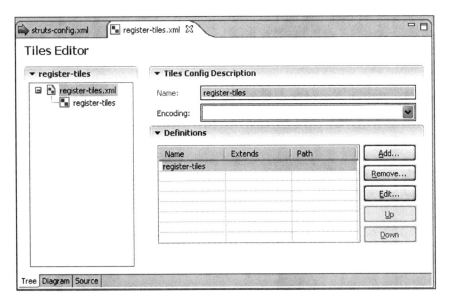

Tree view

This is a tree representation of the new tiles file. From here we can easily create a tiles file structure, as you'll see in the following steps where we create the structure shown previously.

1. Right-click on the **register-tiles** node and select **Rename** from the contextual menu.

2. In the **Rename Definition** window, type **tiles.layout** as the new name. Be sure that the **Update References** checkbox is selected before clicking the **Finish** button.

3. Select the renamed definition node and in the right panel of **Tree** view, type **/WEB-INF/layout.jsp** in the **Path** field. You also may use the **Browse** button from the right of the **Path** field, but in this case the layout.jsp must exist, because you should be able to navigate to it from the **Edit Path** window that appears.

4. Right-click on the **register-tiles.xml** node (root node) and select **Add Definition** option from the contextual menu.

5. In the **Add Definition** window, you should recognize the attributes list for the <definition> elements of the tiles files. Note that the only mandatory attribute is name (the **Name** field), so type here a name for the new definition; as per our example, type **tiles.register**. Usually, you will also specify a path (the **Path** field) or an extension (the **Extends** field). In this case, select the **tiles.layout** definition from the **Extends** field. Click on the **Finish** button to generate the new definition.

6. Repeat steps 4 and 5, but this time in the **Name** field type **tiles.success**. This definition extends the **tiles.layout** definition exactly like **tiles.register** definition.

Now, the **Tiles Editor** should look like this:

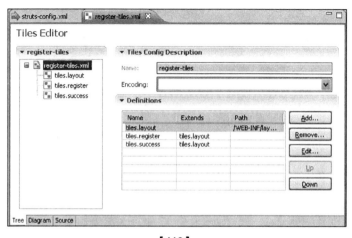

It is time to insert the components of each `<definition>`, and for that we start with **tiles.layout** definition and the following steps:

1. Right-click on the **tiles.layout** icon in the left-panel of **Tree** view.

2. Select the **Add Put** option from the contextual menu.

3. In the **Add Put** window, it is mandatory to specify a name for this component (the **Name** field). For example, type here **tiles.header**. Optionally, you can specify the component's type (the **Type** field) and the component's value (the **Value** field). Because we want to bind this component to the `header.jsp` page, it is necessary to type the path of this page, **/WEB-INF/header.jsp**, in the **Value** field. At the end, just click on the **Finish** button (as shown in the screenshot that follows).

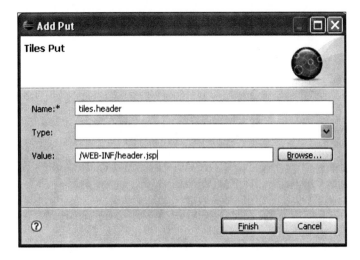

4. Repeat steps 1-3 for adding the component **tiles.footer** with the value **/WEB-INF/footer.jsp**.

5. Repeat steps 1-3 for adding the components **tiles.body** and **tiles.title** with no values set.

6. Repeat steps 1-3, but this time for **tiles.register** definition. Here, add the component **tiles.title** with the value **Provide the following info here:** and the component **tiles.body** with the value **/WEB-INF/registerbody.jsp**.

7. Repeat steps 1-3, but this time for **tiles.success** definition. Here, add the component **tiles.title** with the value **The provided info are:** and the component **tiles.body** with the value **/WEB-INF/successbody.jsp**.

Now the entire tiles file should have been created and its tree representation should look as shown in the following screenshot:

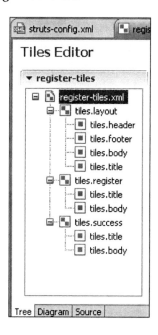

Now, let's edit the source code for JSPs that are related to these tiles. You can use the JBoss Tools Palette for generating the following source codes:

- `layout.jsp` (use the Struts Common, HTML Core, and Struts Tiles tag libraries of JBoss Tools Palette):

```
<%@ taglib uri="/WEB-INF/struts-tiles.tld" prefix="tiles" %>
<html>
<head>
   <title>
      <tiles:getAsString name="tiles.title"/>
   </title>
</head>
 <body>
   <tiles:insert attribute="tiles.header"></tiles:insert>
   <tiles:getAsString name="tiles.title"/>
   <tiles:insert attribute="tiles.body"></tiles:insert>
   <tiles:insert attribute="tiles.footer"></tiles:insert>
 </body>
</html>
```

- `header.jsp` (use HTML Table tag library of JBoss Tools Palette):

```
<table bgcolor="#c0c0c0" border="1" width="100%">
    <tr>
        <th>
            Register Form
        </th>
    </tr>
</table>
```

- `footer.jsp` (use HTML Table tag library of JBoss Tools Palette):

```
<table bgcolor="#c0c0c0" border="1" width="100%">
    <tr>
        <th>
            Copyright 2008
        </th>
    </tr>
</table>
```

- `successbody.jsp` (use Struts Common, HTML Table, and Struts Bean tag libraries of JBoss Tools Palette):

```
<%@ taglib uri="/WEB-INF/struts-bean.tld" prefix="bean" %>
<table bgcolor="#c0c0c0" border="1" width="100%">
    <tr>
        <td>
          Inserted name:<bean:write name="registerFormBean"
                                    property="name"/>
        </td>
        <td>
          Inserted zip:<bean:write name="registerFormBean"
                                   property="zip"/>
        </td>
        <td>
          Inserted e-mail:<bean:write name="registerFormBean"
                                      property="email"/>
        </td>
    </tr>
</table>
```

Diagram view

If the **Tree** view is not exactly your favorite method of creating a tiles file, then probably it is better to use the **Diagram** view. Here, the tiles file is represented as a diagram:

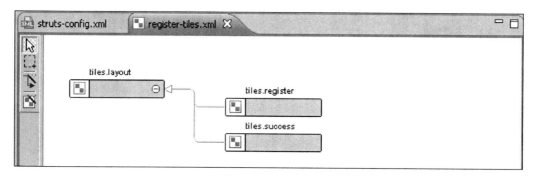

Nevertheless, notice that in this diagram you can't see the components of definitions and you can't create such components. In this case, you can do is create a complex structure of definitions. Probably it is a better solution to create most of this structure in the diagram mode and then switch to the tree mode to add the subcomponents. Feel free to choose what is best for you!

Creating a new definition can be done by right-clicking inside the **Diagram** surface and selecting the **New Definition** option from the contextual menu. Another way to create a new definition is to select the **Definition Template** icon (the bottom) icon from the toolbar placed in the top-left corner of the **Diagram** view and, click inside the **Diagram** view surface.

Creating a new connection between two definitions can be accomplished by selecting the **Create New Connection** icon (third from top) from the toolbar placed in the top-left corner of the **Diagram**. This will change the current cursor into an arrow cursor with a two-pronged plug at the arrow's bottom. First, click on the definition from where you want to start the connection and then click on the definition where you want to end it.

If you want to modify a definition's properties then right-click on it and select the **Properties** option from the contextual menu.

Source view

At any moment, you can check the source code of tiles file by selecting the **Source** view.

Create a start page for the registerStruts application

At this moment, we know that our application's start point is the `register.jsp` page. But this page can be found by a web browser only if it is explicitly specified in the browser, like `http://localhost:8080/registerStruts/pages/register.jsp`. A simple solution is to create an `index.jsp` page and to use our global forward (`start`), to redirect the flow control to `pages/register.jsp`. The browser will find the `index.jsp` and it will be automatically redirected to the `register.jsp` page.

For this, begin by right-clicking on the **registerStruts | WebContent** node in the **Package Explorer** view and select **New | JSP File** from the context menu (or try, **File** menu **| New | Other | JBoss Tools Web | JSP File** path). Type **index** in the **Name** field of the **New File JSP** window and click on the **Finish** button.

Now that you have created the `index.jsp` page, you should redirect it to the `register.jsp` page. For this, we will use the global forward created in the section *Creating a Global Forward*. Use JBoss Tools Palette (use Struts Common and Struts Logic tag libraries) to generate the following source code for `index.jsp`:

```
<%@ taglib uri="/WEB-INF/struts-logic.tld" prefix="logic" %>
<logic:redirect forward="start"></logic:redirect>
```

Testing registerStruts application

Finally, it's time for the first test of our `registerStruts` project. For this, start the **JBoss 4.2 Server** server (do this from **JBoss AS View**) and deploy the application on this server (do this by right-clicking on the project name in **Package Explorer** view and selecting the **Run As | Run On Server** option).

The application will start in **Eclipse Internal Web Browser**, but you may also open it in your own web browser by accessing the `http://localhost:8080/registerStruts/` URL. The following screenshot shows three captures of the application:

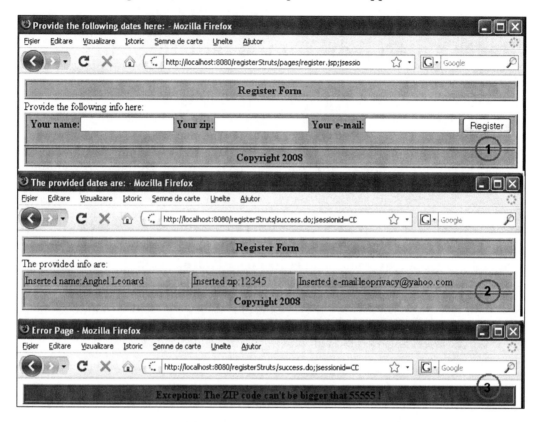

Struts Tools and validation aspects

An important component of Struts is the **Struts Validator Framework**. This framework is used to validate the data on the user's browser as well as on the server side. On the client side, the validation errors are reported through JavaScript message boxes, while on server side they are usually embedded in the JSPs' pages using the `<html:errors/>` tag. If any of the validations fail, the application redisplays the HTML form so that the invalid data can be corrected. In this section, you will learn how to use the **Struts Validator Framework** to validate the user inputs on the client browser.

For starting, we have to turn on the automatic validator and create a properties file.

Turning on the automatic validator

Add the `<plug-in>` element in `struts-config.xml`, for turning on the automatic validator. This can be accomplished in at least two ways:

- Switch to **Project Explorer** view and expand **registerStruts | Web Resources | Configuration | default | struts-config.xml** node. Right-click on the **plug-ins** node and select **Create Special Plug-ins | Validators** option from the contextual menu.

- Open the `struts-config.xml` editor and select the **Tree** view. Right-click on the **plug-ins** node (left panel) and select **Create Special Plug-ins | Validators** option from the contextual menu.

Both solutions will add up in the `struts-config.xml` the following source code:

```
<plug-in className="org.apache.struts.validator.ValidatorPlugIn">
  <set-property property="pathnames" value="/WEB-INF/validator-rules.
xml, /WEB-INF/validation.xml"/>
</plug-in>
```

Creating the properties file for validation purposes

Instead of having hard coded error messages in the framework, the validator allows us to specify a key to a message in a properties file that should be returned if a validation fails. The validator will use them from there on and we can easily change them to fit our needs. Each validation routine in the `validator-rules.xml` file specifies an error message key with the validator tag's `msg` attribute.

In the properties file, we can edit:

- "error" entries for formatting error messages

- standard "validator" error messages

- messages that will be substituted into error messages for {0}, {1}, {2}, ...

We have a few error messages to report, so we should create a properties file. Creating the properties file can be accomplished like this:

1. Switch to the **Project Explorer** view.

2. Right-click on the **registerStruts | Web Resources | Resource Bundles** and select **New | Properties File** from the contextual menu.

3. In the **New Properties File** window, click on the **Browse** button next to the **Folder** field.

4. Navigate to **registerStruts | Java Sources | register** directory.

5. Select this directory and click the **OK** button.

6. Back in the **New Properties File** window, type **errorsProperties** into the **Name** field and click on the **Finish** button (screenshot follows).

7. In the **Outline** view (usually this view is active, but it also can be activated from **Window** menu | **Show View** option), right-click on the **errorsProperties.properties** entry and select the **Add | Default Error Messages** option from the contextual menu. You should see something similar to that shown in the following screenshot (a default set of validation error messages comes prepackaged with Struts example applications. Each message key corresponds to those specified by the validation routines in the `validator-rules.xml` file, which also comes prepackaged with Struts):

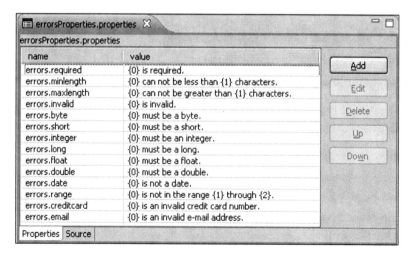

Next, we have to decide what the desired restrictions for the `registerFormBean` properties are. Therefore, a possible validation scenario is:

- `registerFormBean.name` — it can't be omitted (use the predefined validator **required**).
- `registerFormBean.zip` — it can't be omitted and has to be made of five digits (use the predefined validators **required** and **mask**).
- `registerFormBean.email` — it can't be omitted and has to be a well-formed email (use the predefined validators **required** and **email**).

To provide the corresponding error messages to our application, we start by adding new entries in the `errorsProperties.properties` file like this:

1. Open in editor the `errorsProperties.properties` file.
2. Click on the **Add** button from the right side of the **Properties** view.
3. In the **Add Property** window, type **registerFormBean.name** in the **Name** field and *Name* in the **Value** field. Click on **Finish**.
4. Repeat steps 2-3 until you have added all of the following entries:
   - **registerFormBean.zip=ZIP code (5 digits)**
   - **registerFormBean.email=This e-mail**
   - **errors.header=<ul>**
   - **errors.prefix=<li><font color="red">**
   - **errors.suffix=</font></li>**
   - **errors.footer=</ul>**
5. Save the changes!

The last thing that we have to do is to place a `<message-resources>` element in `struts-config.xml`. To do this, open the `struts-config.xml` in editor mode and switch to **Tree** view. In the left panel, expand the **struts-config.xml** node, right-click on **resources** node, and select the **Define Message Resources** option from the contextual menu. In the **Add Message Resource** window, just type **register.errorsProperties** in the **Parameter** field (this is the only mandatory field). Click on the **Finish** button. A new line was added in `struts-config.xml`, and it looks like this:

```
<message-resources parameter="register.errorsProperties"/>
```

Graphical editor for validation files

The `validation.xml` file is used to declare sets of validations that should be applied to form beans. A form bean that is validated has its own definition in this file. Inside that definition, you specify the validations you want to apply to the form bean's fields.

We start by editing the `validation.xml` file. For this, you have to double-click on the **registerStruts | Web Resources | Validation | validation.xml** node in the **Project Explorer** view. This will open the file in the **JBoss Tools XML Editor**.

As you can see, this editor is made of five different views as follows:

- **Formsets** view – from this view you can edit the validation rules (`<formset>` elements)
- **Validators** view – from here you can create new validators
- **Constants** view – from this you can define constants
- **Tree** view – this is a tree representation of `validation.xml`
- **Source** view – this is the source code of `validation.xml`

Next, we will create and populate a new `<formset>` element by following these steps:

1. In the **Formsets** view, click on the **Create Formset** button (first button from up-left).
2. You should see the **Add Formset** window. Because we want to create a default `<formset>` element, we just clicked on the **Finish** button.
3. You should see that the new default formset was added as a node inside the **Formsets** panel. Right-click on this node, and select the **Create Form** option from the contextual menu (as shown in the following screenshot).

4. In the **Add Form** window, type **registerFormBean** in the **Name** field and click on the **Finish** button.

5. Right-click on the **registerFormBean** node and select the **Create Field** option from the contextual menu (as shown in the screenshot below).

6. In the **Add Field** window, type **name** in the **Property** field. Click on the **Finish** button.

7. Repeat steps 5-6 for inserting the `zip` and `email` properties.

Now, if you fully expand the **formset** node, you should see something resembling that shown in the following screenshot:

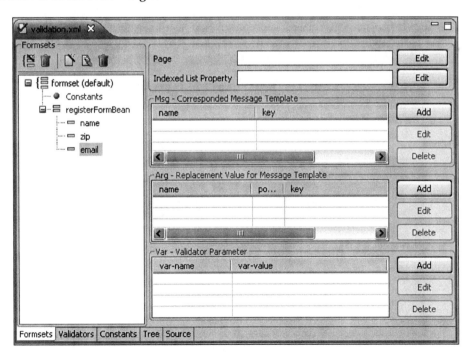

It is time to specify our validation rules for the three properties of `registerFormBean` and for that we follow these steps:

1. Be sure that the **Formsets** view is the current view.

2. Right-click on the **name** property and select the **Add Validation Rule** option from the contextual menu (screenshot shown below).

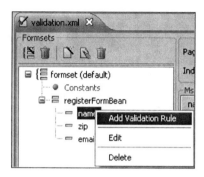

3. In the **Edit Validation Rules List** window, look in the **File** field if the `/validator-rules.xml` file is selected. If not, use the **Browse** button from the left to navigate to this file.

4. Select from the **Available Rules** panel (left side) the **required** rule, and click the **Add** button to copy it into the **Selected Rules** panel (right side). This is shown in the following screenshot. Click on the **OK** button.

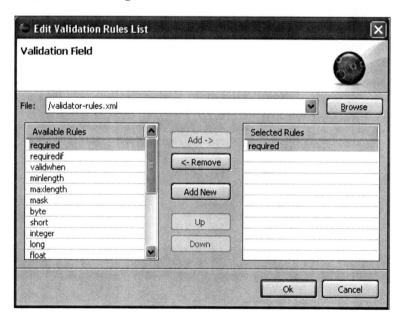

5. Repeat steps 2-4 for the `zip` and `email` properties. For the `zip` property, add the **required** and **mask** rules, and for the `email` property, add the **required** and **email** rules.

Now, the **Formsets** panel of the **Formsets** view (left side) should look like the following:

In the next approach, we will add our custom messages for **required**, **mask**, and **email** standard rules. For this, here are the steps:

Custom message for the name property (required rule)

1. Switch to the **Tree** view of the `validation.xml` file.

2. Completely expand the **validation.xml** node.

3. Right-click on the **name** node and select **Add Arg** from the contextual menu (as shown in the following screenshot).

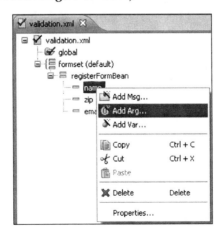

4. In the **Add Arg** window we are especially interested on the mandatory **Key** field. Click on the **Browse** button from the right of the **Key** field and open the **Key** window (as shown in the following screenshot). Be sure that in the **Path to Resource** field the `register.errorsProperties` file is present (if not use the **Browse** button from the right to navigate to this file). After that, select the entry **registerFormBean.name** from the properties list and click on the **OK** button.

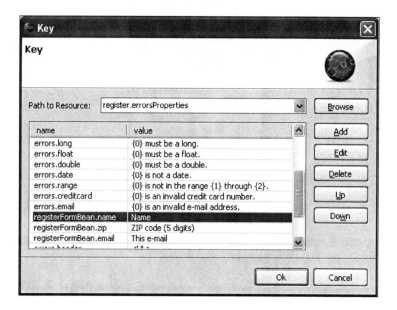

5. Come back to the **Add Arg** window and simply click on the **Finish** button.

Custom message for the zip property (required and mask rules)

Repeat steps 3-5 as above, but this time select from the **Key** window the **registerFormBean.zip** entry. After that, continue with these steps:

1. Right-click on the **zip** node and select **Add Var** from the contextual menu.

2. In the **Add Var** window, type *mask* as the var-name (**Var-Name** field) and $^\wedge\backslash d\{5\}\$$ as the var-value (**Var-Value** field). This is shown in the following screenshot. Click on the **Finish** button.

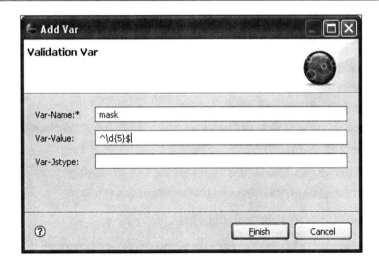

Custom message for the email property (required and email rules)

Repeat steps 3-5 used for the name property but this time select from the **Key** window the **registerFormBean.email** entry.

At the end, the **Tree** view should look like this:

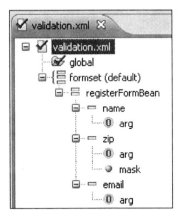

Client-side validation

As you know, Struts supports client and server side validation. On the client side, Struts uses the JavaScript scripting language and on the server side, the validation is implemented in a server component.

In this section, we will activate the client-side validation by following these steps:

1. Edit the `registerbody.jsp` page by selecting it from **Package Explorer** view (**registerStruts | WebContent | WEB-INF** node).

2. Use the JBoss Tools Palette (Struts HTML tag library) or hand typing to insert the highlighted line code from below:

```
<%@ taglib uri="/WEB-INF/struts-html.tld" prefix="html" %>
<html:javascript formName="registerFormBean"/>
```

3. Modify the `<html:form>` tag by inserting this attribute:

```
onsubmit="return validateRegisterFormBean(this)"
```

The `registerbody.jsp` should look like this:

```
<%@ taglib uri="/WEB-INF/struts-html.tld" prefix="html" %>
<html:javascript formName="registerFormBean"/>
<table bgcolor="#c0c0c0" border="1" width="100%">
    <tr>
        <th>
        <html:form action="/success.do" onsubmit="return
                                    validateRegisterFormBean(this)">
            Your name:<html:text property="name"/>
            Your zip:<html:text property="zip"/>
            Your e-mail:<html:text property="email"/>
            <html:submit value="Register">
            </html:submit>
        </html:form>
        </th>
    </tr>
</table>
```

Now, save the modifications and run the application (see the *Testing registerStruts application* section discussed earlier in this chapter). Note that if you don't provide valid info, you will get some JavaScript alerts as shown in the following screenshot:

Server-side validation

To successfully accomplish our last task regarding the `registerStruts` application, it is important to make a small effort and clean up (delete or comment) the `registerbody.jsp` page as it was before the *Client-side validation* section. Once you have done that, it is time to activate the server-side validation as shown in the following steps:

1. Re-open the `registerbody.jsp` page.

2. Add an `<html:errors/>` tag before the `<html:form>` tag (type it manually or use the Struts HTML tag library of JBoss Tools Palette).

3. In the **Project Explorer** view, expand the node under **registerStruts | Web Resources | Configuration | default | struts-config.xml | action-mappings** node and right-click on the **/success** node. From the contextual menu, select the **Properties** option.

4. In the **Edit Properties** window, click on the button from the **value** column, next to the **input** row (as shown in the following screenshot). Browse or type the **/pages/register.jsp** path and click **OK**. Click the **Close** button to close the window.

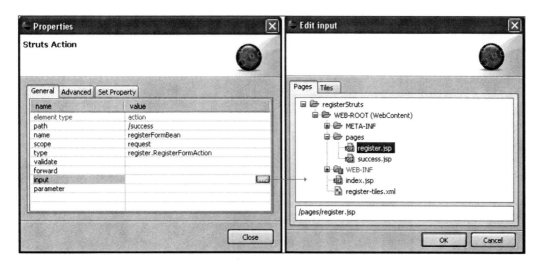

5. Edit the `RegisterFormBean.java` source code.

6. Change the class that it extends from: `org.apache.struts.action.ActionForm` to `org.apache.struts.validator.ValidatorForm`.

7. Put in `/**/` comments the `validate` method.

In the end, the form bean should look like this:

```java
package register;
import javax.servlet.http.HttpServletRequest;
import org.apache.struts.action.ActionMapping;
public class RegisterFormBean extends
 org.apache.struts.validator.ValidatorForm {
    private String name="";
    private String zip="";
    private String email="";
     public RegisterFormBean () {
     }
     public String getName() {
       return name;
    }
    public void setName(String name) {
       this.name = name;
    }
    public String getZip() {
       return zip;
    }
    public void setZip(String zip) {
       this.zip = zip;
    }
    public String getEmail() {
       return email;
    }
    public void setEmail(String email) {
       this.email = email;
    }
    public void reset(ActionMapping actionMapping, HttpServletRequest
request) {
        this.name="";
        this.zip="";
        this.email="";
    }
/*
    public ActionErrors validate(ActionMapping actionMapping,
HttpServletRequest request) {
        ActionErrors errors = new ActionErrors();
        return errors;
    }
*/
}
```

It is the time to test the application once again! Note how the inserted info is validated on server side and how the error messages are exposed to the application's user. The following screenshot represents some captures of errors:

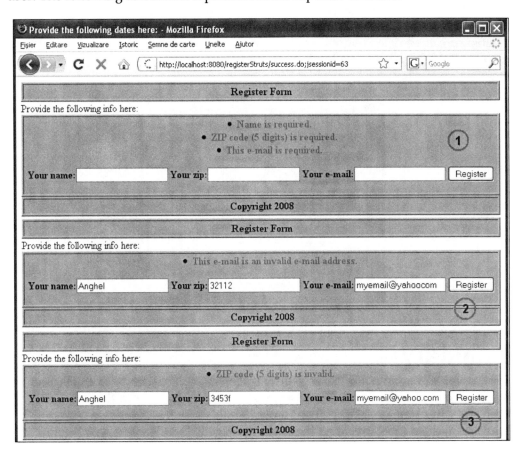

Debugging support for Struts projects

Debugging support for Struts project consists of adding break points for Struts actions and/or pages and then starting the server in debug mode (more details about which are in Chapter 2). For adding a break point, you have to open the struts-config.xml in **Diagram** view, right-click on a Struts action or page and select the **Add Breakpoint** option from the contextual menu (as shown in the following screenshot).

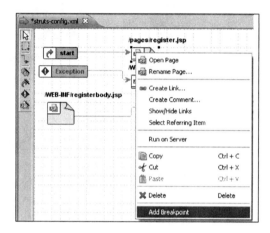

Summary

This chapter was a sample of "how to develop Struts applications with an elegant and modern approach". Struts Tools can prove that in software development, and especially when you are talking about tools, details make the difference between a tool and a super-tool. Revealing the entire power of Struts Tools is now in your hands because complex Struts projects is exactly what Struts Tools takes as its breakfast. Improving your skills in Struts Tools will seriously increase the speed of development, generate a clean and easy-to-maintain source code, and allow you to be more focused on other major aspects of your applications.

6
Seam Tools

In this chapter, you will see how to exploit Seam Tools for developing Seam projects in a visual approach. You will see how to create and configure different kinds of Seam projects, how to use the database reverse engineering technique for developing a Seam application, how to deploy in WAR and EAR formats, and how to run unit tests using TestNG. Before exploring all these goodies, let's see what we are going to develop next.

In this chapter, we will use Seam Tools to accomplish four things. They are as follows:

First step: We will generate a simple Seam application using Seam Tools wizards. Among other things, we will set the Seam runtime, add JSF capabilities, and configure a database for a Seam project. Also, we will deploy and test our first Seam application on JBoss AS.

Second step: This step has, as a main scope, getting you familiar with the Seam Tools wizards used to generate Seam components. We will generate a Seam Action, Form, Entity, and Conversation and you will see how test them on JBoss AS.

Third step: We will run the **TestNG** test for our Seam Action. The test class will be generated by Seam Tools, and all we have to do is to run it and analyze the test output.

Fourth step: Probably the most useful part of Seam Tools is presented in this last step. We will generate a complete Seam application from an existing database using the reverse engineering technique. This feature will help you to develop Seam projects very quickly and easily.

Overview of Seam

We can describe Seam as a lightweight framework for JEE5 that unifies JSF and EJB3 models. Released in 2006, it is based on annotations/EL language and it integrates different technologies, like JSF, Drools, JPA, POJOs, jBPM, AJAX, and so on. Among Seam features (or, why to use Seam?), we mention that (see `http://docs.jboss.org/seam/latest/reference/en-US/html/Book-Preface.html`):

- It defines a uniform component model for all the business logic in your application.

- It does not make a distinction between presentation tier components and business logic components.

- It may simultaneously access state associated with the web request and state held in transactional resources, without the need of manual propagation of the web request state.

- Seam unifies the component models of JSF and EJB3 without extra code. Now, the developer can focus more on business logic, instead of gluing JSF and EJB3.

- SeamJBoss RichFaces and ICEfaces. These solutions let you add AJAX capability without the need to write any JavaScript code.

- Seam provides transparent business process management via jBPM.

- Declarative application state management is made possible by the richness of the context model defined by Seam. Seam extends the context model defined by the servlet specification with two new contexts, conversation, and business process, which are more meaningful from the point of view of the business logic.

- Seam uses bijection, which differs from Inversion of Control in that it is dynamic, contextual, and bidirectional. It is a mechanism for aliasing contextual variables (names in the various contexts bound to the current thread) to attributes of the component. Bijection allows auto-assembly of stateful components by the container. It even allows a component to safely and easily manipulate the value of a context variable, just by assigning it to an attribute of the component.

- Seam applications let the user freely switch between multiple browser tabs, each associated with a different, safely isolated, conversation.

- Seam extends the annotations provided by EJB 3 with a set of annotations for declarative state management and declarative context demarcation. This lets you eliminate the noisy JSF managed bean declarations and reduce the required XML to just that information which truly belongs in XML (the JSF navigation rules).

- Seam provides for testability of Seam applications as a core feature of the framework. You can easily write JUnit or TestNG tests that reproduce a whole interaction with a user, exercising all components of the system apart from the view (the JSP or Facelets page).

Every single bullet from above can be the subject of a tutorial and requires a strong programming background in JEE5 and related technologies. Obviously, these features sound more like a TV commercial and are meant to make you curious regarding Seam's performances. After you read them, you may say that Seam is "too good to be true". Well, there is only one way to find out: develop your next web project using Seam! And, to maximize productivity, try JBoss Seam Tools over Seam framework. You will be amazed as to how easily you can develop complex JEE5 applications.

Preparations

There are two important software requirements that you should satisfy, as follows:

- *Download and install Seam runtime* (as shown in the following screenshot):

  Before starting, it is important to check if you have a Seam runtime installed on your computer (`jboss-seam.zip` archive is representative for Seam distributions). If you don't have a Seam distribution, then you should download one from the `http://seamframework.org/Download` link (for this chapter, it is recommended to download the JBoss Seam 2.1 distribution).

Seam Releases

Package	Version	Category	Size	Released	License		
JBoss Seam 2.1	2.1.1.GA	Production	106 MB	22.12.2008	LGPL	Notes	Download
JBoss Seam 2.1	2.1.0.SP1	Production	102 MB	29.10.2008	LGPL	Notes	Download
JBoss Seam 2.0	2.0.3.CR1	Preproduction	84 MB	13.06.2008	LGPL	Notes	Download
JBoss Seam 2.0	2.0.2.SP1	Production	84 MB	28.05.2008	LGPL	Notes	Download
JBoss Seam 1.2	1.2.1 GA	Production	73 MB	27.03.2007	LGPL	Notes	Download

After downloading, extract the archive in your favorite place and keep this location in mind for later use.

- *Download and install PostgreSQL:*

  For this chapter, you will also need the PostgreSQL RDBMS. This can be downloaded from `http://www.postgresql.org/download/`. After download, you can install it by following the provided setup.

  In addition to this, create an empty database named `accounts` using the following SQL statement (this database will be used later in this chapter):

  ```
  create database accounts;
  ```

Creating a new Seam project

In this section, we will develop a Seam project stub. Actually, this project will be the simplest functional application that Seam Tools can generate in just a few steps. Once we finish developing this application, we will continue by adding to it a set of Seam components. The main scope of this section is to get you familiar with Seam Tools wizards dedicated to developing from scratch Seam projects and components.

Creating a Seam project is a multi-step process as follows:

1. From the **File** main menu, select the **New | Other** option.

2. In the **New** window, expand the **Seam** node and select the **Seam Web Project** leaf (as shown in the following screenshot). Click on the **Next** button.

3. Now, the **New Seam Project** wizard is available (as shown in the following screenshot). Here, you can specify the project name (**Project name** field), the project location (use the **Browse** button to select a new location if you don't agree with the default one), the runtime (**Target Runtime** field) used for building and compiling the application, and the server where the application will be deployed (**Target Server** field). Finally, you have to select one of the predefined configurations (**Configurations** field). Depending

on Seam runtime version (1.2 or 2), you can choose between two types of configurations. In the following screenshot, you can see an example of how we filled-up the **New Seam Project** wizard at this step (click on the **Next** button).

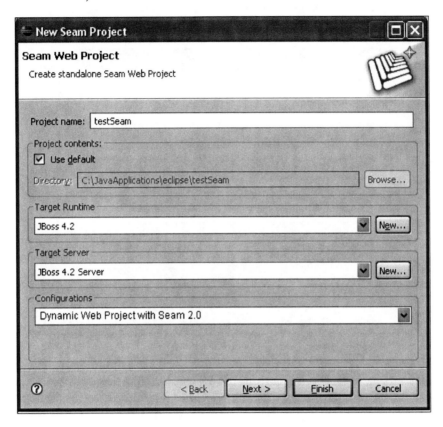

 If you don't have a compatible target runtime and/or a target server, you can see how to install and configure them in Chapter 2, *JBoss AS Tools*.

4. At this step, you should configure the web module settings. Note that all the fields are pre-filled with the default values for our project. Most of the time these settings are very convenient, therefore leave everything unchanged and click on the **Next** button. Nevertheless, it is a good practice to check every time whether the **Generate Deployment Descriptor** is selected (as shown in the following screenshot):

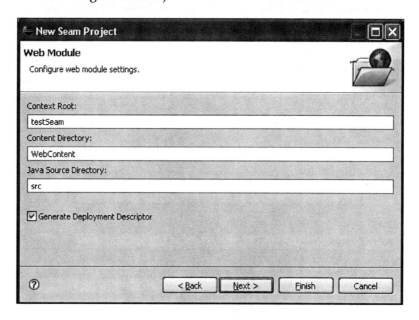

5. It is time to add JSF capabilities to our project! You should leave everything set to its defaults (**Server Supplied JSF Implementation** radio checked) because JBoss AS provides its own JSF implementation and we will be using that for this project. If you have a project where your application server does not provide a default JSF implementation, then you have to explicitly specify one. For this, you should select the lower radio button and click on the **New** button (as shown in the following screenshot). This action will open the **Create JSF Implementation Library** window, where you can easily add the JARs of your JSF implementation by using the **Add** button (as shown in the following screenshot). The last option allows us to edit a path for the JSF configuration file, a name for the JSF servlet, the JSF servlet classname. It also changes the URL mapping patterns. At the end, click on the **Next** button.

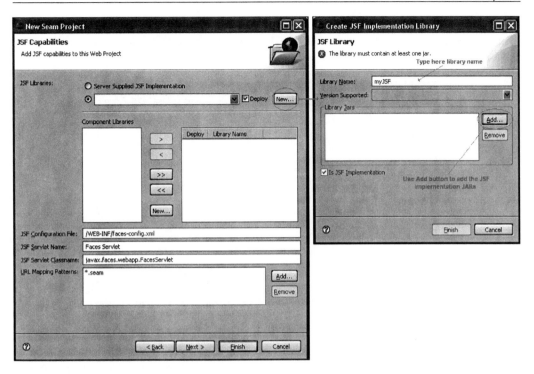

6. This step is the last and most complex in creating a Seam project stub. The current window is made of three sections, namely:

- General section
- Database section
- Code Generation section.

General section

The **General** section allows us to point a Seam runtime by indicating the Seam home folder and by selecting the deploy type (WAR or EAR). For pointing a Seam runtime, you should start by clicking on the **Add** button, next to the **Seam Runtime** field.

This button will open the window as shown in the next screenshot. Here, you should specify a name for the new Seam runtime (**Name** field), its home folder (**Home Folder** field), and its version (**Version** field). Remember that, at the start of this chapter, you have downloaded and installed a Seam 2.0 distribution. The folder where you have unzipped the Seam 2.0 distribution is the **Home Folder** that should be selected for the new runtime by using the **Browse** button from the right.

The **Name** will reflect this folder name (but you can change it by typing a new one) and the version should be automatically detected. When everything is set, click on the **Finish** button.

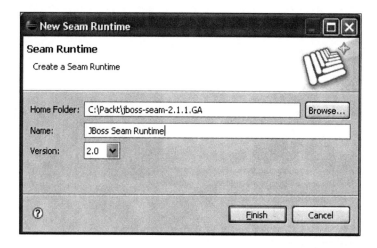

Now that you have a Seam runtime, it is time to select a **WAR** or **EAR** deployment type by checking the corresponding radio button. When you make this choice, it is important to know that EAR projects support EJB 3.0 and require Java Enterprise 5 and WAR doesn't support EJB 3.0, but may be deployed to a J2EE environment. We have selected the **WAR** because it is easy to understand and more popular, but you may also select **EAR** because JBoss AS 4.2 supports EJB 3.0.

At this point, the **General** field is ready and should look like the following:

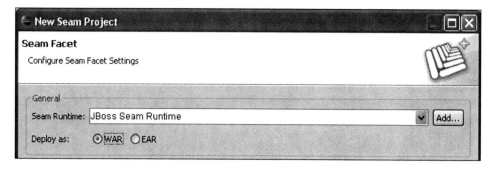

Database section

Next, you should select a database type, which will be used by Seam as a persistent storage for Seam entities. This can be any database type that is available in the **Database Type** list. In this chapter, we will use a PostgreSQL database, so for testing purposes it is recommended to have a PostgreSQL distribution installed on your machine. If you choose to use another database type, then, in the next steps, just adjust the connection/driver information accordingly. Note that the base structure of the next steps is not affected by the database type selection. Select the **PostgreSQL** option in the **Database Type** field.

We continue by configuring a connection profile, which means that we will indicate the RDBMS type, JDBC drivers, database name, database credentials, and so on. Therefore, focus on the **New Connection Profile** field. To start, click on the **New** button, near this field. In this wizard's page, select the **PostgreSQL** connection profile and type a name and a description for it. Click on the **Next** button (screenshot shown below).

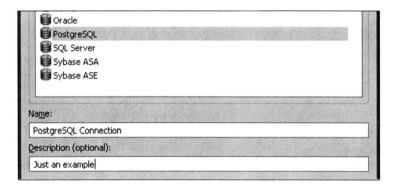

It is time to delve deeper and to configure some details for the connection profile. We will start by indicating the connection driver definition. Since we are here for the first time, the **Drivers** list is empty. Therefore, click on the **New Driver Definition** button (as shown in the following screenshot).

Clicking on the **New Driver Definition** button will open the wizard's page responsible for driver name, location, and properties. Select the **Name/Type** tab and expand the **Database** node (this node will reveal a set of driver templates). From the available templates, select the **PostgreSQL JDBC Driver** type. In the **Driver** name field, type something suggestive like, **My PostgreSQL Driver**.

Next, switch to the **Jar List** tab. Here, we have to indicate the driver's JARs/ZIPs physical location. Start by clicking on the **Add JAR/Zip** button and navigate to the corresponding JARs/ZIPs. For PostgreSQL, the drivers are found in the {PostgreSQL_HOME}/jdbc/ directory. In our example, we have used the driver selected in the screenshot below:

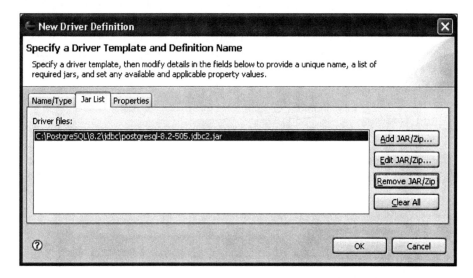

Finally, switch to the **Properties** tab. Here, we have to specify the connection's details like connection URL, database name, and database login credentials. These dates are provided in the **Properties** table (as shown in the next screenshot). In our example, the database URL is **jdbc:postgresql:accounts**, the database name is **accounts**, and the login credentials are **postgres** (user) and **_my_pass** (password). Click on the **OK** button.

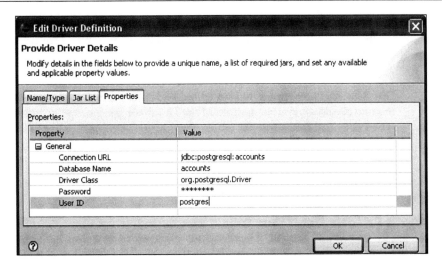

Now, close all wizard's pages—by pressing the **OK** button—until the **New JDBC Connection Profile** page. In this page, click on the **Test Connection** button to see if everything was configured correctly (don't forget to start the PostgreSQL server). If you get a **Ping succeeded!** message, then the connection works fine and it's time to click on the **Finish** button (as shown in the following screenshot).

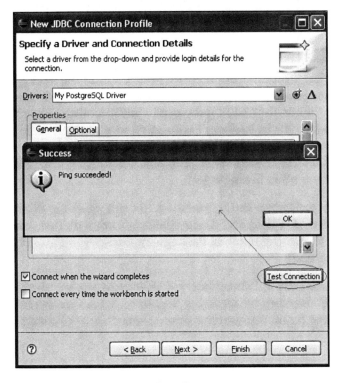

Now, you have a connection profile under *PostgreSQL Connection* name. Select it as your current profile connection. Note that you can easily access it and modify it by clicking on the **Edit** button, near the **New** button.

 Our database, accounts, has no tables, and thus we don't select any of the two checkboxes at the bottom of the **Database** section. Nevertheless, when your databases contain tables, don't forget to select/deselect these checkboxes according to your needs.

Code Generation section

As you can see, the **Code Generation** section was automatically filled with the default values for our Seam project. These values were auto-detected by Seam Tools based on our previous selections. You can leave them exactly as they are or you can choose to change them according to your needs. Since these are just the names of packages, you can change them as you want, as long as you respect the Java package names syntax. When you are pleased, just click on the **Finish** button.

Now, a progress bar will monitor the creation process and in the end, a new Seam project named testSeam is ready to take shape. You can see it in the **Package Explorer** view of the **Seam** perspective that was automatically activated.

Test testSeam project

Note that the project structure contains two node-roots in the **Package Explorer** view, named testSeam (contains the project files) and testSeam-test (contains TestNG tests). In the case of EAR deployment, the structure of testSeam project will have four node-roots in **Package Explorer** view, named testSeam (contains the project files), testSeam-ear (contains EAR specific files), testSeam-ejb (contains EJB specific files), and testSeam-test (contains TestNG test). You can extrapolate this structure for any other Seam project.

At this point, the application can be executed. For this, start the *JBoss 4.2 Server* server (do this from **JBoss AS View**) and deploy the application on this server (do this by right-clicking on the project name in **Package Explorer** view and selecting **Run As | Run On Server** option).

The application will start in Eclipse Internal Web Browser, but you also may open it in your own web browser by accessing the http://localhost:8080/testSeam/ URL. The following figure represents a screenshot of the application running inside Eclipse:

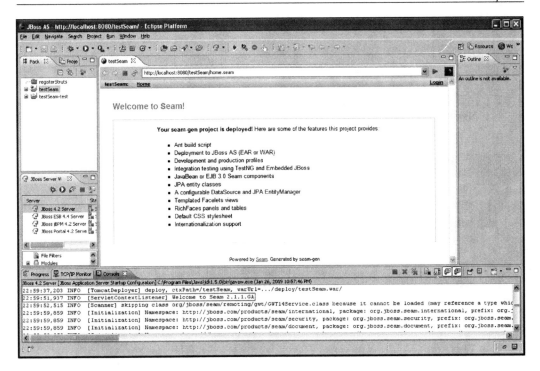

Congratulations! You have successfully finished and tested your first Seam application using Seam Tools.

Note that the base Seam application contains a **Login** option. Actually, the project wizard does not only create the login, it also connects the login to a business object in your root package called simply `Authenticator.java`. This can be very useful because you can write your login validation in `Authenticator.java` and depending on whether it is successful or not, return true or false.

Creating Seam components

As you know, a Seam application flow is made of different components, such as **Seam Action, Seam Form, Seam Conversation**, and **Seam Entity**. As you are a Seam developer, there is no need to tell you what these components do or how to put them together into an application, but we can show you how to create them through Seam Tools. Now that we have the `testSeam` application, it can serve as a "container" for the components stubs generated in the next sections. Therefore, you will see how to generate stubs for a **Seam Action**, a **Seam Form**, a **Seam Conversation**, and a **Seam Entity** without manually touching the source code. Once you know how to generate these stubs, you are free to exploit your Seam knowledge to create your own Seam projects.

Creating a Seam Action

Creating a **Seam Action** can be done like this:

1. Be sure that the **Seam** perspective is the current perspective.

2. In the **Package Explorer** view, right-click on the project name and select the **New | Seam Action** option from the contextual menu.

3. In the **New Seam Action** window, you have to specify names for Seam component, POJO class, method, and page. Also, you can specify a project name or a package name using the **Browse** buttons. When you type the Seam component name, fields below it will be automatically filled for the **POJO class name**, **method name**, and **page name**. You can modify these names as you like and click on the **Finish** button. The following screenshot is an example of how to configure a Seam action:

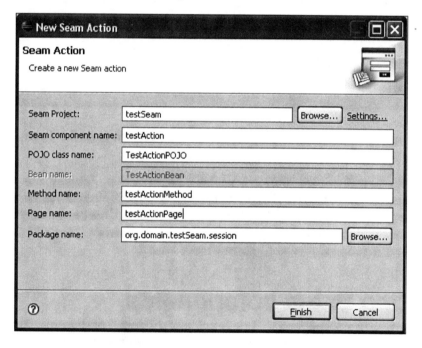

After you click on the **Finish** button, the new Seam action is created and the POJO component source code is listed in the editor:

```
package org.domain.testSeam.session;

import org.jboss.seam.annotations.Name;

@Name("testAction")
public class TestActionPOJO
{
    @Logger private Log log;

    @In StatusMessages statusMessages;

    public void testActionMethod()
    {
        // implement your business logic here
        log.info("testAction.testActionMethod() action called");
        statusMessages.add("testActionMethod");
    }

    // add additional action methods

}
```

The Seam action main page is named `testActionPage.xhtml` and you can find it in the **WebContent** directory of the project. If you double-click on it, you will see the following page in the **JBoss Tools HTML Editor**:

```
<!DOCTYPE composition PUBLIC "-//W3C//DTD XHTML 1.0 Transitional//EN"
    "http://www.w3.org/TR/xhtml1/DTD/xhtml1-transitional.dtd">
<ui:composition xmlns="http://www.w3.org/1999/xhtml"
    xmlns:s="http://jboss.com/products/seam/taglib"
    xmlns:ui="http://java.sun.com/jsf/facelets"
    xmlns:f="http://java.sun.com/jsf/core"
    xmlns:h="http://java.sun.com/jsf/html"
    xmlns:rich="http://richfaces.org/rich"
    xmlns:a="http://richfaces.org/a4j"
    template="layout/template.xhtml">

<ui:define name="body">
```

Running the Seam Action is a simple task that can be accomplished by right-clicking on the **testActionPage.xhtml** node (in **Package Explorer** view) and selecting the **Run As | Run On Server** option. Note that you don't need to restart the server because the Seam action was hot-deployed. The following figure is a screenshot of what you should see in the internal browser of Eclipse:

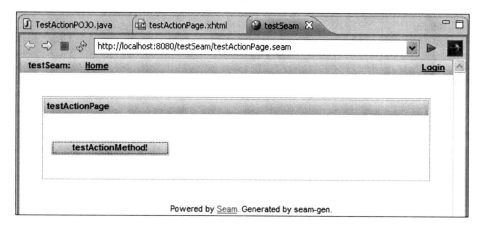

Creating a Seam Form

Creating a Seam Form can be done like this:

1. Be sure that the **Seam** perspective is the current perspective.

2. In the **Package Explorer** view, right-click on the project name and select the **New | Seam Form** option from the contextual menu.

3. In the **New Seam Form** window, you have to specify names for Seam component, POJO class, and page. Also, you can specify a project name and/or a package name using the **Browse** buttons. When you type the Seam component name, the fields below it will be automatically filled for the POJO class name, method name, and page name. You can modify these names as you like before completing by clicking on the **Finish** button. The following screenshot is an example of how to configure a Seam form:

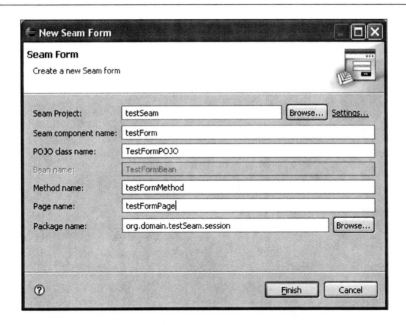

After you click on the **Finish** button, the new Seam Form is created and the POJO component source code is listed in the editor (as shown in the following screenshot).

```java
package org.domain.testSeam.session;

import org.jboss.seam.annotations.Name;

@Name("testForm")
public class TestFormPOJO
{
    @Logger private Log log;

    @In StatusMessages statusMessages;

    private String value;

    public void testFormMethod()
    {
        // implement your business logic here
        log.info("testForm.testFormMethod() action called with: #{testForm.value}");
        statusMessages.add("testFormMethod #{testForm.value}");
    }

    // add additional action methods
    @Length(max = 10)
    public String getValue()
    {
        return value;
    }

    public void setValue(String value)
    {
        this.value = value;
    }
}
```

The Seam Form main page is named `testFormPage.xhtml` and you can find it in the **WebContent** directory of the project (by default, the Form contains only one field). If you double-click on it, you will see this page in the **JBoss Tools HTML Editor** (as shown in the following screenshot):

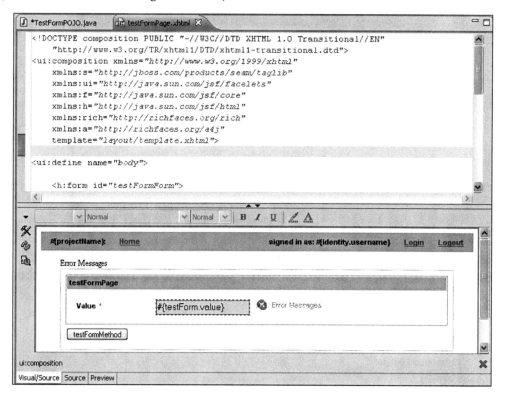

Running the Seam Form is a simple task that can be accomplished by right-clicking on the **testFormPage.xhtml** node (in **Package Explorer** view) and selecting the **Run As | Run On Server** option. Note that you don't need to restart the server because the Seam Form was hot-deployed. Next, is a screenshot of what you should see in the internal browser of Eclipse:

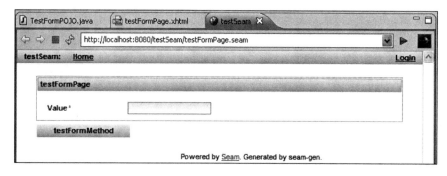

Creating a Seam Conversation

Creating a **Seam Conversation** can be done like this:

1. Be sure that the **Seam** perspective is the current perspective.

2. In the **Package Explorer** view, right-click on the project name and select the **New | Seam Conversation** option from the contextual menu.

3. In the **New Seam Conversation** window, you have to specify names for Seam component, POJO class, method, and page. You can also specify a project name and/or a package name using the **Browse** buttons. When you type the **Seam component name**, the fields below will be automatically filled for the **POJO class name**, **method name**, and **page name**. You can modify these names as you like and click on the **Finish** button. Following is an example of how to configure a Seam Conversation:

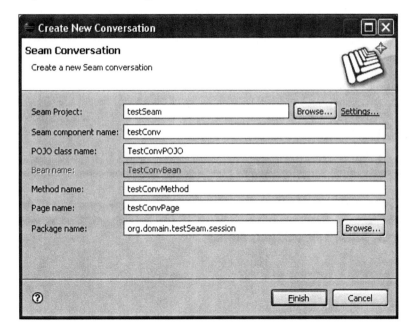

After you click on the **Finish** button, the new Seam Conversation is created and the POJO component source code is listed in the editor (as shown in the following screenshot).

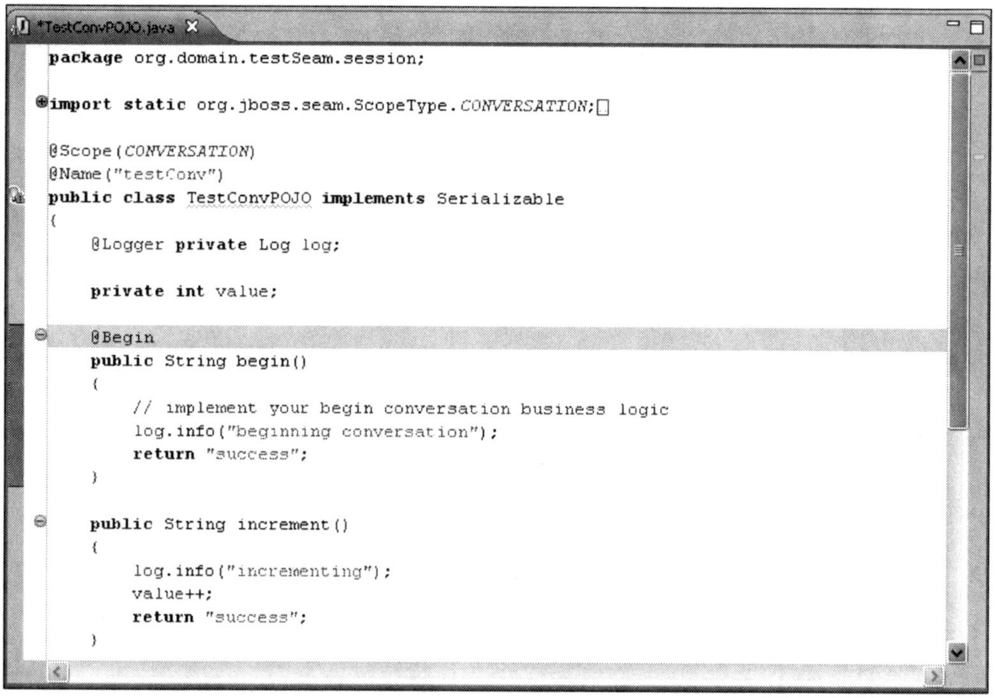

```java
package org.domain.testSeam.session;

import static org.jboss.seam.ScopeType.CONVERSATION;

@Scope(CONVERSATION)
@Name("testConv")
public class TestConvPOJO implements Serializable
{
    @Logger private Log log;

    private int value;

    @Begin
    public String begin()
    {
        // implement your begin conversation business logic
        log.info("beginning conversation");
        return "success";
    }

    public String increment()
    {
        log.info("incrementing");
        value++;
        return "success";
    }
```

The Seam Conversation main page is named `testConvPage.xhtml` and you can find it in the **WebContent** directory of the project. If you double-click on it, you will see this page in the **JBoss Tools HTML Editor**:

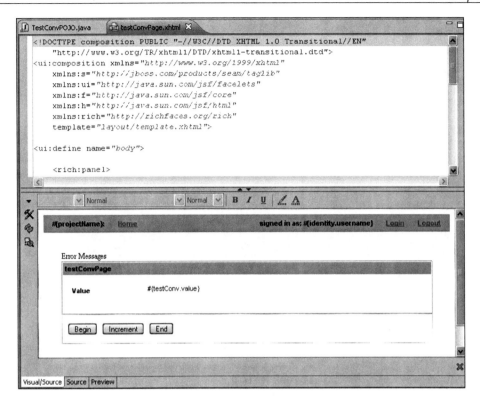

Running the Seam Conversation is a simple task that can be accomplished by right-clicking on the **testConvPage.xhtml** node (in **Package Explorer** view) and selecting the **Run As | Run On Server** option. Note that you don't need to restart the server because the Seam conversation was hot-deployed. Following is a screenshot of what you should see in the internal browser of Eclipse (use the **Increment** button to increment the value):

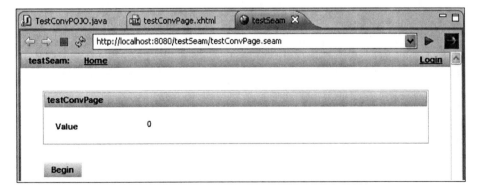

Creating a Seam Entity

Creating a **Seam Entity** can be done like this:

1. Be sure that the **Seam** perspective is the current perspective.

2. In the **Package Explorer** view, right-click on the project name and select the **New | Seam Entity** option from the contextual menu.

3. In the **New Seam Entity** window, you should provide a name for the entity class (**Seam entity class name** field), for a master page (**Master page name** field), and for a page (**Page name** field). Also, you may specify a package name and/or a project name by using the corresponding **Browse** button or hand typing. Following is an example of how to configure a Seam entity:

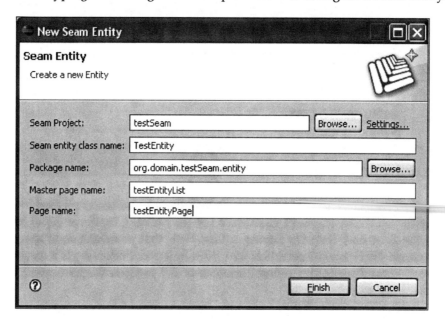

 By default, the name of the table associated with the entity will be exactly the same as the **Seam Entity** class name (some RDBMS, like PostgreSQL, will convert this name in lowercase). For example, in our case the table name will be `testentity`.

If everything is ok, you should see in the **JBoss Tools HTML Editor** the `testEntityPage.xhtml` page (as shown in the following screenshot). This page and the master page (`testEntityList.xhtml`) can be found in the **WebContent** folder of the `testSeam` project.

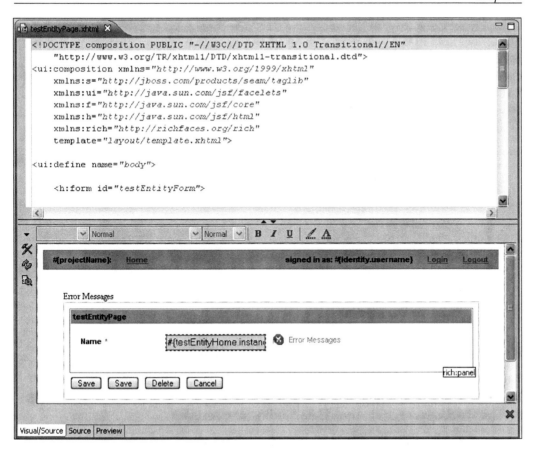

Running the Seam Entity is a simple task that can be accomplished by right-clicking on the **testEntityPage.xhtml** node (in **Package Explorer** view) and selecting the **Run As | Run On Server** option (this time it is recommended to restart the server, because, normally, entities aren't hot-deployed). Following is a screenshot of what you should see in the internal browser of Eclipse:

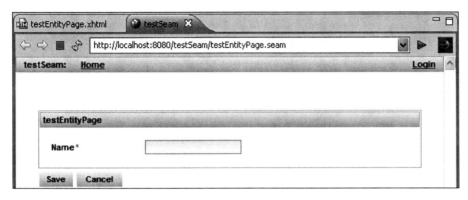

Now, create three rows in the `accounts` database (`testentity` table) by using the **Name** text field of the `testEntityPage.xhtml` page (for example, insert the names **Mike**, **Susan**, and **Tom**). For maintaining every person's name, you should press the **Save** and **Cancel** buttons after each one is typed. Also, use the **Create testEntity** button to create a new row, after a row is persisted. When a row is successfully created, you should see something like this:

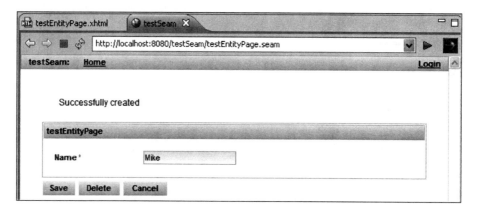

If you want, you can delete a record by clicking on the **Delete** button.

After you close the internal browser of Eclipse, you can see the table with the inserted dates by following the next steps (of course, you also can use a specialized tool for databases, such as Aqua Data Studio, for example):

1. Select the **Database Development** perspective.

2. In the **Data Source Explorer** view, right-click on the **PostgreSQL Connection** node and select the **Connect** option from the contextual menu.

3. After the connection is successfully done, expand the **accounts | Catalogs | accounts | Schemas | public | Tables** node.

4. Right-click on the **testentity** node and select **Data | Edit** from the contextual menu.

You should see a new tab named **testentity** (screenshot shown below). This is a data editor that can be used to modify the existing table rows or to add/delete rows:

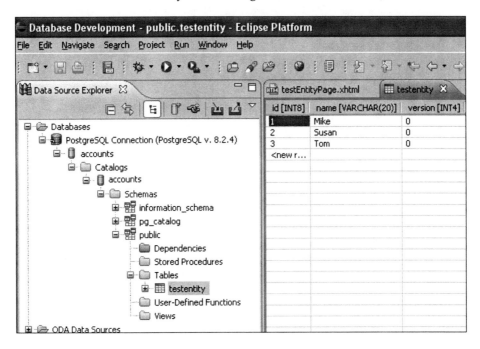

Seam views

In this section, we will discuss the **Seam Components** view and the **Project Explorer** view. Both of them can help us with important information while we develop Seam projects.

Seam Components view

This view is available by default in the Seam perspective and, as the name suggests, it displays a list of Seam Components. For example, if you select the testSeam project in the **Package Explorer** view, you can see that in the **Seam Components** view, a tree of components that belongs to this project appears.

It is shown in the following screenshot:

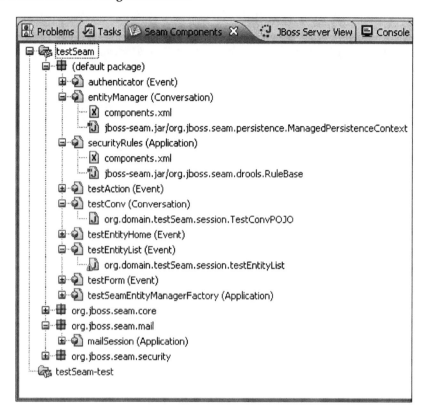

Project Explorer view

Project Explorer is a view that is activated by default when you choose **Seam** perspective as the current perspective. It can be used as an alternative to the **Seam Components** view. In the next screenshot, you can see the testSeam project in the **Project Explorer** view:

Using TestNG for Seam projects

As you have seen earlier, when creating a new Seam project, a project named
`{seam_project_name}-test` (for WAR and EAR formats) appears in the **Package Explorer** view. This project was configured, by default, to run TestNG against the corresponding libraries and server runtime libraries.

 Before any tests, check that the TestNG plug-in for Eclipse is installed on your Eclipse distribution. If you don't have it, you should install it. Go to `http://testng.org/doc/download.html` and follow the installation guide.

Starting a test can be done by following these steps:

1. In the **Package Explorer** view, extend the **testSeam-test | test-src | org.domain.testSeam.test** node.

2. Right-click on the **TestActionPOJOTest.java** node and select **Run As | TestNG test** option from the contextual menu (screenshot shown below).

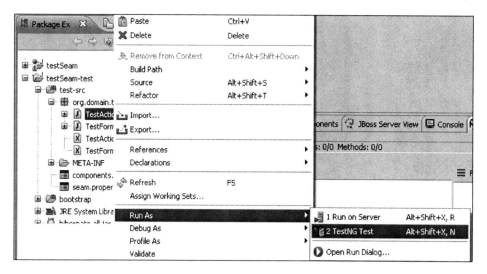

Now, the test will start running. Take a look in the **Console** view to see the test log (as shown in the following screenshot).

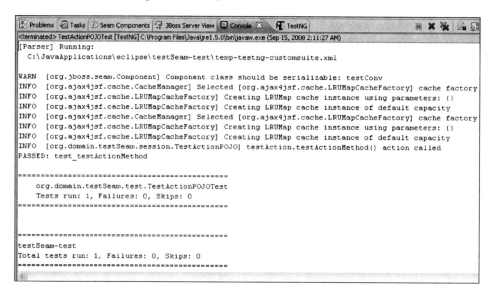

Also, take a look at the **TestNG** view:

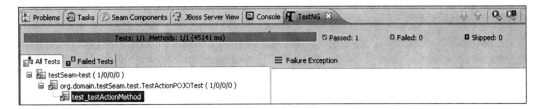

The test output can be seen by expanding the **testSeam-test | test-output** node in the **Package Explorer** view (if you don't see this node click on the *F5* key to refresh the **Package Explorer** view content). Double-click on the **index.html** node:

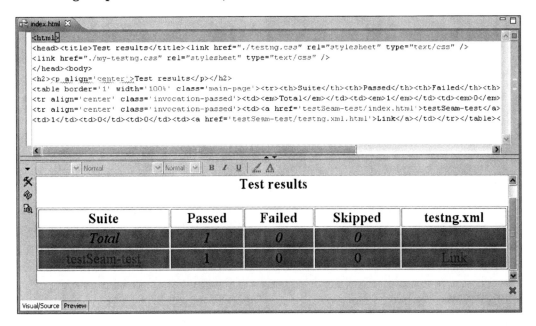

If you want to see more details about the TestNG test, you can open `index.html` in a web browser and follow the links from the page.

If your test does not run and you get a *Bad version number…* error then try to switch from Java 6 to Java 5 and repeat the test.

Generating a Seam project from an existing database

A great facility of Seam Tools is generating a Seam project from an existing database. Practically, Seam Tools will generate a CRUD web application based on the indicated database (CRUD is the acronym for the four basic types of SQL statements: Create, Read, Update, Delete). In this section you will see how to accomplish this goal, but to start with, we have to increase the complexity of the example and, for this, we will add a new table in the `accounts` database.

At this point, the `accounts` database should have a single table, named `testentity`. Next, you should create a new table by running the following SQL commands:

```
CREATE TABLE "public"."details" (
    "id" int NOT NULL,
    "fid" int NOT NULL,
    "email" varchar(25) NULL,
    "pass"    varchar(25) NULL,
    "zip" varchar(25) NULL,
    PRIMARY KEY("id"))
ALTER TABLE "public"."details"
    ADD CONSTRAINT "fid"
    FOREIGN KEY("fid")
    REFERENCES "public"."testentity"("id")
```

This command will create the `details` table, which is related to the `testentity` table through the `fid` foreign key. In the `testentity` table, we keep people's names (`name` column); in the details table we will keep some details for each person's name: email (email column), password (pass column), and zip code (zip column). It is a simple database, similar to those that you have probably used many times in your projects!

Now, it is time to see how to generate a Seam project for the `accounts` database. For this, you have to follow these steps:

1. Create a new project by following the steps 1-6 from the Creating a new Seam project section. At step 3, specify another name for the new project (for example, `generateSeam`). At step 6 you don't need to recreate the *JBoss Seam Runtime* Seam runtime and the *PostgreSQL Connection* connection profile, since they already exist.

2. Launch the **Database Development** perspective.

3. In the **Data Source Explorer** view, expand the **Databases** node.

4. Under the **Databases** node, you should see a leaf named **PostgreSQL Connection**. Right-click on it and select the **Connect** option from the contextual menu (screenshot shown below).

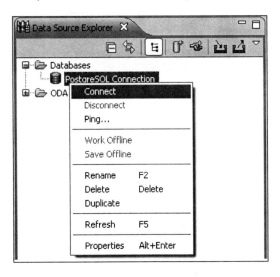

5. In the **Properties** window, just click on the **OK** button and wait for the connection to be established. If everything is ok, the **Data Source Explorer** view should look like the following:

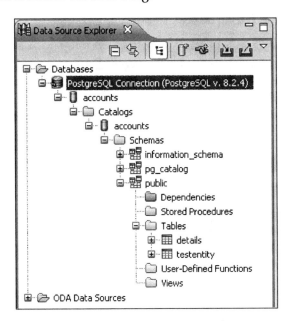

6. Go back to the **Seam** perspective.

7. In the **Package Explorer** view, right-click on the project name (project node) and select the **New | Seam Generate Entities** option from the contextual menu. You should see the **Generate Seam Entities** window as shown in the following screenshot:

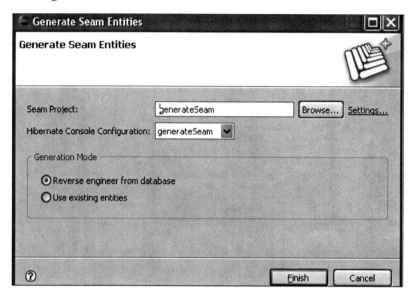

8. Just click on the **Finish** button, without any changes.

After a few seconds, you should see that the new XHTML pages and Java sources were created. You can find them under the **WebContent** and **src/model** nodes in the **Package Explorer** view. For example, in the **WebContent** node, you have the **DetailsList.xhtml** node and in the **src/model** node, you have the **Details.java** node. For a better understanding, take your time and explore all the generated files.

Running the generated Seam application (generateSeam)

At this point, the generated application can be executed. For this, start the *JBoss 4.2 Server* server (do this from **JBoss AS View**) and deploy the application on this server (do this by right-clicking on the project name in **Package Explorer** view and selecting the **Run As | Run On Server** option).

The application will start in the **Eclipse Internal Web Browser**, but you can also open it in your own web browser by accessing the `http://localhost:8080/generateSeam/` URL. The following screenshot represents the start page of the application:

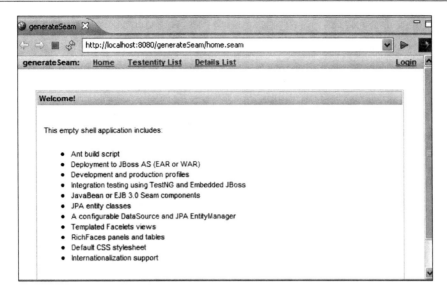

Start by clicking on the **Testentity List** link to display a table with the person's names that are in the `testentity` table (remember that in the section *Creating a Seam Entity* we have inserted in this table three names: **Mike**, **Susan**, and **Tom**). As you can see from the next screenshot, this page contains a table with the three names and also contains a search field for helping us to find a person by his/her name in an easy manner:

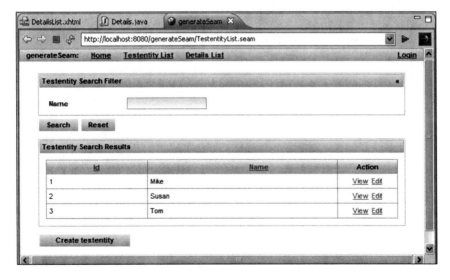

From this point forward, follow your intuition and navigate through the application's pages. Try to get familiar with the common operations such as, search, insert, delete, and so on.

Modify Seam preferences

You can modify Seam preferences during the development of Seam projects by following these steps:

1. From the Eclipse **Window** main menu, select the **Preferences** option.

2. In the **Preferences** window, left panel, expand the **JBoss Tools | Web | Seam** node. If you click on the **Seam** node, you will see the window shown in the following screenshot (from here you can **add/edit/remove** a Seam runtime).

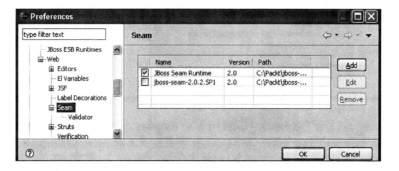

3. If you click on the **Validator** leaf (under **Seam** node), you will see a window as shown in the following screenshot (from here, you can modify the severity level for different problems).

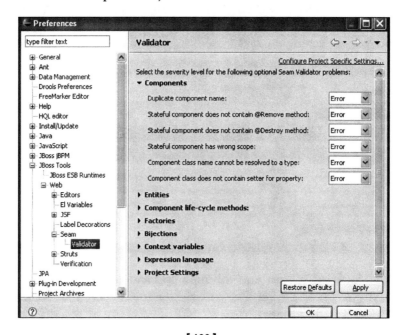

Another set of preferences can be modified by following these steps:

1. In the **Project Explorer** view, right-click on a Seam project node (**testSeam**, for example) and select the **Properties** option from the contextual menu.

2. In the **Properties** window, left panel, click on the **Seam Settings** node (as shown in the following screenshot).

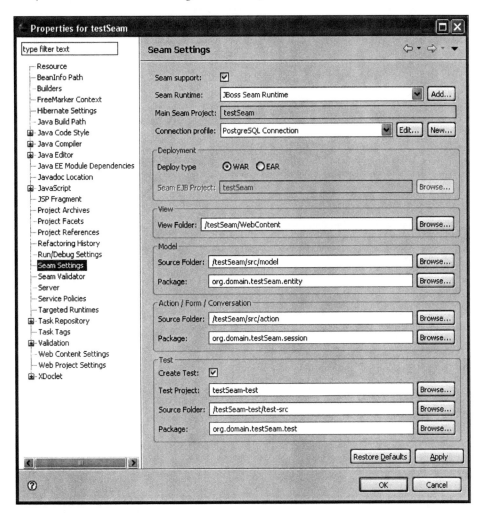

You should recognize all the sections of this window, so no details are needed.

Summary

In this chapter, you have seen how to use Seam Tools for creating complete Seam projects. We have discussed Seam components (Seam Action, Seam Form, Seam Entity, and Seam Conversation), Seam projects deployment (WAR/EAR), TestNG over Seam projects, and reverse engineering for generating Seam applications from existing databases. It is now up to you to explore and exploit Seam Tools in your software production process.

7
Hibernate Tools

In this chapter, we will discuss the most complete tool-set dedicated to the most powerful object/relational persistence and query service. Yes! ... we will be talking about the Hibernate Tools for the Hibernate 3 framework (`http://www.hibernate.org/`).

Hibernate Tools will guide you through the development process of Hibernate projects and help you to create Hibernate configuration files, create mapping files, speed up the development process by code generation (including DAO classes), run Ant tasks, visualize the Hibernate entities in a diagram manner, take advantage of reverse engineering technique, write HQL statements, and so on. Hibernate Tools will help us to implement the Hibernate layer with a minimum amount of effort and time, even when the database's architecture is very complex and difficult to manage.

In the following sections we will use Hibernate Tools to develop a set of Hibernate artifacts that are usually present in any web application that uses the Hibernate framework. Therefore, among other futures, you will see how to:

- Create a Hibernate Mapping file (`.hbm.xml`)
- Create a Hibernate Configuration file
- Use reverse engineering and code generation techniques
- Execute HQL statements in a visual approach
- Generate a `reveng.xml` document
- Use Hibernate Tools for Ant.

Overview of Hibernate

For a start, let's have a short overview about Hibernate's main characteristics and features.

It seems that these days you are not a complete Java developer until you try Hibernate. Most of the time it is love at first sight; Hibernate will gain your trust right from the start. It is as robust as a tank, as fast as a cobra, solves problems that you didn't even think about, and is very modest. This is the essence of the answer that you will get from all of the Hibernate users to the question, "How do you define Hibernate?" To be more technical, Hibernate is an **Object-Relational Mapping (ORM)** library for the Java language, providing a framework for mapping an object-oriented domain model to a traditional relational database. From the Hibernate particularities and facilities, we mention that:

- The main scope of Hibernate is in mapping from Java classes to database tables (and from Java data types to SQL data types).

- Hibernate provides data query and retrieval facilities.

- Hibernate is the mapping of Java classes to the database table through an XML configuration file or by using Java annotation.

- Hibernate supports one-to-many and many-to-many relationships between classes.

- Hibernate supports the mapping of custom value types.

- Hibernate provides transparent persistence for **Plain Old Java Objects (POJOs)**.

- Hibernate provides its own SQL language, called **Hibernate Query Language (HQL)**. It allows SQL-like queries to be written against Hibernate's data objects.

- Hibernate provides an alternative to HQL, named **Hibernate Criteria Queries**.

- Hibernate can be used in standalone Java applications and Java EE.

- Hibernate provides a set of tools that provide Ant tasks and Eclipse plug-ins for performing reverse engineering, code generation, visualization, and interaction with Hibernate. These tools are known as Hibernate Tools, and can be downloaded as a standalone tool-set or integrated in JBoss Tools.

- Hibernate is based on a model known as the **Hibernate Meta Model (HMM)**. Hibernate Meta Models contain information about tables, columns, classes, etc. and are used by the Hibernate Core to perform its object-relational mapping. The start point is `org.hibernate.mapping.Configuration` class.

The model represented by this class and supported by Hibernate Tools can be created in the following four different ways:

- ○ **Core Configuration** (uses Hibernate Core)—known as **core** in Eclipse and `<configuration>` in Ant, requires a `hibernate.cfg.xml` file, and supports reading `.hbm.xml` files.

- ○ **Annotation Configuration** (uses Hibernate Annotations)—known as **annotations** in Eclipse and `<annotationconfiguration>` in Ant, requires a `hibernate.cfg.xml` file, and supports `.hbm.xml` files and annotated classes.

- ○ **JPA Configuration** (uses Hibernate Entity Manager)—known as **JPA** in Eclipse and `<jpaconfiguration>` in Ant, requires a `META-INF/persistence.xml` file, and supports `.hbm.xml` and annotated classes.

- ○ **JDBC Configuration** (uses Hibernate Tools reverse engineering)—used by Eclipse/Ant for reverse engineering tasks based on a JDBC connection (in Ant, it is known as `<jdbcconfiguration>`). It needs reverse engineering files (`reveng.xml`) and JDBC metadata.

Obviously, this brief overview won't help very much without a dedicated technical tutorial. You can start from the `http://www.hibernate.org/5.html` address. Here, you will find detailed documentation for Hibernate Core for Java, Hibernate Annotations, Hibernate Validator, Hibernate Tools, and so on.

Preparations

For proving the power of Hibernate Tools (for Eclipse and Ant), we will build a set of examples based on a real situation. From these examples, you can easily extrapolate to other tasks, configurations, and application goals. For this, we will need some preparations, like an RDBMS, a database ready to be used, and an Eclipse Java project (J2SE, J2EE, Dynamic Web Project, and so on). Let's assume:

- You have a Java project named `testHibernate` (since we use this project only as a support for a Hibernate project, you can choose any type of Java project you like, but for compatibility with our examples, it is recommended to choose an empty **Dynamic Web Project**).

- You have PostgreSQL running on port 5432 (or other RDBMS, like MySQL for example).

- You have a database named `family`, with two tables (`Child` and `Parent`), created with the following SQL statement:

```sql
CREATE TABLE "public"."parent" (
    "id" int NOT NULL,
    "parent_name" varchar(25) NOT NULL,
    "parent_surname"varchar(25) NOT NULL,
    PRIMARY KEY("id")
)
CREATE TABLE "public"."child" (
    "id"        int NOT NULL,
    "fid"       int NOT NULL,
    "child_name" varchar(25) NOT NULL,
    "child_surname" varchar(25) NOT NULL,
    "child_age" int NOT NULL,
    PRIMARY KEY("id")
)
ALTER TABLE "public"."child"
    ADD CONSTRAINT "fid"
    FOREIGN KEY("fid")
    REFERENCES "public"."parent"("id")
INSERT INTO public.parent(id, parent_name, parent_surname)
    VALUES(0, 'Ruby', 'Bundy')
INSERT INTO public.parent(id, parent_name, parent_surname)
    VALUES(1, 'Ella', 'Summer')
INSERT INTO public.parent(id, parent_name, parent_surname)
    VALUES(2, 'Olivia', 'Hannah')
INSERT INTO public.child(id, fid, child_name, child_surname,
child_age)
    VALUES(0, 0, 'Jane', 'Bundy', 3)
INSERT INTO public.child(id, fid, child_name, child_surname,
child_age)
    VALUES(1, 0, 'Mike', 'Bundy', 5)
INSERT INTO public.child(id, fid, child_name, child_surname,
child_age)
    VALUES(2, 1, 'Lee', 'Summer', 4)
INSERT INTO public.child(id, fid, child_name, child_surname,
child_age)
    VALUES(3, 1, 'Kelly', 'Summer', 8)
INSERT INTO public.child(id, fid, child_name, child_surname,
child_age)
    VALUES(4, 1, 'Jo', 'Summer', 8)
INSERT INTO public.child(id, fid, child_name, child_surname,
child_age)
    VALUES(5, 2, 'Franny', 'Hannah', 2)
```

The above two tables are mapping the well-known relation, parent-child. In the `Parent` table, we store parents by name and surname, while the `Child` table will store their children. Every child is characterized by name, surname, and age. In addition to this, the `family` database is pre-populated with a set of records using the corresponding SQL `INSERT` statements.

Now, we are ready to start exploring Hibernate Tools and we start Hibernate Tools for Eclipse.

Hibernate Tools for Eclipse

As you already know, Hibernate Tools is available for Eclipse (starting at version 3.3.x + WTP 2.x) as a JBoss Tools component or as a standalone plug-in. In Chapter 1 we already discussed installing JBoss Tools, so now let's see how we can install Hibernate Tools as a standalone plug-in for Eclipse (if you have downloaded and installed a bundle of all the JBoss Tools plug-ins, then you may want to skip the manual installation procedure).

Manual installation

To manually install the Hibernate Tools standalone plug-in for Eclipse, you can follow these steps:

1. Download Hibernate Tools from `http://www.hibernate.org/6.html`.

2. Extract the ZIP archive content into your Eclipse directory or Eclipse extensions directory (`plugins` and `features` directories).

3. Restart Eclipse with the `-clean` option. For example:

   ```
   C:\>eclipse -clean
   ```

When Eclipse restarts, the new plug-in will be ready to serve you!

 If you are not a big fan of manual installations, then you can use the **Eclipse Software Updates** as you have seen in Chapter 1. This time, select only the Hibernate Tools component from the JBoss Tools set of plug-ins.

Hibernate perspective

Hibernate perspective is the perfect place to start working with Hibernate Tools for Eclipse. For launching this perspective, follow these steps:

1. From the **Window** Eclipse main menu, select the **Open Perspective | Other** option.

2. In the **Open Perspective** window, select the **Hibernate** perspective and click on the **OK** button (note the Hibernate Tools views of **Hibernate** perspective).

Creating a Hibernate mapping file (.hbm.xml)

Hibernate Tools can help us to generate mapping file stubs (.hbm.xml) for the POJOs classes (obviously, we are talking about the POJOs that correlate Java objects with databases). This task can be accomplished before or after creating the corresponding POJO classes.

Let's start with a situation where we have already created the POJO classes. For example, let's suppose that we have the following POJO for Parent and Child tables (Hibernate persistent entities):

- Parent.java—class associated with the Parent table of the family database (save it in the src folder of the testHibernate project):

```java
package mappings;

import java.util.HashSet;
import java.util.Set;
import javax.persistence.CascadeType;
import javax.persistence.Column;
import javax.persistence.Entity;
import javax.persistence.FetchType;
import javax.persistence.Id;
import javax.persistence.OneToMany;
import javax.persistence.Table;

@Entity
@Table(name = "parent", schema = "public")
public class Parent implements java.io.Serializable {
    private int id;
    private String parentName;
    private String parentSurname;
    private Set<Child> childs = new HashSet<Child>(0);

    public Parent() {
    }
```

```java
    public Parent(int id, String parentName, String parentSurname)
{
        this.id = id;
        this.parentName = parentName;
        this.parentSurname = parentSurname;
    }
    public Parent(int id, String parentName, String parentSurname,
            Set<Child> childs) {
        this.id = id;
        this.parentName = parentName;
        this.parentSurname = parentSurname;
        this.childs = childs;
    }
    @Id
    @Column(name = "id", unique = true, nullable = false)
    public int getId() {
        return this.id;
    }
    public void setId(int id) {
        this.id = id;
    }
    @Column(name = "parent_name", nullable = false, length = 25)
    public String getParentName() {
        return this.parentName;
    }
    public void setParentName(String parentName) {
        this.parentName = parentName;
    }
    @Column(name = "parent_surname", nullable = false, length = 25)
    public String getParentSurname() {
        return this.parentSurname;
    }
    public void setParentSurname(String parentSurname) {
        this.parentSurname = parentSurname;
    }
    @OneToMany(cascade = CascadeType.ALL, fetch = FetchType.LAZY,
mappedBy = "parent")
    public Set<Child> getChilds() {
        return this.childs;
    }
    public void setChilds(Set<Child> childs) {
        this.childs = childs;
    }
}
```

- Child.java—class associated to the Child table of the family database (save it in the src folder of the testHibernate project):

```java
package mappings;

import javax.persistence.Column;
import javax.persistence.Entity;
import javax.persistence.FetchType;
import javax.persistence.Id;
import javax.persistence.JoinColumn;
import javax.persistence.ManyToOne;
import javax.persistence.Table;

@Entity
@Table(name = "child", schema = "public")
public class Child implements java.io.Serializable {

    private int id;
    private Parent parent;
    private String childName;
    private String childSurname;
    private int childAge;

    public Child() {
    }

    public Child(int id, Parent parent, String childName, String
childSurname,
            int childAge) {
        this.id = id;
        this.parent = parent;
        this.childName = childName;
        this.childSurname = childSurname;
        this.childAge = childAge;
    }

    @Id
    @Column(name = "id", unique = true, nullable = false)
    public int getId() {
        return this.id;
    }

    public void setId(int id) {
        this.id = id;
    }

    @ManyToOne(fetch = FetchType.LAZY)
    @JoinColumn(name = "fid", nullable = false)
    public Parent getParent() {
        return this.parent;
```

```
    }
    public void setParent(Parent parent) {
        this.parent = parent;
    }
    @Column(name = "child_name", nullable = false, length = 25)
    public String getChildName() {
        return this.childName;
    }
    public void setChildName(String childName) {
        this.childName = childName;
    }
    @Column(name = "child_surname", nullable = false, length = 25)
    public String getChildSurname() {
        return this.childSurname;
    }
    public void setChildSurname(String childSurname) {
        this.childSurname = childSurname;
    }
    @Column(name = "child_age", nullable = false)
    public int getChildAge() {
        return this.childAge;
    }
    public void setChildAge(int childAge) {
        this.childAge = childAge;
    }
}
```

Now, to generate the mapping file stubs for these POJOs, you can follow these steps (for the `Parent` POJO class):

1. Switch to the **Hibernate** perspective.
2. In the **Package Explorer**, expand the **testHibernate | src | mappings** node.
3. Right-click on the **Parent.java** node and select the **New | Other** option.

4. In the **New** window, expand the **Hibernate** node and select the **Hibernate XML Mapping file (hbm.xml)** leaf (as shown in the following screenshot). Click on the **Next** button.

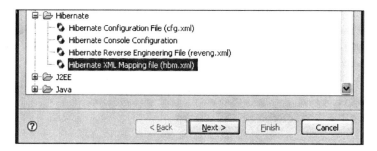

5. Next, you have to indicate the folder where the Hibernate mapping file will be stored, and its name (in general, the name will be the same as the POJO class). We have selected the **src/mappings** folder of the **testHibernate** project and the **Parent.hbm.xml** name (as shown in the following screenshot). Note that these selections were also automatically suggested. Click on the **Next** button.

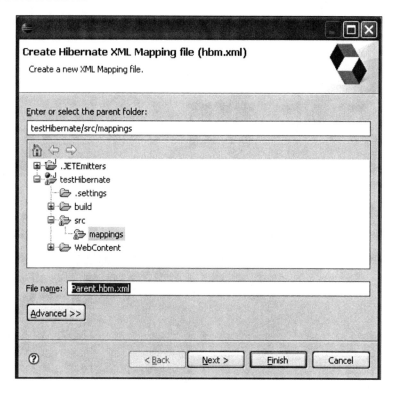

6. It's time to indicate the POJO class that will sit behind this mapping file. If the **Class to map** field wasn't automatically populated, then you should manually insert the fully qualified class name, **mappings.Parent** (as shown in the following screenshot). You may also use the **Browse** button but, in this case, you have to select the class from the **Select class to map** window. At the end, just select it and click on the **OK** button.

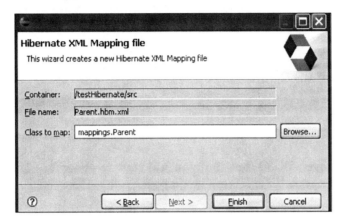

7. Click on the **Finish** button.

Now, you should see the new Hibernate mapping file stub in the **Hibernate XML Editor**, like in the following screenshot:

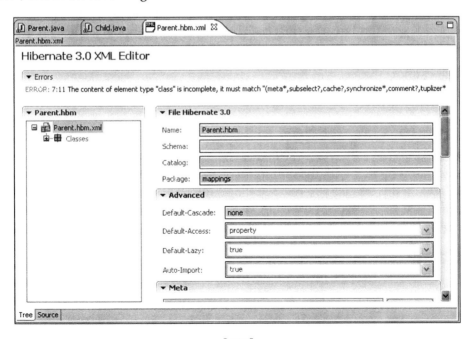

Note that we have errors because this is just an empty stub, not the result of reverse engineering. Fixing this error is a simple task that can be accomplished from the **Source** view, by deleting the generated `<class>` definition. Switching to the **Source** view, you should easily recognize the highlighted code from the following screenshot (just remove it, save the project, and the error should disappear).

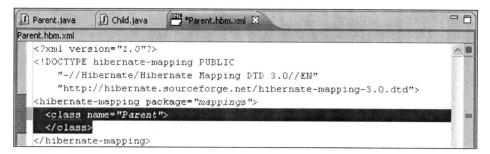

If you don't yet have a POJO class, but you still want to generate a Hibernate mapping file, then launch the Hibernate mapping wizard like this:

1. Switch to **Hibernate** perspective.

2. From the Eclipse **File** main menu, select the **New | Other** option (or right-click on the **testHibernate** project and select the **New | Other** option from the context menu — in this case, the wizard's sections will be pre-filled by using the auto-detection technique).

3. In the **New** window, expand the **Hibernate** node and select the **Hibernate Configuration File (cfg.xml)** leaf (figure given on page 10). Click on the **Next** button.

If you don't know the name of the POJO class, then you can leave it empty in the **Class to map** field, because you can specify/refactor it later.

Hibernate XML Editor

The **Hibernate XML Editor** is a very powerful tool that will help us to create complete mapping files with the minimum of manual interventions over their source code. In this section you will see a brief introduction, which will mark the main tasks that can be accomplished by this editor. First, note that the editor is made up of two main views, named **Tree** and **Source**.

Tree View

The **Tree** view consists of a tree representation of the mappings files. From here, we can modify these mappings files by adding/removing/editing the XML components of those files, such as `<class>`, `<property>`, `<set>`, `<one-to-many>`, and so on.

Next, we will talk about how to create the main XML components of a generic mapping file. Based on the following code, try to reproduce our `Parent.hbm.xml` and `Child.hbm.xml` mapping files using only the features of the **Tree** view. These are the `.hbm.xml` files that correspond to our database, and they can be used as an exercise for getting familiar with the **Tree** view.

The `Parent.hbm.xml` mapping file is:

```
<?xml version="1.0"?>
<!DOCTYPE hibernate-mapping PUBLIC
    "-//Hibernate/Hibernate Mapping DTD 3.0//EN"
    "http://hibernate.sourceforge.net/hibernate-mapping-3.0.dtd">
<hibernate-mapping package="mappings">
 <class name="Parent" table="parent" schema="public">
  <id name="id" type="int">
      <column name="id" />
      <generator class="assigned" />
  </id>
  <property name="parentName" type="string">
      <column name="parent_name" length="25" not-null="true" />
  </property>
  <property name="parentSurname" type="string">
      <column name="parent_surname" length="25" not-null="true" />
  </property>
  <set name="childs" inverse="true">
      <key>
        <column name="fid" not-null="true" />
      </key>
      <one-to-many class="mappings.Child" />
  </set>
 </class>
</hibernate-mapping>
```

The `Child.hbm.xml` mapping file is:

```
<?xml version="1.0"?>
<!DOCTYPE hibernate-mapping PUBLIC
    "-//Hibernate/Hibernate Mapping DTD 3.0//EN"
    "http://hibernate.sourceforge.net/hibernate-mapping-3.0.dtd">
<hibernate-mapping package="mappings">
  <class name="Child" table="child" schema="public">
    <id name="id" type="int">
        <column name="id" />
        <generator class="assigned" />
    </id>
```

```
            <many-to-one name="parent" class="mappings.Parent"
fetch="select">
                <column name="fid" not-null="true" />
            </many-to-one>
            <property name="childName" type="string">
                <column name="child_name" length="25" not-null="true" />
            </property>
            <property name="childSurname" type="string">
                <column name="child_surname" length="25" not-null="true"
                />
            </property>
            <property name="childAge" type="int">
                <column name="child_age" not-null="true" />
            </property>
        </class>
</hibernate-mapping>
```

Adding a <class> element

1. In the **Tree** view, right-click on the *{mapping_file_name}*.**hbm.xml** node and select the **New | Class** option from the contextual menu (note that from this contextual menu, you may also select a **Joined-Subclass** or a **Subclass**).

2. In the **Add Class** window, use the **Search**, **Browse**, or **Recent** tab for locating the desired class. After that, click on the **Finish** button.

Adding an <id> element

1. In the **Tree** view, right panel, select the *{mapping_file_name}*.**hbm.xml** | **Classes** | *{class_name}* | **id** node (note that if you want to configure a new `<generator>` or `<column>` subelement for `<id>` element, then you can right-click on the **id** node and select the corresponding option from the contextual menu).

2. In the left panel (**Properties Editor**), fill in the desired sections for configuring the `<id>` element.

Adding a <property> element

1. In the **Tree** view, right panel, select the *{mapping_file_name}*.**hbm.xml** | **Classes** | *{class_name}*.

2. Right-click on the *{class_name}* node and select the **New | Property** option from the contextual menu (note that from this contextual menu, you can create many other components that help us to configure many details of a mapping file).

3. In the **Add Property** window, type the property name and click on the **Finish** button. A new {*property_name*} node is added under the **Properties** node (**Tree** view, left panel) and is ready to be configured in the right panel (**Property** panel).

Adding a <set> element

1. In the **Tree** view, right panel, select the {*mapping_file_name*}.**hbm.xml** | **Classes** | {*class_name*} node.

2. Right-click on the {*class_name*} node and select the **New | Set** option from the contextual menu (note that from this contextual menu, you may also create `<map>`, `<list>`, `<bag>`, and so on elements).

3. In the **Add Set** window, it is mandatory to indicate the set's name and optionally, the corresponding table name. Click on the **Finish** button.

Adding a <one-to-many> element

This scenario is applicable to all the association mappings.

1. In the **Tree** view, right panel, select a node that is authorized to encapsulate a `<one-to-many>` element.

2. Right-click on this node and select **New | One-to-Many** option from the contextual menu.

3. In the **Add One To Many** window, use the **Search**, **Browse**, or **Recent** tab for locating the desired class. After you select the class, click on the **Finish** button.

At any moment, you can check the source code of mapping files by selecting the **Source** view. Note that manually modifying these files will automatically update the previous view (if you don't see the modifications, then try to save the file/project).

Creating a Hibernate configuration file

Hibernate Core and Hibernate Annotation requires a `hibernate.cfg.xml` or a `hibernate.properties` configuration file. Hibernate Tools can generate a `hibernate.cfg.xml` in just a few steps, as follows (it can't generate a `hibernate.properties`, but it can use one):

1. Switch to the **Hibernate** perspective.

2. From the Eclipse **File** main menu, select the **New | Other** option (or right-click on the **testHibernate** project and select the **New | Other** option from the contextual menu — in this case, the wizard's sections will be pre-filled by using the auto-detection technique).

3. In the **New** window, expand the **Hibernate** node and select the **Hibernate Configuration File (cfg.xml)** leaf (as shown in the following screenshot). Click on the **Next** button.

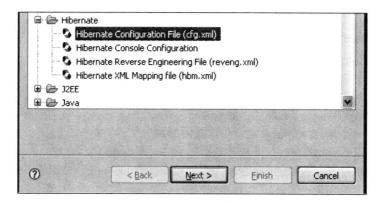

4. Next, you have to indicate the folder where the Hibernate configuration file will be stored, and its name (note that the default name is automatically filled, `hibernate.cfg.xml`). We have selected the `src` folder of the `testHibernate` project and the default name (as shown in the following screenshot). Click on the **Next** button.

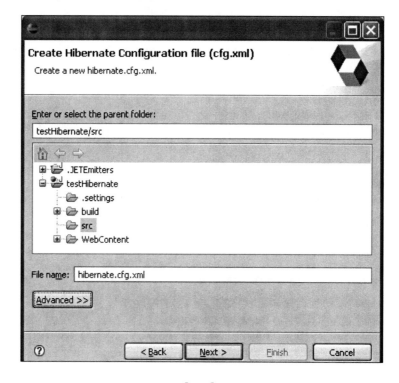

5. This is the main step that fills up the Hibernate configuration file with the desired settings (as shown in the following screenshot). From top to the bottom, we have the following sections (once complete, click on the **Finish** button):

- **Container**—it indicates the folder where the Hibernate configuration file is stored after generation (this field can be modified from the previous step).

- **File name**—it indicates the name of the Hibernate configuration file (this field can be modified from the previous step).

- **Session factory name**—it indicates an optional name for the current session factory. In our example, we left this field empty.

- **Database dialect**—it indicates the database dialect by selecting a RDBMS from the provided list. In our example, we will select the **PostgreSQL** dialect.

- **Driver class**—it indicates the driver's classes available for the selected dialect. For PostgreSQL dialect, there is one driver class, named **org.postgresql.Driver**.

- **Connection URL**—it indicates the database connection URL. You can use one of the provided templates for constructing this URL, or you can manually type the entire URL. In our example, the URL is: `jdbc:postgresql://localhost:5432/family`.

- **Default Schema**—it indicates a database default schema (if you don't need this information, then leave this field empty).

- **Default Catalog**—it indicates a database default catalog (if you don't need this information, then leave this field empty).

- **Username**—it indicates the username for accessing the database (in our example, this is `postgres`, but you have to provide your own username).

- **Password**—it indicates the password for accessing the database (in our example, this is `explorer`, but you have to provide your own password).

- Leave the **Create a console configuration** checkbox unselected. We will discuss later about how to create a Hibernate Console Configuration. For now, just click on the **Finish** button.

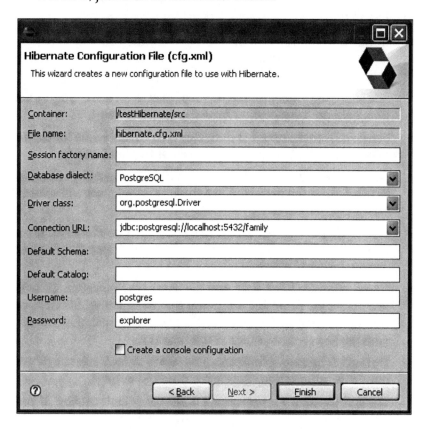

If everything is ok, then you should see that the **hibernate.cfg.xml** file is present under src folder (in **Package Explorer** view) and it is open in the **Hibernate Configuration XML Editor**.

Hibernate Configuration XML Editor

This editor allows us to visualize and modify the Hibernate configuration file in a simple and interactive manner. As you can see from the following screenshot, this editor has three main views: **Session Factory**, **Security**, and **Source**.

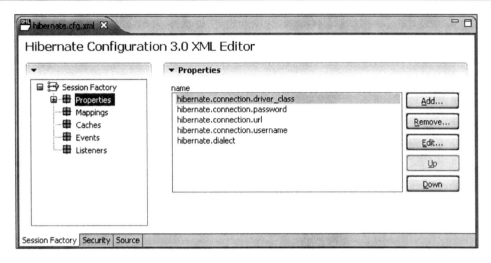

Session Factory view

Session Factory view is a tree representation of the Hibernate configuration file. From here, you can access the main components of this file: properties, mappings, caches, events, and listeners. You can add/remove/edit any of these components by following these three generic steps:

1. Select the component's node from the left panel.

2. Select the desired property, mapping, event, and so on from the middle panel (obviously, when this panel is empty, skip this step).

3. Click on the button that corresponds to the desired action (**Add/Remove/ Edit/Up/Down**).

4. Follow your intuition and Hibernate knowledge to successfully accomplish the selected action.

For example, if we want to add the two mapping files created earlier in this chapter into the configuration file, we can follow these steps (this example is for `Parent.hbm.xml`, but it can be adapted for any other mapping file):

1. Select the **Mappings** node from the left panel, **Session Factory** view.

2. Click on the **Add** button from the right panel to open the **Add Mapping** window.

3. Leave the **Class and Package** field empty and click on the **Finish** button. You should see that an empty mapping was added (as shown below):

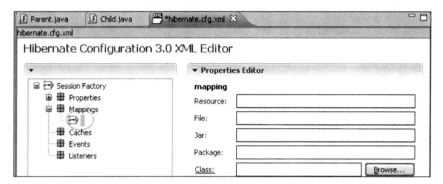

4. Now, in the **Resource** field, type **mappings/Parent.hbm.xml** (for `Child.hbm.xml` file, type **mappings/Child.hbm.xml**). Done!

Now, let's see another example of using the **Session Factory** view. Let's assume we want to add the corresponding event listeners for enabling the use of JAAS authorization. The following steps will show you how:

1. Select the **Listeners** node from the left panel, **Session Factory** view.

2. Click the **Add** button from the right panel to open the **Add Listener** window.

3. In this window, click on the **Browse** button, next to the **Class** field.

4. In the **Edit Class** window, switch to the **Browse** tab and navigate to **org | hibernate | secure | JACCPreLoadEventListener** node. Click on the **OK** button (as shown in the following screenshot).

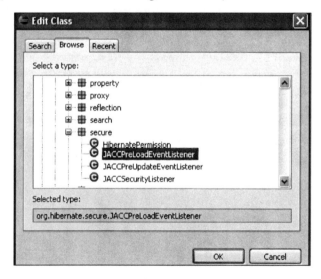

If you don't find the desired listener then you can use the Search tab; type the listener class name into the **Choose a Type** field. All classes that correspond to the inserted one will be displayed under the **Matching types** field.

5. Select the **pre-load** listener in the **Type** field, **Add Listener** window (as shown in the following screenshot).

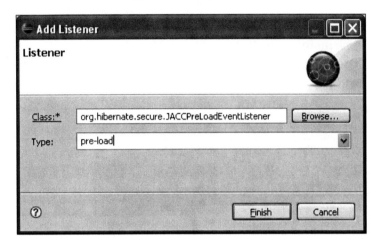

6. Click on the **Finish** button.

Note that the **pre-load** listener was added under the **Listeners** node (screenshot shown below):

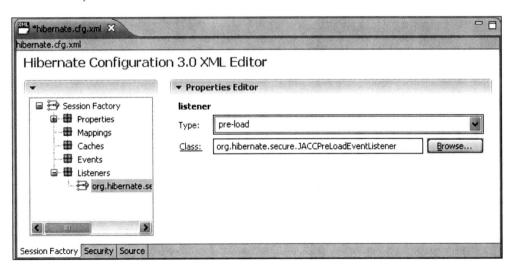

7. Repeat steps 1-6 to add the **pre-delete (org.hibernate.secure. JACCPreDeleteEventListener** class), **pre-update (org.hibernate.secure. JACCPreUpdateEventListener** class) and **pre-insert (org.hibernate.secure. JACCPreInsertEventListener** class) listeners.

Security view

From this view, we can bind permissions to roles. For example, if we want to bind permissions to roles for JAAS authorization, we can follow these steps:

1. Optional, type the security context name in the **Context** field.

2. Right-click on the **Security** node (**Security** left panel).

3. Select the **New | Grant** option from the context menu (screenshot given below).

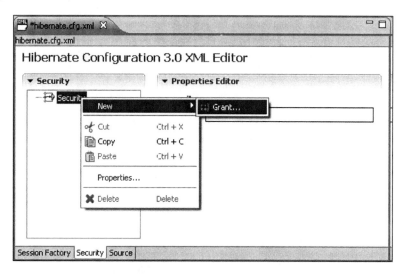

4. In the **Add Grant** window, it is mandatory to specify a role (**Role** field), an entity name (**Entity-Name** field), and the corresponding actions (**Actions** field). The provided roles should be understood by your JACC provider, but, just as an example, you can fill up these fields as shown in the following screenshot (note that multiple actions should be separated by commas). Click on the **Finish** button.

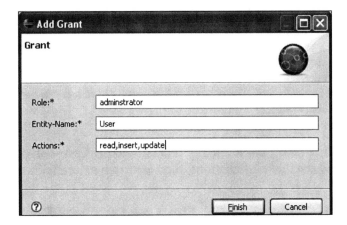

 If you want to allow all possible actions, then use a * in the **Actions** field.

The new grant was successfully added (as shown in the following screenshot):

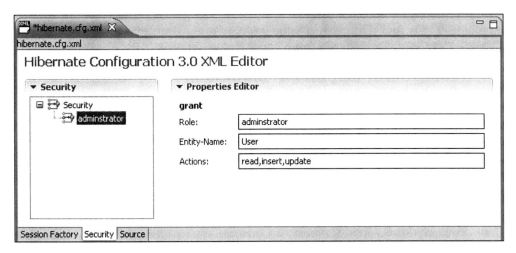

Source view

At any moment, you can check the source code of the Hibernate configuration file by selecting the **Source** view. For example, delete the next fragment of code from this view and save the file (this mean that these settings should not appear in the final code):

```
<listener class="org.hibernate.secure.JACCPreLoadEventListener"
type="pre-load"/>
  <listener class="org.hibernate.secure.JACCPreDeleteEventListener"
type="pre-delete"/>
```

```
  <listener class="org.hibernate.secure.JACCPreUpdateEventListener"
type="pre-update"/>
  <listener class="org.hibernate.secure.JACCPreInsertEventListener"
type="pre-insert"/>
<security context="MyContext">
  <grant actions="read,insert,update" entity-name="User"
role="administrator"/>
</security>
```

Note that modifying these files manually will automatically update the previous two views (if you don't see the modifications, then try to save the file/project).

Creating a Hibernate Console Configuration

A **Hibernate Console Configuration** tells the Hibernate plug-in which configuration files should be used to configure Hibernate, including which classpath is needed to load the POJO's, JDBC drivers, and so on. Reverse engineering, code generation, and query prototyping are the most important facilities that depend on a Hibernate Console Configuration. The associated wizard will help us to indicate the console's details, like configurations file (for example, `.cfg.xml`, `persistence.xml`), additional mappings, POJOs, and JDBC driver's classpath, naming strategy, etc. Before creating a Console Configuration, let's see some general observations:

- You can create as many Console Configurations as you want
- In general, you will need one Console Configuration per project
- If you are coming from the Hibernate configuration file wizard and had checked the **Create Console Configuration** checkbox, then you will see the Hibernate Console Configuration wizard
- If you need to configure a property file, a `persistence.xml` file, a naming strategy, and/or an entity resolver then you should create them before launching the Hibernate Console Configuration wizard
- You can delete/create/modify a Console Configuration anytime, without affecting the project's integrity
- The wizard will auto-detect the current settings and automatically fill up the corresponding fields
- You can see Console Configurations in the **Hibernate Configurations** view

Now, for creating a Console Configuration, you can follow these steps:

1. Switch to **Hibernate** perspective.

2. From the Eclipse **File** main menu, select the **New | Other** option (or right-click on the **testHibernate** project and select the **New | Other** option from the contextual menu — in this case, wizard's fields will be pre-filled by using the auto-detection technique).

3. In the **New** window, expand the **Hibernate** node and select the **Hibernate Console Configuration** leaf (as shown in the following screenshot). Click on the **Next** button.

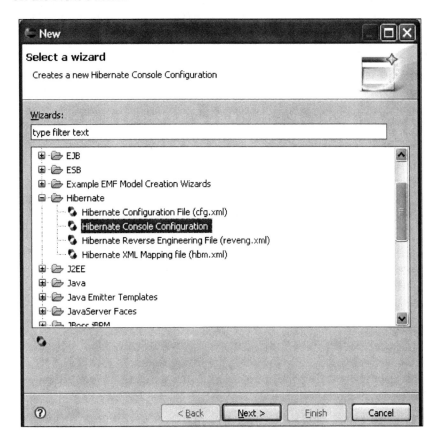

4. The next window allows us to set the main details for our Console Configuration. As you can see, this window contains five tabs (**Main,** **Options, Classpath, Mappings,** and **Common**). Before discussing the content of these tabs, provide a name for our console in the **Name** section (for example, type **testHibernateConsole***)*.

Now, that we have an identification name, let's continue with the tabs:

Main tab

From this tab, fill in the fields as follows:

- **Type** — select from **Core**, **Annotations (jdk 1.5+)**, or **JPA (jdk 1.5+)** types. Note that for the first two you will need a `.cfg.xml` configuration file and for the JPA type, you will need a `persistence.xml` file. Since we have a `.cfg.xml` file, we can select the **Core** type.

- **Project** — this is a mandatory field, indicating the name of the Java project used in this case. For example, type **testHibernate** or use the **Browse** button to navigate to this project.

- **Database connection** — from this field, we can select an existing custom database connection profile, create a new one (by clicking on the **New** button) or leave the default connection profile **[Hibernate configured connection]**, which means that we will provide the connection details through Hibernate property, configuration, or persistence files. Leave it as default!

- **Property file** — indicates the path to a `hibernate.properties` file. By default it may be automatically filled with the first `hibernate.properties` file found in the Java project. We left this field empty, but if you want to test it then you can use the following `hibernate.properties` file:

```
hibernate.connection.driver_class=org.postgresql.Driver
hibernate.connection.url=jdbc:postgresql://localhost:5432/family
hibernate.connection.username=postgres
hibernate.connection.password=explorer
hibernate.dialect=org.hibernate.dialect.PostgreSQLDialect
```

- **Configuration file** — indicates the path to the Hibernate `.cfg.xml` configuration file. By default, it may be automatically filled with the first `hibernate.cfg.xml` file found in the Java project. In our case, type here **\testHibernate\src\hibernate.cfg.xml** or use the associated **Browse** button to navigate to this file.

- **Persistence unit** — indicates the name of a persistence unit (this is getting active if you use the JPA type). By default, it has no value and it lets the Hibernate Entity Manager find the persistence unit. Obviously, because we use a `.cfg.xml` file, we left this field empty, but if you want to test this case then you can start writing a `persistence.xml` from the generic example shown below (don't forget to configure the corresponding JNDI name in JBoss AS server or in your J2EE application server):

```
<persistence>
    <persistence-unit name="{unit_name}">
        <provider>org.hibernate.ejb.HibernatePersistence</provider>
        <jta-data-source>java:/{datasource_name}</jta-data-source>
        <properties>
            ...
        </properties>
    </persistence-unit>
</persistence>
```

At this point, the wizard should look like this (screenshot given below):

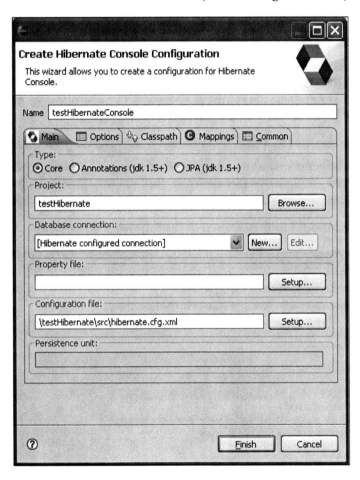

Options tab

Next, switch to **Options** tab for setting:

- **Naming strategy** — indicates a class that implements a custom **NamingStrategy** (the fully qualified name is required). It has no default value. We will leave this field empty.

- **Entity resolver** — indicates a class that implements a custom **EntityResolver** (the fully qualified name is required). Needed only if you have a special XML entity included in your mapping files. It has no default value. We will leave this field empty.

Classpath tab

Switch to the **Classpath** tab for adding additional classpaths to load POJOs and JDBC drivers (not Hibernate JARs!). Note that this is needed only if the default classpath of the project does not contain the required classes. In our example, we have to add the classpath of the JDBC driver for PostgreSQL. The steps are:

1. Click on the **Add External JARs** button to display the **JAR Selection** window.

2. In **JAR Selection** window navigate to `{PostgreSQL_HOME}/jdbc` and select the proper JDBC driver (for example, for PostgreSQL 8.2, we have selected the `postgresql-8.2-505.jdbc2.jar` driver). Click on the **Open** button.

Now, the wizard should look as shown in the following screenshot:

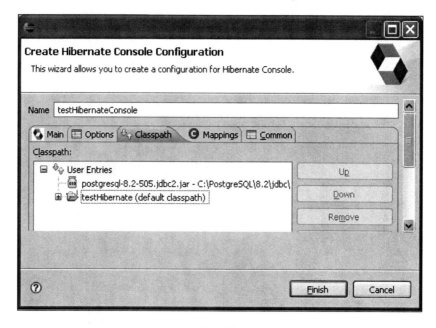

Mappings tab

Switch to the **Mappings** tab for adding additional mapping files. Note that you should only add additional mappings that are not listed in `.cfg.xml` or `persistence.xml` files. Any mapping that is added from here and that is present in these two files will generate a *Duplicate mapping* error. To add a mapping, you can use the **Add** button and, to remove a mapping, you can use the **Remove** button. In our example we don't need any additional mapping, so we will leave this tab as default.

Common tab

This tab contains common settings, like **Save as** and **Standard Input and Output**. Leave everything as default.

Finally, click on the **Finish** button.

Hibernate Configurations view

Now that you have created the console, let's see how to use it. The Hibernate Console Configurations can be seen in the **Hibernate Configurations** view. In case you don't see this view—after creating the Console Configuration as above—then follow these steps to launch it:

1. Select the **Show View | Other** option from the Eclipse **Window** main menu.

2. In the **Show View** window, expand the **Hibernate** node and select the **Hibernate Configurations** leaf (under the **Hibernate** node, you can see all the Hibernate views).

3. Click on the **OK** button.

Now, the **Hibernate Configurations** view should look like the following figure (expand the **testHibernateConsole** node to see more details):

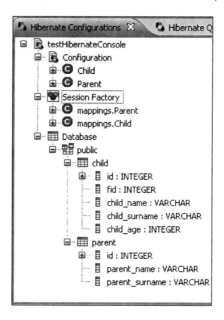

If you right-click on the **testHibernateConsole** node, you can, among other things, rebuild (**Rebuild Configuration** option), edit (**Edit Configuration** option), delete (**Delete Configuration** option), and refresh (**Refresh** option) the current Console Configuration. Note that there are cases when you will need to rebuild/refresh the Console Configuration for seeing the changes.

As you can see, under the **testHibernateConsole** node, we have three main nodes: **Configuration**, **Session Factory**, and **Database**. These nodes provide a list of POJOs, mappings, and databases that characterize this Console Configuration. Next, we will see some of the Hibernate Tools skills that can be used from this view.

Mapping diagram

This feature provides a graphical diagram for the Hibernate entities. It can be very useful when entities have many interdependencies and complex structures, because it helps us to achieve a complete view of the situation. To see the mapping diagram, for our example, right-click on the **Child** node (or **Parent** node) under the **Configuration** node and select the **Open Mapping Diagram** from the contextual menu. You should see something like this:

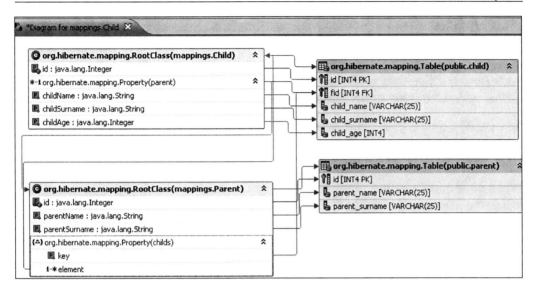

Next, is a set of facilities that are strongly related to the displayed diagram:

- Export the diagram as an image—right-click on the diagram and select the **Export as Image** option from the contextual menu. Now, the image is independent of your project and can be used for other scopes (for example, you can paste it in an article about your project).

- Open the mapping/source file of an entity element—right-click on the desired element and select the **Open Mapping File/Open Source File** option from the contextual menu. The corresponding file will be displayed and the indicated element will be highlighted. Using this facility will help you to open and edit an entity element directly from the diagram.

- Navigate through **Mapping Diagram** in tandem with **Outline** view—launch the **Outline** view (**Window** menu, **Show view | Other** option, **General | Outline** leaf) and see how the navigation in **Mapping Diagram** is reflected in the **Outline** view, and vice versa. The **Outline** view offers two modes of navigation (tree and diagram) that can be switched from the view's toolbar buttons (as shown in the following screenshot). This is a good technique when the diagram is really large and is "heavy" to navigate through.

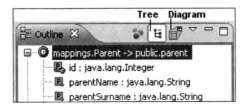

HQL Editor

From the **HQL Editor**, we can execute/prototype queries written in the Hibernate Query Language syntax. Open this editor by right-clicking on the **Configuration** node (or any other node under **testHibernateConsole** node) and select the **HQL Editor** option from the contextual menu (as shown below).

To execute a query, you can click on the **Run HQL** button or press the *Ctrl+Enter* keyboard combination. This button should appear in the upper-left corner of the **HQL Editor** and/or on the main toolbar of Eclipse.

When your queries return many results (over the memory limit), just type a number inside the **Max results** field in the **HQL Editor**. This will reduce the number of returned results to the specified number.

If you select an entity/property from the Console Configuration and open the **HQL Editor**, then you will get the corresponding pre-filled query, as in the example shown below. Otherwise, you will open an empty **HQL Editor**.

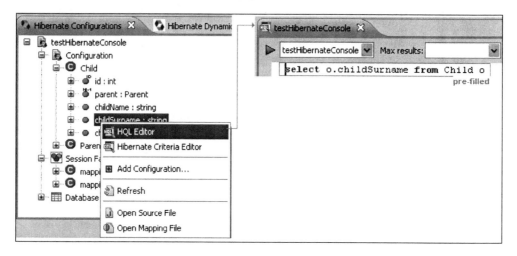

 At any moment, you can get assistance for writing your HQL queries by pressing *Ctrl+Space* keyboard combination inside the **HQL Editor** or by right-clicking and selecting the **ContentAssistProposal.label** option from the contextual menu.

Hibernate Criteria Editor

As you know, Hibernate offers a powerful but limited alternative to HQL, known as Hibernate Criteria API. Hibernate Tools offer us **Hibernate Criteria Editor** that can be used to write criteria search queries based on this API.

Note that many aspects of the **HQL Editor** are also available for this editor, so there is no need to repeat them here.

Open this editor by right-clicking on the **Configuration** node (or any other node under the **testHibernateConsole** node) and selecting the **Hibernate Criteria Editor** option from the contextual menu (as shown in the following screenshot).

If you start the **Hibernate Criteria Editor** from an entity/property, you will get a pre-filled criterion. In the following screenshot, you can see an example:

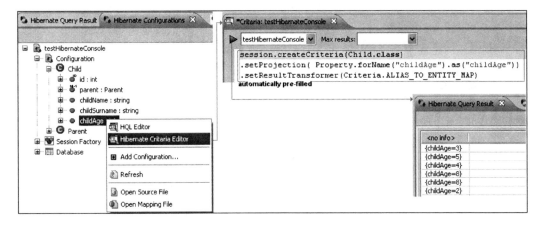

Hibernate Query Result view

Note that the results of the queries are displayed in another Hibernate Tools view, named **Hibernate Query Result**. Next, you can see some HQL examples executed over the Parent and Child tables:

- Select the parent's first names (as shown in the following screenshot):

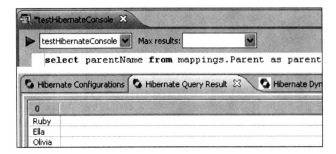

- For Ella Summer parent, select her child's first names and child's ages (screenshot shown below):

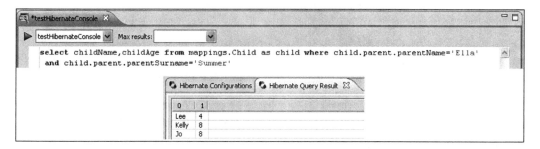

Hibernate Dynamic SQL Preview view

Related to the **HQL Editor,** we have the **Hibernate Dynamic SQL Preview** and **Query Parameters** views. The first one will display the SQL version of the HQL queries written in the **HQL Editor**. For example, for the above two HQL queries, we have the following SQL queries displayed in **Hibernate Dynamic SQL Preview**:

- Select the parent's first names (as shown in the previous screenshot—the HQL query, as shown in the following screenshot—the translated SQL):

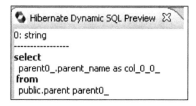

- Select first name and age of the child *Ella Summer* (as shown in the previous screenshot—the HQL query, as shown in the following screenshot—the translated SQL):

Query Parameters view

This view can be used in conjunction with the **HQL Editor** for writing parameterized HQL queries (as you know, a HQL parameter syntax may be of form :p, where p can be replaced with different values before the query is executed). For example, open the **HQL Editor** and type the following HQL query:

```
select parentName from mappings.Parent as parent where parent.id
between :starts and :ends
```

Note that this query contains two parameters, starts and ends. Now, we will switch to the **Query Parameters** view (if this view is not visible, then add it from the Eclipse **Window** main menu, **Show View | Other** option, **Hibernate | Query Parameters** leaf) and we will collect the parameters from the **HQL Editor** by clicking on the first button (from the left to right) placed on the view's toolbar (as shown in the following screenshot). Note that the two parameters are collected and added in the view's list:

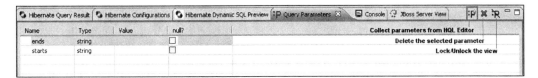

Because our parameters are integers, you have to select the integer type in the **Type** column:

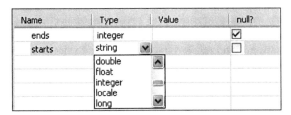

Next, we set the parameter's values. For example, type *0* in the **Value** column for starts parameter and *2* for the ends parameter (as shown in the following screenshot). Remember that our parameters represent an interval for parent.id column.

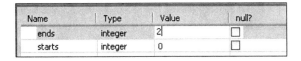

Finally, we can execute the query by pressing the **Run HQL** button of the **HQL Editor**. The output will be displayed into the **Hibernate Query Result** view.

Properties view

After a query is executed, we can see some important details about it in the
Properties view. In the following screenshot, left side, you can see the details of
a query that was successfully executed and in the same figure, right side, you can
see the details of a query that generates errors.

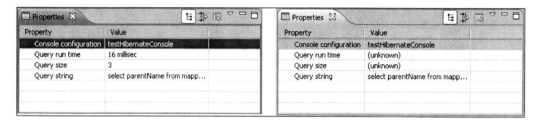

Reverse engineering and code generation techniques

Reverse engineering and code generation techniques support the developers
who want to speed up the process of getting some Hibernate artifacts for their
databases. With just a few mouse clicks, we can obtain all the main parts of a
Hibernate project, such as: POJOs, mapping files, `.cfg.xml` files, documentation
files, DAO sources, and so on.

Before you can take advantage of reverse engineering and code
generation techniques, you have to create at least one Hibernate Console
Configuration. Read more details about this in the section *Creating a
Hibernate Console Configuration*.

Now, let's see how we can use these techniques in a real example. We will try to
generate some Hibernate artifacts for our `family` database. For this, you can follow
these steps:

1. From the main toolbar of Eclipse, select the **Run** menu. Click on the
    small arrow of this menu and select the **Hibernate Code Generation
    Configurations** item for opening the **Hibernate Code Generation
    Configurations** wizard.

2. From this wizard, we can manage *launchers* (take your time and read the
    instructions that appear next to the *launchers* list, which is empty for now).
    We will create a new *launcher* by clicking on the **New launch configuration**
    button (as shown in the following screenshot).

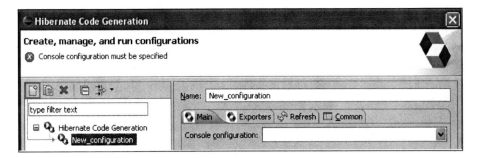

3. A new *launcher* named **New_configuration** was created and added under the **Hibernate Code Generation** node. Now, it is time to configure it and we will start by providing a new name for it in the **Name** field. For example, type **testHibernateCodeGen** and click on the **Apply** button (as shown below).

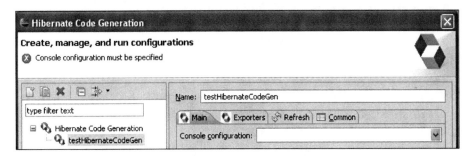

4. Now, we will focus on the four tabs under the **Name** field (after each tab is filled with the desired settings, click on the **Apply** button):

Main tab

This tab contains the following sections (general settings):

- **Console configuration** — hibernate tools will auto-detect the available Console Configurations and pre-fill this list with their names. In this case we have a single **Console configuration**, named **testHibernateConsole**. Select it from the list as the current **Console configuration**. This operation will activate the following sections!

- **Output directory** — indicate the directory's path where the output files will be written. In our case, use the **Browse** button to navigate to \testHibernate\ src directory. Note that all the existing files will be overwritten.

- **Reverse engineer from JDBC Connection** — if this checkbox is selected, then reverse engineering will use the selected Console Configuration and the database schema. If it is not selected, then the existing mappings from Console Configuration will be used. In our case, select this checkbox.

- **Package** — indicates the package's name used for the found entities. For our example, type here **mappings_re**.

- **reveng.xml** — indicates the path for a `reveng.xml` file used to control the reverse engineering process. Later in this chapter you will see how to create such a file using the Hibernate Tools dedicated wizard. For now, leave this field empty.

- **reveng. Strategy** — indicates your own implementation of `ReverseEngineeringStrategy` for providing the finest customization of the reverse engineering process. For now, leave this field empty.

- **Generate basic typed composite ids** — if this checkbox is selected, and there are matching foreign keys, each key column is considered a basic type (`int`, `string`, `float`, etc.). If it is not selected, then `<key-many-to-one>` elements will be used. For our example, select this checkbox.

- **Detect optimistic lock columns** — if this checkbox is selected, then Hibernate Tools will automatically detect optimistic lock columns — check Hibernate documentation for more details (controllable from **reveng. strategy**). For our example, select this checkbox.

- **Detect many-to-many tables** — if this checkbox is selected, then Hibernate Tools will automatically detect many-to-many tables — check Hibernate documentation for more details (controllable from **reveng. strategy**). For our example select this checkbox.

- **Use custom templates (for custom file generation)** — if this checkbox is selected, then you have to specify the templates directory where Hibernate Tools can find custom templates for processing the Hibernate mapping model. For our example, leave this checkbox unselected.

- **Template directory** — indicates the path to the directory that contains custom templates.

The following figure should reflect the setting that we have proposed for the
Main tab:

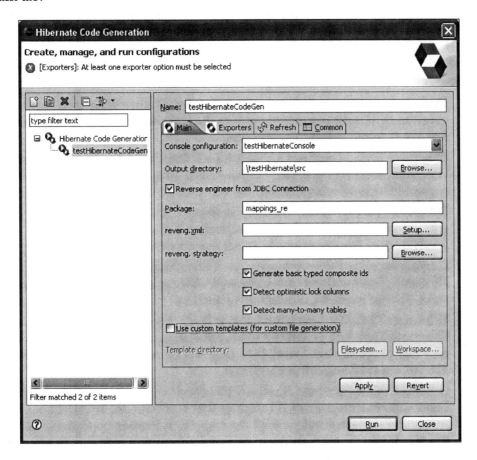

Exporters tab

This tab contains the following sections (code generation settings):

- **Use Java 5 syntax**—if this checkbox is selected, then the generated code will
  respect the Java 5 syntax. For our example, select this checkbox.

- **Generate EJB3 annotations**—if this checkbox is selected, then the generated
  code will contain and respect EJB3 annotations style. For our example, do not
  select this checkbox.

Next, we will indicate which artifacts should be generated for our configuration. We will try to achieve the following artifacts: the corresponding POJO classes, the Hibernate mappings file, the DAO classes, the Hibernate configuration file, and the HTML schema documentation. We don't want to obtain the customizable generic exporter and the DDL file associated with the database schema. Anyway, this is just a scenario, so you are free to test your own. For now, here are the selections that we have to make for our:

- **Domain code (.java)** — if this checkbox is selected, then Hibernate Tools will generate POJOs classes according with the current Hibernate configuration. For our example, select this checkbox.

- **Hibernate XML Mappings (.hbm.xml)** — if this checkbox is selected, then Hibernate Tools will generate Hibernate mappings files according to the current Hibernate configuration. For our example, select this checkbox.

- **DAO code (.java)** — if this checkbox is selected, then Hibernate Tools will generate a set of DAO classes according to the current Hibernate configuration. For our example, select this checkbox.

- **Generic exporter (<hbmtemplate>)** — if this checkbox is selected, then Hibernate Tools will generate a customizable exporter for custom generation tasks. For our example, deselect this checkbox.

- **Hibernate XML Configuration (.cfg.xml)** — if this checkbox is selected, then Hibernate Tools will generate a `hibernate.cfg.xml` configuration file. If new mappings files are found, then they will be added to this configuration file. For our case, select this checkbox.

- **Schema Documentation (.html)** — if this checkbox is selected, then Hibernate Tools will generate a set of HTML files that represent documentation for database schema and some of the mappings. For our example, select this checkbox.

- **Schema Export (.ddl)** — if this checkbox is selected, then Hibernate Tools will generate the DDL file associated the database schema. For our example, deselect this checkbox.

Exporters can have a set of properties that can be indicated in the **Properties** section. You can have predefined or customized properties and you can manage them through the **Add/Remove** buttons. For adding a property, you have to select the desired exporter and click on the **Add** button from the **Properties** section. You will see a list of predefined/customized properties that correspond to the selected exporter. The following list contains all the predefined properties and a short description:

- **Generate Java 5 syntax [jdk5]** — set this property to **true** if you want to have code generated using the Java 5 syntax.

- **Generate EJB3 annotations [ejb3]** — set this property to **true** if you want to have code generated using EJB3 annotations.

- **Template directory [template_path]** — indicates a template directory (you may also use Eclipse variables).

- **Output directory [outputdir]** — indicates an output directory (you may also use Eclipse variables).

- **For each [for_each]** — indicates for which type of model elements the exporter should create a file and run through the templates (accepted values are: **configuration, component,** and **entity**). The values are comma separated!

- **File pattern [file_pattern]** — indicates a path pattern used for the generated files. The default value is ${*package-name*}**/**${*class-name*}**.java**.

- **Executable to run GraphViz [dot.executable]** — indicates executable to run GraphViz. Note that it is optional for schema documentation.

The following figure reflects the settings that we have proposed for the **Exporters** tab:

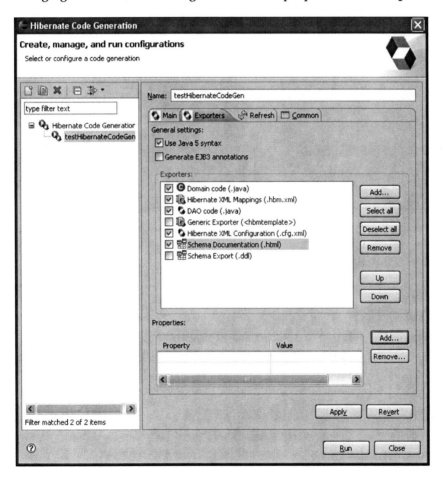

Refresh tab

This tab is used for setting refresh tasks after the code generation process is complete. First, you have to select the **Refresh resources upon completion** checkbox and then you can select one of the radio buttons, depending on your needs. Our selections are shown below:

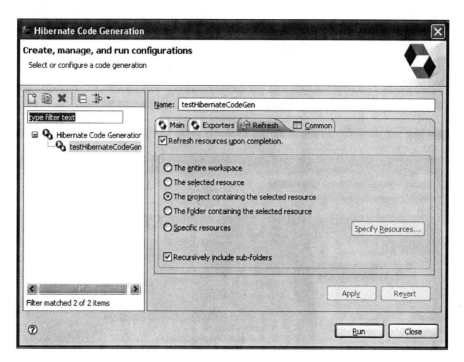

 Refresh tasks can affect sub-folders if you select the **Recursively include sub-folders** checkbox.

Common tab

Contains common settings, like **Save as** and **Standard Input and Output**. As you can see, this tab is pretty intuitive and not very significant in our case, so no details are provided.

Generating Hibernate artifacts

Finally, it is the time to leave Hibernate Tools to accomplish its job and generate the Hibernate artifacts based on the above settings. For this, click on the **Run** button and wait until the process ends.

Now, if you take a look in the **Package Explorer** you will notice that all the required artifacts are there (as shown in the following screenshot):

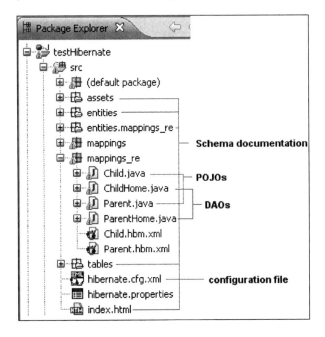

Customize and control reverse engineering (reveng.xml)

In this section we will learn how to generate a reveng.xml file that is used to customize and control the reverse engineering process. Hibernate Tools helps us with a dedicated wizard that supports the development of the main parts of a reveng.xml file, like:

- Include/exclude tables from reverse engineering process
- Map JDBC types to Hibernate types
- Customize table & columns' settings.

Next, we will follow the wizard's steps for obtaining a reveng.xml file without manually typing any code lines. We start by launching the wizard and we will continue to use it until we get a functional reveng.xml document. Here are the steps:

1. Switch to the **Hibernate** perspective.
2. From the Eclipse **File** main menu, select the **New | Other** option (or right-click on the **testHibernate** node and select the **New | Other** option from the contextual menu).

3. In the **New** window, expand the **Hibernate** node and select the **Hibernate Reverse Engineering File** leaf (as shown in the following screenshot). Click on the **Next** button.

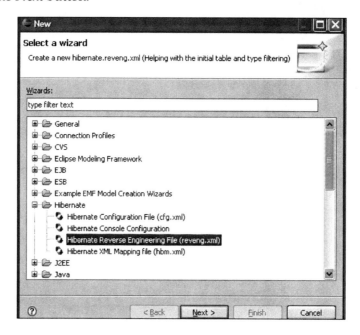

4. At this step, you have to specify a name for reveng.xml file and select a location for it. For example, name it **hibernate.reveng.xml** and place it in **testHibernate/src** folder (as shown in the following screenshot).

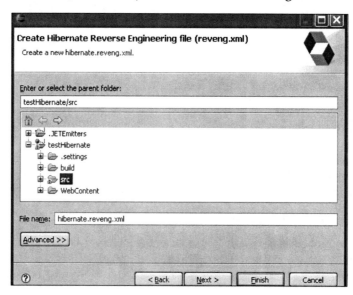

5. We can skip this step since it is not important now. Everything that can be set here can be set later, so click on the **Finish** button (as shown in the following screenshot).

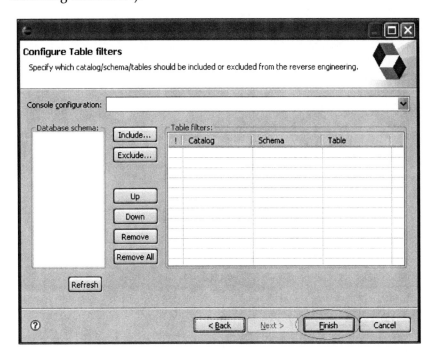

6. Now, you should see the Hibernate reverse engineering editor. This editor contains six views that help us to obtain the desired reveng.xml file.

Next, we will discuss in detail each of these six views.

Overview view

This view has two main sections, **Console Configuration** and **Contents**. From the first section, you can select a Console Configuration from the available list and from the second section, you can access **Type Mappings**, **Table filters**, or **Tables & Columns** view.

Table Filters view

As the view's name suggest, from here we can filter tables. We can include (**Include** button) and exclude (**Exclude** button) in the tables like this:

1. Click on the **Refresh** button for showing the database's tables.
2. Expand the root node (**public**) until you see the **parent** and **child** nodes.

3. Select the **parent** node and click on the **Include** button.

4. Repeat step 3 for **child** node.

You should see something as shown below:

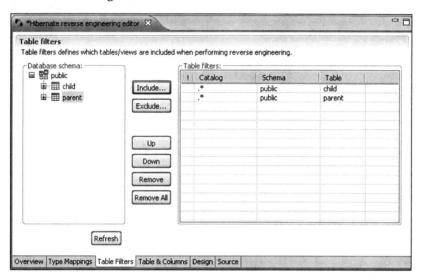

Type Mappings view

For customizing the default process of mapping JDBC types to Hibernate types (predefined and user-defined types), we can use the **Type Mappings** view like this:

1. Click on the **Refresh** button for showing the database's tables.

2. Expose the desired table's columns by expanding the corresponding nodes (for example, expand the **parent** node).

3. Select the desired column and click on the **Add** button (for example, select the **parent_name** column and click the **Add** button).

Note that when you clicked on the **Add** button, the **Type mappings** table was auto-filled with the JDBC type mapping characteristics of the selected column. In this table, you can modify the type of mappings according to your needs. The modifications will be visible in the source of `reveng.xml`.

Table & Columns view

This view allows us to customize table & column settings. We can control default settings and/or specify our settings when the default ones are not applicable. For this, follow these steps:

1. Click the **Add** button.

2. From the **Add Table & Columns** window, select the desired tables and columns and click on the **OK** button (as shown below).

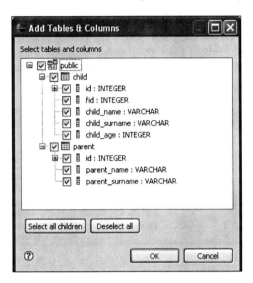

3. Now, the tables and columns have been added into the view, left panel. Select the desired table/column and adjust its settings from the right panel (**Table Details/Column Details**). For tables, you can indicate the catalog name, schema name, table name, and the class name (as shown in the following screenshot, left side). Also, you may add a primary key with a generator. For columns, you can indicate the JDBC type, Hibernate type, and property name. Also, you may exclude a column from reverse engineering by selecting the **Exclude column from reverse engineering** checkbox (as shown below, right side).

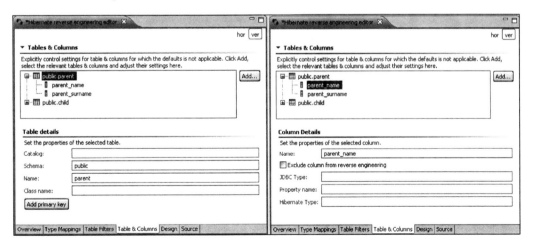

Design view

This is a tree representation of the `reveng.xml` file. From here, you can remove/ edit attributes (right-click on the desired attribute and select **Remove** or **Edit Attribute** option from the contextual menu—as shown below, left side), remove/add attributes/elements/child (right click on the desired attribute and select **Remove/ Add Attribute/Add Child/Add Before/Add After** option from the contextual menu—as shown below, right side).

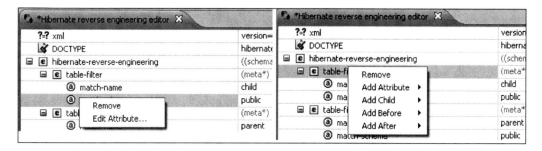

Note that if we place the mouse cursor over **Add Attribute/Add Child/Add Before** or **Add After** option, then Hibernate Tools will provide a sub-menu with the possible XML components that can be processed in this case (as shown below).

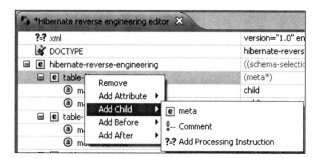

Source view

At any moment, you can check the source code of `reveng.xml` file by selecting the **Source** view. Note that modifying these files manually will automatically update the previous view (if you don't see the modifications, then try to save the file).

Hibernate Tools for Ant

Next, we will discuss the main aspects of Hibernate Tools for Ant. We can download Hibernate Tools as a ZIP archive from `http://www.hibernate.org/6.html` under the name: *Hibernate Tools for Ant and Eclipse*.

Extract this archive on your machine and note that it contains two folders with many JARs and sub-directories related to Eclipse IDE. Since we are not interested in Eclipse, in this section we will follow a simple copy-paste scenario that will help us to extract from here the required JARs that can be used with Ant.

Start by creating an empty directory on your machine and name it testHibernateToolsForAnt. In this directory, we will store the necessary JARs (under a /libs folder) and the examples created in this section (the examples are based on family database—for details see the *Preparations* section). The first JAR library that we will copy into the /libs folder is hibernate-tools.jar. This is the Hibernate Tools core JAR and it can be copied from /plugins/org.hibernate. eclipse_3.2.2.Beta1/lib/tools.

At this moment, the testHibernateToolsForAnt folder will look like this:

The <hibernatetool> Ant Task

Before using Ant tasks for Hibernate Tools, we need to define a <hibernatetool> task. For this, we will use the Ant <taskdef> task that permits us to define different kinds of tasks. In this case, we will define a <hibernatetool> task such as that in the following build.xml file (save this file in the testHibernateForAnt folder):

```
<project name="testHibernateToolsForAnt-hibernatetool" default="">

<!-- Hibernate Tools libraries -->
<property name="hibernate.tools"
          value="./libs/hibernate-tools.jar"/>
<!-- Hibernate Tools libraries paths -->
<path id="libraries">
 <path location="${hibernate.tools}" />
</path>
<!-- Define the "hibernatetool" task -->
<taskdef name="hibernatetool"
         classname="org.hibernate.tool.ant.HibernateToolTask"
         classpathref="libraries" />

</project>
```

Running this Ant script will not reveal any of the capabilities of the Hibernate Tools. You should get only a **BUILD SUCCESSFUL** message, as shown below:

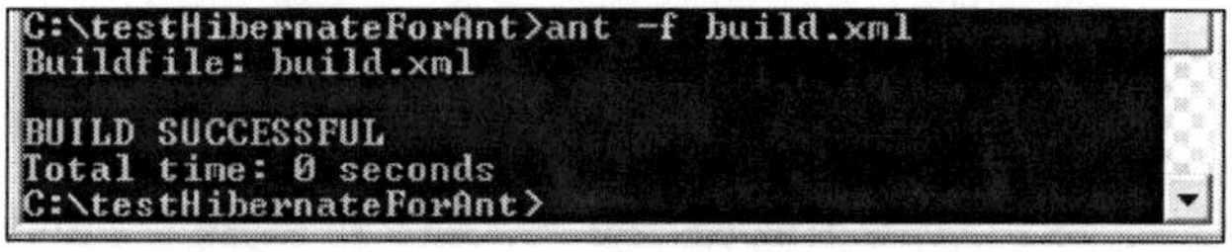

```
C:\testHibernateForAnt>ant -f build.xml
Buildfile: build.xml

BUILD SUCCESSFUL
Total time: 0 seconds
C:\testHibernateForAnt>
```

Adding Hibernate tools dependencies

Before writing Ant scripts that will actually put Hibernate Tools to work, we should provide the dependencies that sustain this goal. These dependencies are JARs that should be copied from their location to our /libs directory. For complete support, you should copy into the /libs folder all the JARs from these locations:

- `plugins/org.hibernate.eclipse_3.2.2.Beta1/lib/annotations`
- `plugins/org.hibernate.eclipse_3.2.2.Beta1/lib/hibernate`
- `plugins/org.hibernate.eclipse_3.2.2.Beta1/lib/tools`

Beside these libraries, we will also need two more JARs in /libs folder, as follows:

- The JDBC driver for our database—since we are using PostgreSQL, we will copy one of the available JDBC drivers (for example, `postgresql-8.2-505.jdbc2.jar`) from {`PostgreSQL_HOME`}/jdbc directory to the /libs directory. If you are using MySQL, SQL Server, or any other RDBMS, then copy the corresponding JAR JDBC driver instead of this.

- The `jboss-archive-browsing.jar`—this JAR can't be found in the Hibernate Tools distribution, but we will need it especially for testing the **Query Exporter**. This archive can be downloaded from the `http://www.java2s.com/Code/Jar/Spring-Related/Downloadjbossarchivebrowsingjar.htm` link.

Hibernate Configurations

There are four types of Hibernate configurations that can be used with Hibernate Tools for Ant. These configurations are:

- **Standard Hibernate Configuration**—known as `<configuration>`; this type reads the mappings from a `.cfg.xml` and/or a fileset. The general syntax of this element is:

```
<configuration
  configurationfile="hibernate.cfg.xml"
  propertyfile="hibernate.properties"
```

```
     entityresolver="your EntityResolver classname"
     namingstrategy="your NamingStrategy classname">
     <fileset...>

</configuration>
```

- **Annotations Configuration** — known as `<annotationconfiguration>`; this type reads the metamodel from EJB3/Hibernate Annotations based POJOs. The general syntax of this element is:

```
<hibernatetool destdir="${build.dir}/generatedfiles">
 <annotationconfiguration
  configurationfile="hibernate.cfg.xml"/>

 <!-- list exporters here -->

</hibernatetool>
```

- **JPA Configuration** — known as `<jpaconfiguration>`; this type reads the metamodel from a `persistence.xml` configuration file. The general syntax of this element is:

```
<jpaconfiguration persistenceunit="your_presistence_unit_name"/>
 <classpath>
  <!--here put classes dir, and/or jpa persistence compliant
   jar -->
  <path location="the_path" />
 </classpath>

 <!-- list exporters here -->
```

- **JDBC Configuration** — known as `<jdbcconfiguration>`; this type performs reverse engineering of the database from a JDBC connection. The general syntax of this element is:

```
<jdbcconfiguration
   ...
   packagename="package.name"
   revengfile="hibernate.reveng.xml"
   reversestrategy="your ReverseEngineeringStrategy classname"
   detectmanytomany="true|false"
   detectoptmisticlock="true|false"
>
   ...
</jdbcconfiguration>
```

Hibernate Tools exporters

It is time to get some real examples that will make our life easier when we talk about obtaining the main Hibernate artifacts. Next, you will see how to write Ant scripts for applying reverse engineering to get the following artifacts:

- Hibernate mapping files (.hbm.xml)
- POJOs (.java)
- Hibernate configuration file (.cfg.xml)
- SQL DDL(.ddl)
- Schema Documentation (.html)
- HQL queries results.

Before going further, we need to place some Hibernate configuration files in our testHibernateToolsForAnt directory, which will be used in different contexts of our examples (note that we are using the PostgreSQL RDBMS and the family database). We will need a hibernate.cfg.xml file, a hibernate.properties file, and a persistence.xml file, as follows:

- hibernate.cfg.xml — save this file in the testHibernateToolsForAnt/cfg directory:

```xml
<?xml version="1.0" encoding="utf-8"?>
<!DOCTYPE hibernate-configuration PUBLIC
"-//Hibernate/Hibernate Configuration DTD 3.0//EN"
"http://hibernate.sourceforge.net/hibernate-configuration-
3.0.dtd">
<hibernate-configuration>
    <session-factory name="">
        <property name="hibernate.bytecode.use_reflection_
         optimizer">
          false
        </property>
        <property name="hibernate.connection.driver_class">
          org.postgresql.Driver
        </property>
        <property name="hibernate.connection.url">
          jdbc:postgresql://localhost:5432/family
        </property>
        <property name="hibernate.connection.username">
          postgres
        </property>
        <property name="hibernate.connection.password">
          explorer
```

```
    </property>
    <property name="hibernate.dialect">
      org.hibernate.dialect.PostgreSQLDialect
    </property>
  </session-factory>
</hibernate-configuration>
```

- `hibernate.properties` — save this file in the `testHibernateToolsForAnt/properties` directory:

```
hibernate.connection.driver_class=org.postgresql.Driver
hibernate.connection.url=jdbc:postgresql://localhost:5432/family
hibernate.connection.username=postgres
hibernate.connection.password=explorer
hibernate.dialect=org.hibernate.dialect.PostgreSQLDialect
```

- `persistence.xml` — save this file in `testHibernateToolsForAnt/persistence/META-INF` directory:

```xml
<?xml version="1.0" encoding="UTF-8"?>
  <persistence
    xmlns="http://java.sun.com/xml/ns/persistence"
    xmlns:xsi="http://www.w3.org/2001/XMLSchema-instance"
    xsi:schemaLocation="http://java.sun.com/xml/ns/persistence
    http://java.sun.com/xml/ns/persistence/persistence_1_0.xsd"
    version="1.0">
    <persistence-unit name="unitTest">
    <properties>
      <property name="hibernate.connection.driver_class"
                value="org.postgresql.Driver"/>
      <property name="hibernate.connection.url"
                value="jdbc:postgresql://localhost:5432/family"/>
      <property name="hibernate.connection.username"
                value="postgres"/>
      <property name="hibernate.connection.password"
                value="explorer"/>
      <property name="hibernate.dialect"
                value="org.hibernate.dialect.PostgreSQLDialect"/>
    </properties>
  </persistence-unit>
  </persistence>
```

Now, the `testHibernateToolsForAnt` directory has this structure:

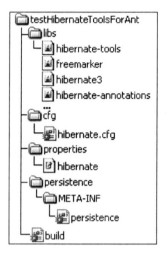

Hibernate Mapping Files Exporter

Hibernate Mapping Files Exporter is known as `<hbm2hbmxml>` and it generates a set of `.hbm.xml` files based on any kind of configuration. In the next example, we will use the JDBC Hibernate Configuration (`<jdbcconfiguration>`) to obtain the `Parent.hbm.xml` and `Child.hbm.xml` files for the `family` database, based on our `hibernate.cfg.xml` configuration file. Following is the Ant script that will do this job. Name it `build_hbm2hbmxml.xml` and save it in the `testHibernateToolsForAnt` directory. After running this script, the generated output will be saved in the `testHibernateToolsForAnt/hbm2hbmxml` directory.

```xml
<project name="testHibernateToolsForAnt-hbm2hbmxml" default="">

<!-- Hibernate Tools libraries -->
<property name="hibernate.tools"
          value="./libs/hibernate-tools.jar"/>
<property name="hibernate.3"
          value="./libs/hibernate3.jar"/>
<property name="freemarker"
          value="./libs/freemarker.jar"/>
<property name="commons.logging"
          value="./libs/commons-logging-1.0.4.jar"/>
<property name="dom4j"
          value="./libs/dom4j-1.6.1.jar"/>
<property name="commons.collections"
          value="./libs/commons-collections-2.1.1.jar"/>
```

```xml
<property name="jtidy"
          value="./libs/jtidy-r8-20060801.jar"/>
<!-- PostgreSQL JDBC driver -->
<property name="jdbc.driver"
          value="./libs/postgresql-8.2-505.jdbc2.jar"/>
<!-- Directory where the generated .hbm.xml files are saved (it
will be automatically created) -->
<property name="build.dir.hbm2hbmxml" value="./hbm2hbmxml"/>
<!-- Hibernate Tools libraries paths -->
<path id="libraries">
 <path location="${hibernate.tools}" />
 <path location="${hibernate.3}" />
 <path location="${freemarker}" />
 <path location="${commons.logging}" />
 <path location="${dom4j}" />
 <path location="${commons.collections}" />
 <path location="${jtidy}" />
 <path location="${jdbc.driver}" />
</path>
<!-- Define the "hibernatetool" task -->
<taskdef name="hibernatetool"
         classname="org.hibernate.tool.ant.HibernateToolTask"
         classpathref="libraries" />
<!-- Generating .hbm.xml files via hbm2hbmxml from a basic
hibernate.cfg.xml -->
<hibernatetool destdir="${build.dir.hbm2hbmxml}">
 <classpath>
  <path location="."/>
 </classpath>
 <jdbcconfiguration configurationfile="cfg/hibernate.cfg.xml" />
 <hbm2hbmxml/>
</hibernatetool>

</project>
```

When you run this Ant script use the –f option to indicate that we don't use the `build.xml` default name:

```
{root}/testHibernateToolsForAnt>ant -f build_hbm2hbmxml.xml
```

POJOs Exporter

The **POJOs Exporter** is known as `<hbm2java>` and it generates a set of POJO files. In the next example, we will use the JDBC Hibernate Configuration (`<jdbcconfiguration>`) to obtain the `Parent.java` and `Child.java` files for the `family` database, based on our `hibernate.cfg.xml` configuration file. The Ant script that will do this job is listed below. Name it `build_hbm2java.xml` and save it in the `testHibernateToolsForAnt` directory. After running this script, the generated output will be saved in `testHibernateToolsForAnt/hbm2java` directory.

```xml
<project name="testHibernateToolsForAnt-hbm2java" default="">

<!-- Hibernate Tools libraries -->
<property name="hibernate.tools"
          value="./libs/hibernate-tools.jar"/>
<property name="hibernate.3"
          value="./libs/hibernate3.jar"/>
<property name="freemarker"
          value="./libs/freemarker.jar"/>
<property name="commons.logging"
          value="./libs/commons-logging-1.0.4.jar"/>
<property name="dom4j"
          value="./libs/dom4j-1.6.1.jar"/>
<property name="commons.collections"
          value="./libs/commons-collections-2.1.1.jar"/>

<!-- PostgreSQL JDBC driver -->
<property name="jdbc.driver"
          value="./libs/postgresql-8.2-505.jdbc2.jar"/>

<!-- Directory where the generated POJOs are saved (it will be
automatically created) -->
<property name="build.dir.hbm2java" value="./hbm2java"/>

<!-- Hibernate Tools libraries paths -->
<path id="libraries">
 <path location="${hibernate.tools}" />
 <path location="${hibernate.3}" />
 <path location="${freemarker}" />
 <path location="${commons.logging}" />
 <path location="${dom4j}" />
 <path location="${commons.collections}" />
 <path location="${jdbc.driver}" />
</path>

<!-- Define the "hibernatetool" task -->
<taskdef name="hibernatetool"
          classname="org.hibernate.tool.ant.HibernateToolTask"
```

```
                classpathref="libraries" />
    <!-- Generating pojo's via hbm2java from a basic hibernate.cfg.xml
    -->
    <hibernatetool destdir="${build.dir.hbm2java}">
     <classpath>
      <path location="."/>
     </classpath>
     <jdbcconfiguration configurationfile="cfg/hibernate.cfg.xml" />
     <hbm2java/>
    </hibernatetool>

    </project>
```

When you run this Ant script, use the –f option to indicate that we don't use the `build.xml` default name:

{root}/testHibernateToolsForAnt>ant -f build_hbm2java.xml

The above Ant script will generate traditional POJO classes. If you want to generate POJOs that respect the JDK 5 syntax and features or EJB3 features, then you can use the following attributes:

- `jdk5` — if is set to `true` then the generated POJOs will respect JDK 5 syntax. By default, it is set to `false`. For example:

  ```
  <hbm2java jdk5="true"/>
  ```

- `ejb3` — if it is set to `true` then the generated POJOs will respect the EJB3 syntax. By default, it is set to `false`. For example:

  ```
  <hbm2java ejb3="true"/>
  ```

Hibernate Configuration File Exporter

The **Hibernate Configuration File Exporter** is known as `<hbm2cfgxml>` and it generates a Hibernate configuration file, `hibernate.cfg.xml`, based on any kind of configuration. In the next example, we will use the Standard Hibernate Configuration (`<configuration>`) to obtain the `hibernate.cfg.xml` file for the `family` database, based on our `hibernate.properties` configuration file. The Ant script that will do this job is listed below. Name it `build_hbm2cfgxml.xml` and save it in the `testHibernateToolsForAnt` directory. After running this script, the generated output will be saved in `testHibernateToolsForAnt/hbm2cfgxml` directory.

```
<project name="testHibernateToolsForAnt-hbm2cfgxml" default="">

<!-- Hibernate Tools libraries -->
<property name="hibernate.tools"
          value="./libs/hibernate-tools.jar"/>
```

```xml
<property name="hibernate.3"
        value="./libs/hibernate3.jar"/>
<property name="freemarker"
        value="./libs/freemarker.jar"/>
<property name="commons.logging"
        value="./libs/commons-logging-1.0.4.jar"/>
<property name="dom4j"
        value="./libs/dom4j-1.6.1.jar"/>
<property name="commons.collections"
        value="./libs/commons-collections-2.1.1.jar"/>
<property name="jtidy"
        value="./libs/jtidy-r8-20060801.jar"/>

<!-- PostgreSQL JDBC driver -->
<property name="jdbc.driver"
        value="./libs/postgresql-8.2-505.jdbc2.jar"/>

<!-- Directory where the generated .cfg.xml file is saved (it will be
automatically created) -->
<property name="build.dir.hbm2cfgxml" value="./hbm2cfgxml"/>

<!-- Hibernate Tools libraries paths -->
<path id="libraries">
 <path location="${hibernate.tools}" />
 <path location="${hibernate.3}" />
 <path location="${freemarker}" />
 <path location="${commons.logging}" />
 <path location="${dom4j}" />
 <path location="${commons.collections}" />
 <path location="${jtidy}" />
 <path location="${jdbc.driver}" />
</path>
<!-- Define the "hibernatetool" task -->
<taskdef name="hibernatetool"
        classname="org.hibernate.tool.ant.HibernateToolTask"
        classpathref="libraries" />

<!-- Generating hibernate configuration file via hbm2cfgxml from a
basic hibernate.properties -->
<hibernatetool destdir="${build.dir.hbm2cfgxml}">
 <classpath>
  <path location="."/>
 </classpath>
 <configuration propertyfile="properties/hibernate.properties">
  <fileset dir=".">
    <include name="**/*.hbm.xml"/>
```

```
    </fileset>
   </configuration>
  <hbm2cfgxml/>
 </hibernatetool>

</project>
```

When you run this Ant script, use the –f option to indicate that we don't use the `build.xml` default name:

{root}/testHibernateToolsForAnt>ant –f build_hbm2cfgxml.xml

The above Ant script will generate a traditional `hibernate.cfg.xml` file, which means that the `.hbm.xml` files will be mapped using the `<mapping resource="{name.hbm.xml}"/>` syntax. If you want to use the `<mapping class="{name.hbm.xml}"/>` instead, then use the `ejb3` attribute as shown below (by default, this attribute's value is `false`):

```
<hbm2cfgxml ejb3="true"/>
```

In the next example, we will use the JPA Configuration (`<jpaconfiguration>`) to obtain the `hibernate.cfg.xml` file for the `family` database, based on our `persistence.xml` configuration file. The Ant script that will do this job is listed below. Name it `build_hbm2cfgxml_jpa.xml` and save it in the `testHibernateToolsForAnt` directory. After running this script, the generated output will be saved in the `testHibernateToolsForAnt/hbm2cfgxml_jpa` directory.

```
<project name="testHibernateToolsForAnt-hbm2cfgxml_jpa" default="">

<!-- Hibernate Tools libraries -->
<property name="hibernate.tools"
          value="./libs/hibernate-tools.jar"/>
<property name="hibernate.3"
          value="./libs/hibernate3.jar"/>
<property name="freemarker"
          value="./libs/freemarker.jar"/>
<property name="commons.logging"
          value="./libs/commons-logging-1.0.4.jar"/>
<property name="dom4j"
          value="./libs/dom4j-1.6.1.jar"/>
<property name="jtidy"
          value="./libs/jtidy-r8-20060801.jar"/>
<property name="ejb3.persistence"
          value="./libs/ejb3-persistence.jar"/>
<property name="hibernate.entitymanager"
          value="./libs/hibernate-entitymanager.jar"/>
<property name="hibernate.annotations"
```

```
                value="./libs/hibernate-annotations.jar"/>
    <property name="hibernate.commons.annotations"
                value="./libs/hibernate-commons-annotations.jar"/>
    <property name="jboss.archive.browsing"
                value="./libs/jboss-archive-browsing.jar"/>

    <!-- PostgreSQL JDBC driver -->
    <property name="jdbc.driver"
                value="./libs/postgresql-8.2-505.jdbc2.jar"/>

    <!-- Directory where the generated .cfg.xml file is saved (it will be
    automatically created) -->
    <property name="build.dir.hbm2cfgxml_jpa" value="./hbm2cfgxml_jpa"/>

    <!-- Hibernate Tools libraries paths -->
    <path id="libraries">
     <path location="${hibernate.tools}" />
     <path location="${hibernate.3}" />
     <path location="${freemarker}" />
     <path location="${commons.logging}" />
     <path location="${dom4j}" />
     <path location="${jtidy}" />
     <path location="${ejb3.persistence}" />
     <path location="${hibernate.entitymanager}" />
     <path location="${hibernate.annotations}" />
     <path location="${hibernate.commons.annotations}" />
     <path location="${jboss.archive.browsing}" />
     <path location="${jdbc.driver}" />
    </path>

    <!-- Define the "hibernatetool" task -->
    <taskdef name="hibernatetool"
                classname="org.hibernate.tool.ant.HibernateToolTask"
                classpathref="libraries" />

    <!-- Generating hibernate configuration file via hbm2cfgxml from a
    basic persistence.xml -->
    <hibernatetool destdir="${build.dir.hbm2cfgxml_jpa}">
    <classpath>
      <path location="./persistence"/>
     </classpath>
     <jpaconfiguration persistenceunit="unitTest"/>
     <hbm2cfgxml/>
    </hibernatetool>

    </project>
```

Database Schema Exporter

The **Database Schema Exporter** is known as `<hbm2ddl>` and it generates the appropriate SQL DDL file. In the next example we will use the JDBC Hibernate Configuration (`<jdbcconfiguration>`) to obtain the SQL DDL file for the `family` database, based on our `hibernate.cfg.xml` configuration file. The Ant script that will do this job is listed below. Name it `build_hbm2ddl.xml` and save it in the `testHibernateToolsForAnt` directory. After running this script, the generated output (`sql.ddl`) will be saved in `testHibernateToolsForAnt/hbm2ddl` directory. Note that the `hbm2ddl` directory must be manually created!

```
<project name="testHibernateToolsForAnt-hbm2ddl" default="">

<!-- Hibernate Tools libraries -->
<property name="hibernate.tools"
          value="./libs/hibernate-tools.jar"/>
<property name="hibernate.3"
          value="./libs/hibernate3.jar"/>
<property name="commons.logging"
          value="./libs/commons-logging-1.0.4.jar"/>
<property name="dom4j"
          value="./libs/dom4j-1.6.1.jar"/>
<property name="commons.collections"
          value="./libs/commons-collections-2.1.1.jar"/>

<!-- PostgreSQL JDBC driver -->
<property name="jdbc.driver"
          value="./libs/postgresql-8.2-505.jdbc2.jar"/>

<!-- Directory where the generated DDL file is saved (it will not be
automatically created) -->
<property name="build.dir.hbm2ddl" value="./hbm2ddl"/>

<!-- Hibernate Tools libraries paths -->
<path id="libraries">
 <path location="${hibernate.tools}" />
 <path location="${hibernate.3}" />
 <path location="${commons.logging}" />
 <path location="${dom4j}" />
 <path location="${commons.collections}" />
 <path location="${jdbc.driver}" />
</path>

<!-- Define the "hibernatetool" task -->
<taskdef name="hibernatetool"
         classname="org.hibernate.tool.ant.HibernateToolTask"
         classpathref="libraries" />
```

```
<!-- Generating DDL file via hbm2ddl from a basic hibernate.cfg.xml
-->
<hibernatetool destdir="${build.dir.hbm2ddl}">
 <classpath>
  <path location="."/>
 </classpath>
 <jdbcconfiguration configurationfile="cfg/hibernate.cfg.xml" />
 <hbm2ddl export="false" outputfilename="sql.ddl" format="true"
delimiter=";"/>
</hibernatetool>

</project>
```

Documentation Exporter

The **Documentation Exporter** is known as `<hbm2doc>` and it generates the appropriate HTML documentation for database schema. In the next example we will use the JDBC Hibernate Configuration (`<jdbcconfiguration>`) to obtain the HTML documentation for the `family` database, based on our `hibernate.cfg.xml` configuration file. The Ant script that will do this job is listed below. Name it `build_hbm2doc.xml` and save it in the `testHibernateToolsForAnt` directory. After running this script, the generated output will be saved in the `testHibernateToolsForAnt/hbm2doc` directory.

```
<project name="testHibernateToolsForAnt-hbm2doc" default="">

<!-- Hibernate Tools libraries -->
<property name="hibernate.tools"
          value="./libs/hibernate-tools.jar"/>
<property name="hibernate.3"
          value="./libs/hibernate3.jar"/>
<property name="freemarker"
          value="./libs/freemarker.jar"/>
<property name="commons.logging"
          value="./libs/commons-logging-1.0.4.jar"/>
<property name="dom4j"
          value="./libs/dom4j-1.6.1.jar"/>
<property name="commons.collections"
          value="./libs/commons-collections-2.1.1.jar"/>

<!-- PostgreSQL JDBC driver -->
<property name="jdbc.driver"
          value="./libs/postgresql-8.2-505.jdbc2.jar"/>

<!-- Directory where the generated documentation is saved (it will be
automatically created) -->
<property name="build.dir.hbm2doc" value="./hbm2doc"/>
```

```
<!-- Hibernate Tools libraries paths -->
<path id="libraries">
 <path location="${hibernate.tools}" />
 <path location="${hibernate.3}" />
 <path location="${freemarker}" />
 <path location="${commons.logging}" />
 <path location="${dom4j}" />
 <path location="${commons.collections}" />
 <path location="${jdbc.driver}" />
</path>

<!-- Define the "hibernatetool" task -->
<taskdef name="hibernatetool"
        classname="org.hibernate.tool.ant.HibernateToolTask"
        classpathref="libraries" />

<!-- Generating documentation file via hbm2doc from a basic hibernate.
cfg.xml -->
<hibernatetool destdir="${build.dir.hbm2doc}">
 <classpath>
  <path location="."/>
 </classpath>
 <jdbcconfiguration configurationfile="hbm2cfgxml/hibernate.cfg.xml"
/>
 <hbm2doc/>
</hibernatetool>

</project>
```

Query Exporter

The **Query Exporter** is known as `<query>` and it allows us to execute HQL statements over a database. In the next example, we will use the JDBC Hibernate Configuration (`<jdbcconfiguration>`) to obtain the result of a simple HQL query (`select childName from Child as child`) for the `family` database, based on our `hibernate.cfg.xml` configuration file. The Ant script that will do this job is listed below. Name it `build_query.xml` and save it in the `testHibernateToolsForAnt` directory. After running this script, the generated output (`hql.txt`) will be saved in the `testHibernateToolsForAnt/hqlquery` directory.

```
<project name="testHibernateToolsForAnt-query" default="">

<!-- Hibernate Tools libraries -->
<property name="hibernate.tools"
        value="./libs/hibernate-tools.jar"/>
<property name="hibernate.3"
        value="./libs/hibernate3.jar"/>
```

```
<property name="freemarker"
         value="./libs/freemarker.jar"/>
<property name="commons.logging"
         value="./libs/commons-logging-1.0.4.jar"/>
<property name="dom4j"
         value="./libs/dom4j-1.6.1.jar"/>
<property name="commons.collections"
         value="./libs/cglib-2.1.3.jar"/>
<property name="cglib"
         value="./libs/commons-collections-2.1.1.jar"/>
<property name="asm"
         value="./libs/asm.jar"/>
<property name="jta"
         value="./libs/jta.jar"/>
<property name="antlr"
         value="./libs/antlr-2.7.6.jar"/>

<!-- JDBC driver -->
<property name="jdbc.driver"
         value="./libs/postgresql-8.2-505.jdbc2.jar"/>

<!-- Directory where the query's results are saved (it will be
automatically created) -->
<property name="build.dir.hql" value="./hqlquery"/>

<!-- Hibernate Tools libraries paths -->
<path id="libraries">
 <path location="${hibernate.tools}" />
 <path location="${hibernate.3}" />
 <path location="${freemarker}" />
 <path location="${commons.logging}" />
 <path location="${dom4j}" />
 <path location="${commons.collections}" />
 <path location="${cglib}" />
 <path location="${asm}" />
 <path location="${jta}" />
 <path location="${antlr}" />
 <path location="${jdbc.driver}" />
</path>

<!-- Define the "hibernatetool" task -->
<taskdef name="hibernatetool"
         classname="org.hibernate.tool.ant.HibernateToolTask"
         classpathref="libraries" />

<!-- Executing the HQL query -->
<hibernatetool destdir="${build.dir.hql}">
 <classpath>
```

```
    <path location="."/>
    <path location="./hbm2java"/>
    <path location="./hbm2hbmxml"/>
  </classpath>
  <jdbcconfiguration configurationfile="cfg/hibernate.cfg.xml">
  </jdbcconfiguration>
  <query destfile="hql.txt">
    <hql>select childName from Child as child</hql>
  </query>
</hibernatetool>

</project>
```

 For placing more HQL queries in the same Ant script, use multiple `<hql>` elements.

Import all libraries dependencies

As you saw in the above Ant scripts, we have always imported from /libs only the libraries that sustained a particular example. If you don't want to spend time with this aspect, then you can import all the libraries from /libs by using the following code:

```
<!-- Hibernate Tools libraries -->
<property name="librariesdir" value="./libs"/>
...
<!-- Hibernate Tools libraries paths -->
<path id="libraries">
  <fileset dir="${librariesdir}">
   <include name="*.jar"/>
  </fileset>
</path>
```

Summary

In this chapter we have learnt how to use Hibernate Tools for Eclipse and Ant. We saw how to manage different kind of configurations, how to use the available wizards for speeding up the process of getting Hibernate artifacts, how to take advantage of reverse engineering, how to execute HQL queries, how to convert HQL to SQL queries without any effort, and how to control and customize different Hibernate Tools processes. In other words, we have learnt to exploit and control the tremendous power of Hibernate from a great dedicated tool-set named Hibernate Tools.

8
jBPM Tools

In this chapter, we will discuss the jBPM Tools. As you probably know, jBPM is the acronym for **Java Business Process Management**, and it represents a JBoss workflow management system. The term "business process management" typically refers to a set of actions meant to optimize business processes for adapting them to dynamic environments. jBPM executes business processes expressed in BPEL or in its own process definition language, jPDL.

If you are not familiar with the jBPM paradigm, then before going further, it is advisable that you read the jBPM manual, which is available online at `http://docs.jboss.org/jbpm/v3/userguide/` (if you download a jPDL Runtime, then this documentation is also available in the `/doc` folder of the received distribution).

Next, you will see how to configure a proper environment for developing and running/testing jBPM processes. After that, we will develop a jBPM process through jBPM Tools, and we will run it on a JBoss server with jBPM support. We will finish by developing a JUnit test for our jBPM process.

In this chapter, following the learning by example technique, we will develop a simple jBPM process meant to get you familiar with the jBPM Tools. The base idea is to reproduce the "road" followed by an invoice, from submission to the moment when it is resolved. Starting from this idea, here is our process scenario:

1. Author of an article is submitting an invoice to the publisher.
2. The invoice arrives at the publisher financial department, where a financial controller checks the invoice for any mistakes.
3. The financial controller may accept or reject the invoice.
4. If the invoice is rejected, than the author receives a notification by email with the contact phone number.
5. If the invoice is accepted, then it is registered (stored in electronic format) and the author is paid the fee through an online payment system (such as PayPal).
6. The invoice "road" ends up here.

In the figure below you can see a UML sketch of what we have just discussed above:

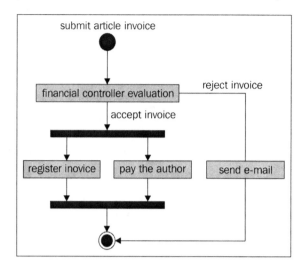

Downloading and installing the JBoss jBPM Suite

To start working with the jBPM Tools, it is mandatory to install the JBoss jPDL Runtime. Also, for testing the tasks, we will need a server that supports jBPM, such as the JBoss server with jBPM included, known as JBoss jBPM Server. For accomplishing these tasks with minimum effort, we will download the jPDL Suite from `http://www.jboss.org/jbossjbpm/jpdl_downloads/` (as shown in the following screenshot). The advantage of downloading jPDL Suite, instead of jPDL Runtime, is that the suite contains complete jBPM support, including the runtime and the JBoss jBPM server (pre-configured JBoss installation). This server contains jBPM inside the console web application, which is packaged as a web archive (`jbpm-console.war`) that can be used by jBPM administrators and process participants.

jBPM Downloads						
Name	Version	Size	Released	License		
jPDL Suite	3.2.3	85.1 MB	2008-06-16	LGPL	Download	Notes
jPDL Runtime	3.2.3	18.3 MB	2008-06-16	LGPL	Download	Notes
jBPM BPEL	1.1	13.9 MB	2007-11-29	CPL	Download	Notes
jBPM GPD	3.1.4	9.6 MB	2008-09-10	LGPL	Download	Notes
PVM	1.0.alpha2	7 MB	2008-04-30	LGPL	Download	Notes

If you don't see the jPDL Suite, then click on the **All jPDL Downloads** link. A SourceForge.net page should be displayed with all the jPDL releases. Among them, you should find the jPDL suite.

Next, extract the ZIP archive (`jbpm-jpdl-suite-3.2.3.zip`) in your favorite location (for example, we extracted it in the `C:\Packt\jbpm-jpdl-3.2.3` folder). It is time to configure the JBoss jBPM Server and the JBoss jPDL Runtime under Eclipse IDE. Configuring the JBoss jBPM Server is a goal that can be accomplished by following the example from the *Adding a WTP Runtime in Eclipse* and *Adding a WTP Server in Eclipse* sections, in the *JBoss AS Tools* chapter. Anyway, here are some clues that you may find useful during this job (adjust the following paths and names according to your favorites):

- For the jPDL Suite version 3.2.3, the JBoss jBPM Server version is 4.2.2, so in Eclipse, you should select a **JBoss 4.2 Runtime** from the available runtimes.
- Use the **JBoss jBPM 4.2** name for the JBoss 4.2 Runtime.
- The home directory of **JBoss 4.2 Runtime** is `C:\Packt\jbpm-jpdl-3.2.3\server`.
- Use the **JBoss jBPM 4.2 Server** name for the JBoss jBPM Server.
- The deploy directory of JBoss jBPM Server is `C:\Packt\jbpm-jpdl-3.2.3\server\server\jbpm\deploy`.

If you have correctly configured the JBoss jBPM Server in Eclipse, then the **JBoss Server View** should display the new server as in the following screenshot:

Now, let's focus on how to configure the jPDL Runtime in Eclipse. The jBPM Designer is already included in the JBoss Tools distribution, but to make it work we need the jPDL Runtime, which may be configured like this:

1. Launch the Eclipse IDE.
2. In the mail menu of Eclipse, go to **Window** and select the **Preferences** option.
3. In the **Preferences** window, expand the **JBoss jBPM** node (left panel) and select the **Runtime Locations** leaf.

4. In the same window, right panel, click on the **Add** button to open the **Edit Location** window (screenshot shown below). In this window, type any name you like for this runtime instance (**Name** field) and use the **Search** button to navigate to the folder where you have extracted the ZIP archive representing the JBoss jPDL Runtime. Now, click on the **OK** button.

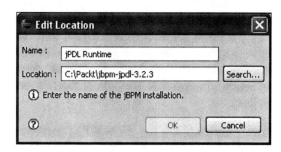

5. Note that the new runtime is added in the **Preferences** window, right panel. Select the checkbox next to the added runtime and click on the **Apply** and **OK** buttons.

Creating a jBPM stub project

Our process, as any other jBPM process, needs a "frame" that will sustain the process definitions. In our case, this "frame" is a jBPM project that can be generated through jBPM Tools like this:

1. From the Eclipse File main menu, select the **New | Other** option.

2. In the **New** window, expand the **JBoss jBPM** node and select the **Process Project** leaf.

3. Click on the **Next** button (as shown in the following screenshot).

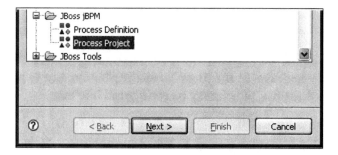

4. At this step we have to indicate the project name (**Project name** field) and the project location (**Location** field). By default, this location is your Eclipse workspace, but it can be modified by de-selecting the **Use default location** checkbox and using the **Browse** button to navigate to the new location. We named the project **article-invoice** and we selected the default Eclipse workspace (screenshot given below). Click on the **Next** button.

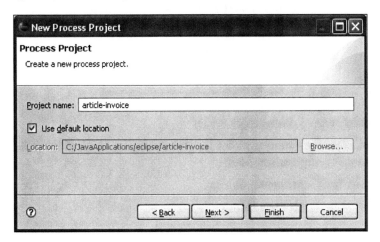

5. Now, we should indicate which jPDL Runtime we want to use. From the runtime list, select the jPDL Runtime (installed earlier) and click on the **Finish** button (as shown in the following screenshot).

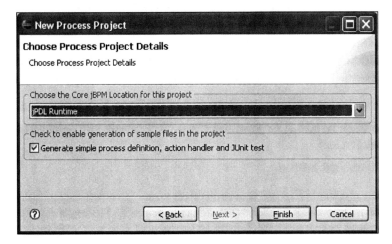

After a few seconds the project stub is generated, and it's available in the **Project Explorer** view. Here, we have four generated folders as follows (screenshot given below):

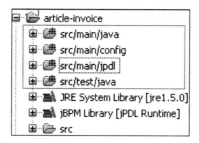

- **src/main/java** – Java sources folder
- **src/main/config** – resources folder (for example, **properties** files and Hibernate configuration files)
- **src/main/jpdl** – processes folder
- **src/test/java** – unit tests folder

Creating a jBPM process definition

As you probably know, process definitions are the core of jBPM. They are packaged in process archives and are executed by the jPDL process engine. For this, the jPDL engine must "read" the process graph, execute the defined actions, maintain the process flow, and report the process events. Following the jBPM paradigm, we can now create the process definition for our case. Next, we will create an empty process definition for the jBPM stub project created above, and we will name it **article-invoice-pd**. The steps are listed below:

1. From the Eclipse **File** main menu, select the **New | Other** option.
2. In the **New** window, expand the **JBoss jBPM** node and select the **Process Definition** leaf.
3. Click the **Next** button.

We now have to indicate the process definition name (**Process name** field) and the process definition source folder (**Source folder** field). For example, type **article-invoice-pd** as the process definition name and select `article-invoice/src/main/jpdl` as the source folder (use the **Browse** button to navigate to this folder) as per shown in the following screenshot. Click on the **Finish** button.

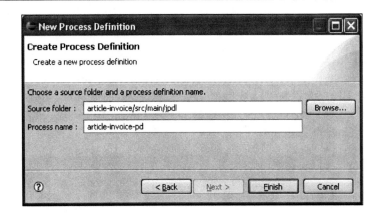

After a few seconds the process definition is created and the **jBPM Graphical Process Designer** (jBPM GPD) editor is launched.

After the process definition is created, the **Package Explorer** view will reveal two XML documents named **gpd.xml** and **processdefinition.xml**. The first one contains the graphical information for the process definition editor and the second one contains process definition information without the graphical information (formal description of the process' components such as nodes, transitions, actions, etc.). See the following screenshot.

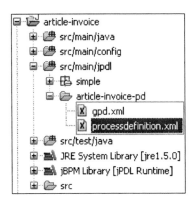

Launching the jBPM JPDL perspective

Now that we have a jPBM project and an empty process definition, we can almost start creating the process itself. Before this, let's bring in front another facility of jBPM Tools that will make our life easier in the following sections. This facility is the **jBPM JPDL** perspective, which can be launched from the **Window | Open Perspective** option | **Other** option | **jBPM JPDL** perspective. This perspective contains three views as follows:

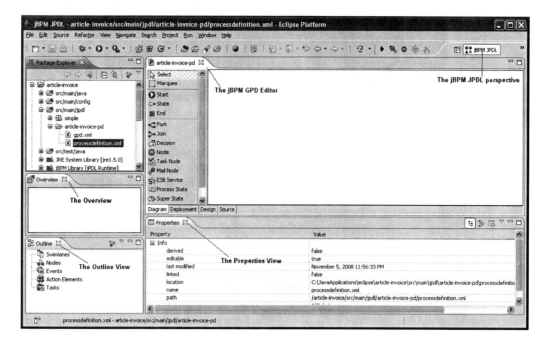

- **Overview**—here we will see a scrollable thumbnail of the entire process. This is very useful when the process structure is large and the navigation becomes difficult.

- **Outline** view—here we will see a tree structure representing the process outline.

- **Properties** view—here we will see/modify the main properties of the selected items from **jBPM GPD Editor** (every item has its own set of properties).

For example, the first thing that you can do to see how the **Properties** view works is to give a name to the process definition graph. This name will be used to recognize our process in the JBoss jBPM Server console. For this, click inside the **jBPM GBD Editor** and then type **INVOICE-PD** in the **Properties** view, **General** tab (screenshot shown below).

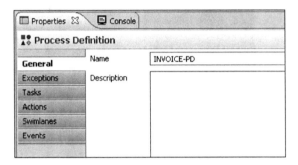

jBPM GPD Editor

A process definition is based on a graph that contains **nodes**, **transitions**, **actions**, one **start-state,** and one **end-state**. In this model, the execution starts from the start-state, flows through the graph and stops at the end-state. Nodes are commands executed when they are encountered, and transitions are the highways of the graph, directing the flow execution between nodes. Actions are pieces of Java code that are executed by the jPDL engine for following a specific logic. Most of the time, actions are encountered in nodes, but they can also be placed in transitions.

All these components can be easily developed through the **jBPM GPD Editor**, which can assist us to create the desired graph. From here, we can create process definitions, attach action handlers to events, edit definition source, create process archives, test process definitions, and so on.

This designer contains four views (tabs): **Diagram**, **Deployment**, **Design**, and **Source**. Next, we will discuss each one of these and see how to exploit them for our process definition.

Diagram view

We can use this view to manage the process's components in a graphical manner. As you can see from the screenshot given below, the **Diagram** view contains a set of tools (left side) and a canvas (right side). The basic idea of creating a process' component consists of selecting the desired tool from the tools-set and clicking on the canvas.

After that, we can arrange the components on the canvas and configure the desired properties.

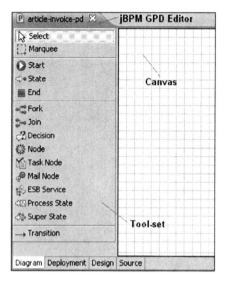

 By default, the **Diagram** view canvas looks like a blank sheet of paper. For obtaining a "good looking" graph, we may use a grid that helps us to get a nice alignment of the graph's components. The grid can be activated by selecting the **Show Grid** option from the Eclipse **View** menu (screenshot given below).

Adding states

According to jBPM, every process definition must have a start-state and an end-state. These nodes are the boundaries of the process and they mark the beginning and the end of the process flow. Therefore, we will begin the graph drawing with these two components. These states can be added through the **Diagram** view, by selecting the **Start** and **End** states from the tools-set, and clicking on the canvas after each selection (this logic is applicable for all tools from this tool-set). The result should resemble that in the screenshot given below:

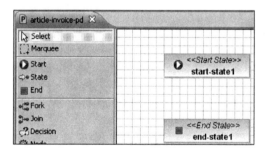

In our case, the start-state will have a double role. First, it will serve as a start point (its default goal) and second, it will be the point where the article's author will fill up the invoice fields, before sending it to the financial controller.

We now have a clear definition for our process definition, and it is thus time to "feed" the graph with more components.

Adding task-nodes

When the article's author sends the invoice it arrives with the financial controller. This is an important step in our process definition, because the financial controller will accept or reject the invoice based on a closer look at the invoice's fields (he/she will check for any errors that may invalidate the invoice). As you can see, this is an action performed by a human, which means that at this point the execution should be stopped until the human gives the verdict. Depending on human decision, the flow will follow the indicated transition to the next node. This situation is known as a "wait state" and, in JBPM, is accomplished by a task-node.

Just select the **Task Node** tool from the tool-set and place the task-node on the canvas between the start and end states (as shown in the following screenshot).

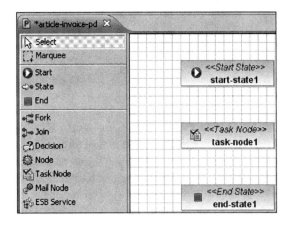

If the invoice is rejected, then the process definition will inform the author about this action and finish the process definition execution. Otherwise, the invoice should be registered (electronic stored) and the author should get the fee online through an electronic system like PayPal.

Adding nodes

Practically, if we arrive here, it means that the financial controller has accepted the invoice. Now, we need to register the invoice in our dedicated database and send the fee to the author through an online payment system. These goals can't be accomplished by jBPM, they must be hard coded in Java API and executed at the proper moment (these pieces of Java code are known as actions). What jBPM can do is offer us a component named **node**, which was especially designed to serve us when we want to write our own code. The idea is that we associate the node with an action, and the action is executed when the flow arrives in the node. Later, we will see how to write an action, but for now, let's add two nodes to our process definition. For this, select the **Node** tool from the tools-set and place the nodes on the canvas, between the task-node and the end-state (as shown in the following screenshot).

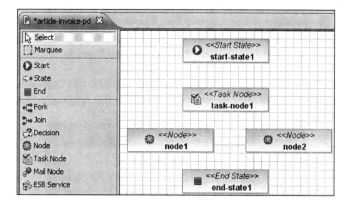

Adding a fork-join system

In the previous section we have added two nodes that will sustain us to register the invoice and to pay the article's author fee. Because these two actions are not related, (none of them should expect the other one to end before it can be executed) we can try to optimize the process definition by executing them concurrently. For these kind of goals, jBPM provide the **fork-join** system, which splits one path of execution into multiple concurrent paths of execution. Actually, the jBPM **fork** component is responsible for splitting, while the jBPM **join** component reunites the fork's transitions into one transition. The join will end every token that arrives in it, and, when all sibling tokens are ended, it will propagate the executing further.

Select the **Fork** tool from the tool-set and place the fork on the canvas between the task-node and the two nodes. After that, select the **Join** tool and place the join between the nodes and the end-state (as shown in the following screenshot).

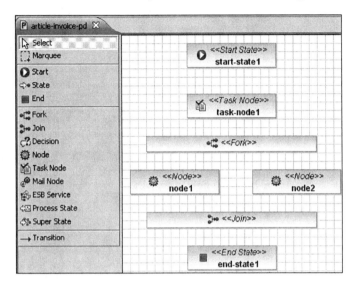

Adding a mail node

As we said earlier, the financial controller may reject an invoice for a variety of reasons that are not relevant here. What matters is that the process definition should inform the article's author about this decision. For example, a simple solution consists in sending him/her an email of the type "Sorry, but your invoice was rejected by the financial controller. For details please contact Mr. ... ". This issue can be accomplished by jBPM through a **mail-node** that maps a defined action for sending an email.

 Beside mail-node, jBPM also may send emails using a mail action (nothing appears in the graph), task assign mails (a notification email can be sent when a task gets assigned to an actor), and task reminder mail (an email can be sent periodically to an actor to remind them of something).

Select the **Email Node** tool and place a mail-node on the canvas next to the two nodes (as shown in the following screenshot).

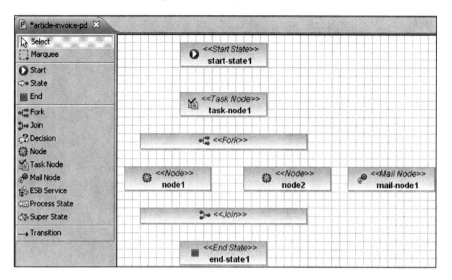

Adding transitions

So far, it is like we have a map (the graph) with eight cities (the nodes), but we don't have any idea of how to travel from one city to another, because there are no visible roads (transitions). Obviously, this makes the map useless, so in this section we will see how to sketch roads and what particularity they may have.

In jBPM, the roads are named **transitions** and they are characterized by a source node (represented by the **from** property), a destination node (represented by the **to** property) and, optionally, they can have a unique name. We can add a transition to our graph like this:

1. Select the **Transition** tool from the tool-set.
2. Click on the source node (per example, on the **start-state**).
3. Click on the destination node (per example, on the **task-node**).

Repeat steps 1-3 from above until your graph looks like the one in the following screenshot (note that for uniqueness, some transitions will get a default name). Keeping in mind what we have said in previous sections, you should have no problem in understanding the logic of our transitions (note how we sketched the transitions in the fork-join system). Anyway, if you think that is a little too abstract for you, then the following sections will surely help to clear things.

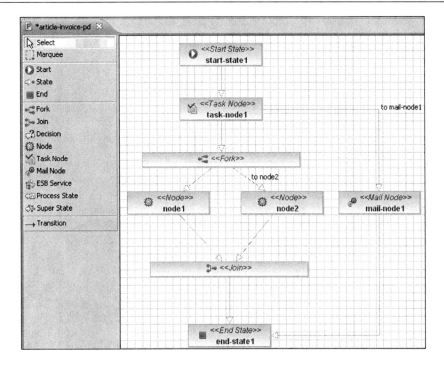

Now, the jPDL engine will use the transitions to traverse the graph.

Customizing node names

As you can see from the above screenshot, jBPM has generated a set of generic names for our nodes (for example, task-node1, node1, node2, etc.). Obviously, humans are not very impressed by these names, as they don't suggest anything and intuition is useless in this case. This is why it is a good idea to rename the nodes accordingly to our scopes. For this, we can proceed in at least two ways:

1. Click on the node's name inside the diagram and type the new name here.

2. Click on the node's rectangle and type the new node's name in the **Properties** view, **General** tab, **Name** field.

Try to accomplish this goal and obtain the names such as in the following screenshot:

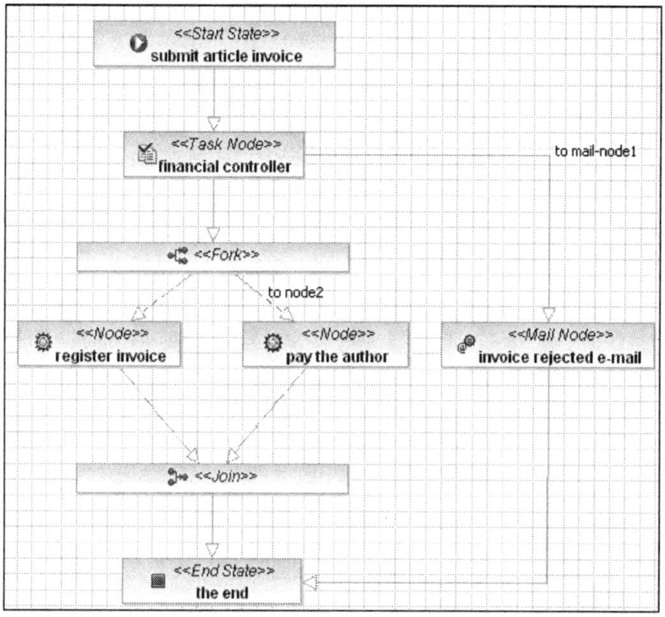

Customizing transition's names

A transition can optionally have a name. A good technique is to specify a unique name for every transition because most of the jBPM features depend on transition's names and their uniqueness. Even though transition's names are optional, they are strongly recommended!

The easiest way to specify a transition's name consists of the following steps:

1. Select the transition using the **Select** tool from the tool-set.
2. Type the new name in the **Properties** view, **General** tab, **Name** field.

In the following screenshot you can see the names that we have associated to our transitions:

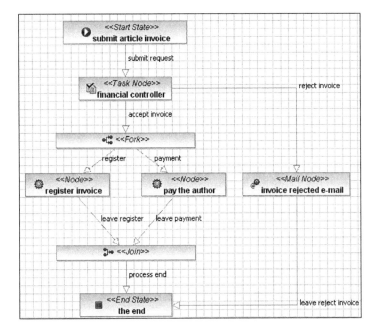

Defining swimlanes

According to our process definition scenario, we have different goals for different people. For example, we know that the invoice is sent by the article's author and it is accepted or rejected by the financial controller. In jBPM terminology, these persons are known as **actors** and their job is to accomplish tasks (don't understand from here that tasks can be accomplished only by actors!). A task may be explicitly assigned to an actor (using the assignment element in processdefinition.xml) or it can point to a process role or a swimlane (using the swimlane attribute in processdefinition.xml).

A swimlane is a facility of jBPM used to indicate that multiple tasks should be accomplished by the same actor (also, they may be accomplished by **pooled actors, handlers** or **expressions**). The advantage of using this facility is that the actor is remembered for all tasks that are in the same swimlane. Note that all tasks that reference a swimlane should not be explicitly assigned to an actor.

Even if in our case we only have two actors, using swimlanes is a good technique, especially if in the future we decide to extend our process definition and add more actors and tasks. In this time, swimlanes will sustain a clean process, easy to understand and maintain.

Now, let's create two swimlanes for our actors. Follow these steps:

1. Click inside the canvas (not on the graph) to activate the process definition properties in the **Properties** view.

2. Switch to **Swimlane** tab in the **Properties** view.

3. Right-click inside the swimlane's list and select the **New Swimlane** option from the contextual menu (by default, this list is empty).

4. Now, two more tabs should be visible at the right of the swimlane's list. In the **General** tab, **Name** field, type **authors** as the swimlane's name.

5. Switch to **Assignment** tab and choose **Actor** 0.

6. An **Actor** field should appear! Type here **article's author** as the actor's ID.

Repeat steps 1-6, but this time type **financialdepartment** as the swimlane's name and **financialemployees** as the actor's ID.

Now, you should see something like this:

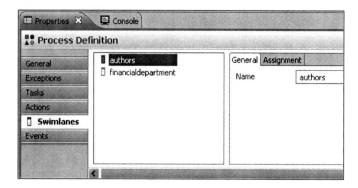

Defining a task for the start-state

It is time to make our actors do some work! For this, we have to assign them **tasks**. In jBPM terminology, tasks define how **task instances** must be created and assigned during process executions, while a task instance may be assigned to an actor, swimlane, etc. The number and type of task instances that are created depends on the task definitions that are configured. Every actor may have zero, one or more tasks that must be successfully accomplished for sustaining the fluency of the process execution flow.

Per example, the article's author must submit the invoice in the process. This is a task that can be configured like this:

1. Select the process definition start-state by clicking on the corresponding node in the graph. Note that we are selecting the start-state because the invoice must be submitted when the process execution starts. In particular, you should know that the start-state may have only one task associated.

2. In the **Properties** view, switch to the **Task** tab.

3. Select the **Configure Task** checkbox to activate the tool. An embedded tabbed form will appear, with tab pages for the different categories of properties.

4. In the **General** tab, type **submit invoice task** in the **Name** field. This is an identification name associated to this task (tasks names must be unique in the whole process definition). Optionally, you can write a description of the task in the **Description** field. (The screenshot is given below).

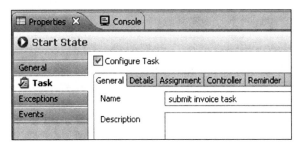

5. Switch to **Details** page. Here we have to indicate a due date (**Due Date** field) for setting the date on which the task should be accomplished. For example, we set it to **5 business days**. Optionally, we can set a task's priority, which can be useful in creating tasks hierarchies based on priorities. Per example, we know that this task should be the first in the process, so we can set it to the highest priority. Also, we can indicate that the process will not be able to continue if this task is still unaccomplished by selecting the **Blocking** checkbox. Selecting the **Signalling** and **Notify** checkboxes will indicate that the process will continue when the task is accomplished and that the assignee will be notified by email when the task is assigned. In the following screenshot, you can see what selections we have made at this step:

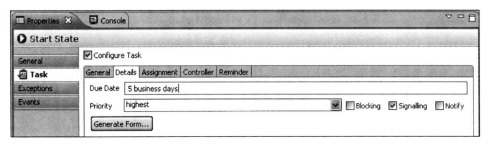

6. If you ask yourself how exactly the article's author is submitting the invoice, then at this step, you will get the answer. The invoice is submitted through an XHTML form, which is designed based on JSF and JSTL capabilities (note that this is not just a simple HTML form, it's a task form that can be rendered by the jBPM console and it is certainly pretty understandable to the uninitiated). In our case, the author's form may contain multiple fields like: the author's name, the article's name, the article's URL, an email address, and the article's fee. After the author fills up these fields, he/she will press a form button that will propagate the process execution following the `submit request` transition. Note that this form can be generated by the jBPM Tools by following these steps:

6.1 In the **Details** tab, click on the **Generate Form** button. This will open the **Generate Task Form** window.

6.2 This window contains two separate sections—the first one section allows us to add the form fields and the second one section allows us to add the form buttons. Before adding form fields, you should know that a form field is characterized by an internal variable used by the process (this variable stores the user's input), a label displayed to the form user (this label suggests to the user what to input in the field), and three attributes: **read**, **write**, and **required** (it is trivial what these attributes mean, so no supplementary details are needed). All these properties are available in the table from the **Define the form fields** field. Next, try to use the **Add** button and this table to reproduce the following screenshot:

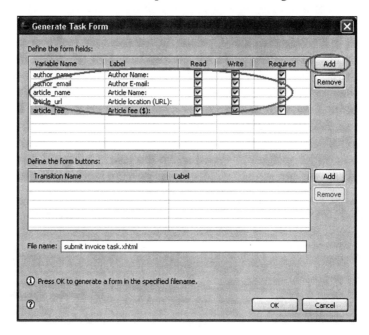

When typing the **Variable Name** and **Label**, you must use the *Enter* key or the new text is not registered (the *Tab* key will not retain the field's settings).

6.3 Now, we will add to our form a button that will act as a signal for the process. This button should be pressed by the author for submitting the invoice. Pressing this button will propagate the execution by purchasing the invoice to the financial controller. These kinds of buttons are characterized by a label, and a transition name used to indicate which execution path should be followed to leave this task and go further to the next destination (in our case, the `submit request transition`). Note that, by default, jBPM Tool will add to this form a **Save** and a **Cancel** button. The first one will update the form variables states and the second one will cancel them. In conclusion, our form will have three buttons: **Save**, **Cancel**, and our button, named **Evaluate**. To add the **Evaluate** button, use the **Add** button and the table from the bottom of the window. The following screenshot shows what you should get:

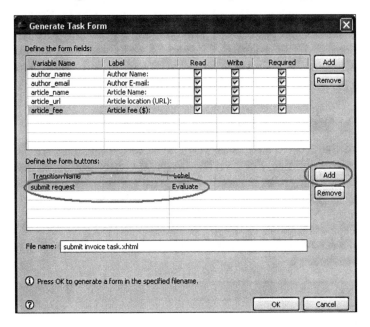

6.4 The last thing to do is to specify a name to the XHTML document that encapsulates our form. By default, this name reflects the task name, and is auto-filled into the **File name** field of the **General Task Form** window. This step is optional and not really relevant, so we prefer to use the default name.

6.5 Click on the **OK** button. The XHTML document will be saved in **src/main/ jpdl/article-invoice-pd** folder. Double-click on it if you want to open it in the JBoss Tools HTML Editor. Note that using this editor and the JBoss Tools Palette, you can add more fields to your forms, like checkboxes, drop-down lists, radio buttons, etc., that are not available in the **Generate Task Form** window.

7. The task is almost ready! Next, we will have to assign it to the swimlane **authors**. For this, you have to switch to the **Assigment** tab, select the **Swimlane** option from the drop-down list, and type **authors** in the **Swimlane Name** field (as shown in the following screenshot).

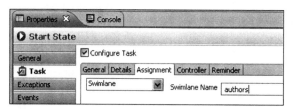

Now, our task is ready, but as you can see, there are two more tabs that we didn't use, named **Controller** and **Reminder**. You can find a good introduction about task controllers in the jBPM jPDL manual, Chapter 12 and about the **task reminder** in the same manual, Chapter 17. Using this knowledge and your intuition you shouldn't have too many problems understanding how these two tabs work.

Defining a task for the task-node

At this moment, the process execution stops until the financial controller accepts or rejects the submitted invoice. For this, the financial controller should see the invoice fields, check if everything was correctly filled, and come, with a verdict. In other words, we need to define a task for the **financial controller** task-node.

Based on what we have learnt in the previous section, this goal should be a piece of cake. First, create a new task for the task-node and name it **financial controller task** (screenshot given below).

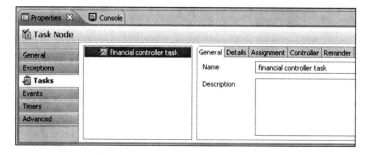

Second, set a due date of **2 business days**, a **normal** priority and check only the **Sigalling** checkbox in the **Details** tab (screenshot given below).

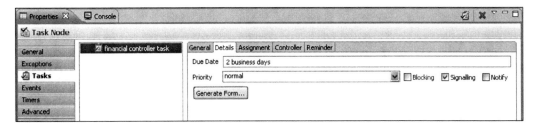

Third, we have to generate a new XHTML form that will reveal the submitted invoice. For this, our new form will display the submitted variables. Because the financial controller should see the submitted invoice, without the possibility of modifying it, the form's fields will be read only.

Depending on the decision of the financial controller, the path of execution will follow the **accept invoice** or **reject invoice** transition. This choice is made by the financial controller by clicking on the **Accept Invoice** button or the **Reject Invoice** button. These two buttons are added in the form exactly as we have learnt in the previous section, when we have added the **Evaluate** button.

What follows is a screenshot of the **Generate Task Form** for this form (try to reproduce it):

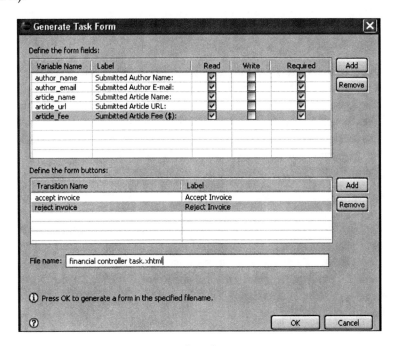

Finally, we end this task configuration by assigning it to the **financialdepartment** swimlane (screenshot given below).

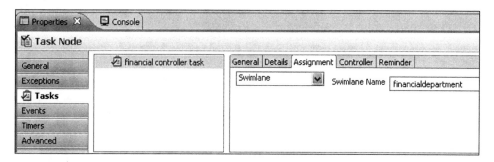

Decorating graph with actions

Let's suppose that the financial controller has accepted the submitted invoice. Conforming to the **accept invoice** transition, the execution will flow to the next node, which is a fork. As we can see from the graph, the fork will split the execution path following two transitions, **register** and **payment**, which propagate the execution further to the **register invoice** and **pay the author** nodes.

Because these two nodes should execute goals that are beyond the jBPM graph capabilities, we have to decorate them with pieces of Java code. In jBPM terminology, these pieces of Java code are named **actions classes** or **actions** that are executed upon events in the process execution. Note that there are two kinds of actions: actions placed in events and actions placed in nodes. Next, we will use actions placed in nodes.

For the **register invoice** node, we may create an action that will save the submitted invoice into a database, an XML file, text file, or something that keeps some evidence of accepted invoices. Next, we will skip the Java code that is actually doing that, and will focus more on the Java code used to create an action handler and to extract the information from the invoice fields. Putting this information into a database, XML file, text file etc. can be done in many ways, and it is beyond the scope of this chapter to show you how to do that.

Therefore, the steps of generating an action are:

1. In case we don't have a package to put our actions in, a good technique is to start by creating one. For this, expand the **article-invoice | src/main/java** node, under the **Package Explorer** view. Right-click on this node and select the **New | Package** option from the contextual menu. In the **New Java Package** window, type **articles.invoices.actions** in the **Name** field and click on the **Finish** button.

2. It is now time to create an action, but before this you should know that a jBPM action can be of type **handler** or **expression**. A handler action is a Java class that implements the **ActionHandler** interface and that can execute some user code during the execution of a jBPM process. This interface contains one method named **execute** that should be implemented by every action of type handler. On the other hand, in actions, assignments and decision conditions can be written as a jPDL expression, which is a language similar to the JSF expression language. Keeping this in mind, we will now create an action of type handler, named **RegisterInvoiceAction.java**. Start by right-clicking on the new package name and select the **New | Class** option from the contextual menu. You should be familiar with creating a Java class through Eclipse wizard, so we have not gone into the details now. The only particularity consists in adding the interface **org.jbpm.graph.def.ActionHandler** in the **Interfaces** field, as you can see from the following screenshot.

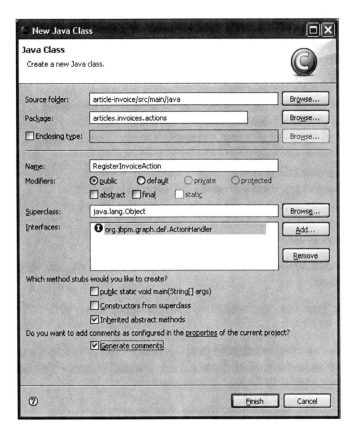

3. Click on the **Finish** button.

A new action stub of type handler was created and it looks like this:

```
package articles.invoices.actions;
import org.jbpm.graph.def.ActionHandler;
import org.jbpm.graph.exe.ExecutionContext;
public class RegisterInvoiceAction implements ActionHandler {
public void execute(ExecutionContext executionContext) throws
Exception {
    // TODO Auto-generated method stub
  }
}
```

Now, we can write our code in the TODO section of the **execute** method. First, we extract the invoice information using the **ExecutionContext** object and display them:

```
String author_name = String.valueOf (executionContext.
getContextInstance().getVariable("author_name"));
String author_email = String.valueOf (executionContext.
getContextInstance().getVariable("author_email"));
String article_name = String.valueOf (executionContext.
getContextInstance().getVariable("article_name"));
String article_url = String.valueOf (executionContext.
getContextInstance().getVariable("article_url"));
String article_fee = String.valueOf (executionContext.
getContextInstance().getVariable("article_fee"));

System.out.println("Author name:"+author_name);
System.out.println("Author e-mail:"+author_email);
System.out.println("Article name:"+article_name);
System.out.println("Article URL:"+article_url);
System.out.println("Article fee:"+article_fee);
```

Next, we add a comment—replace it with any Java code that you want to process the invoice information:

```
//store the invoice information into a database, XML file, text file,
etc.
```

At the end, actions are responsible to propagate the execution further. For this, we can call the **leaveNode** method and pass it the transition name that will be followed. In our case, this transition is leave register:

```
executionContext.leaveNode("leave register");
```

Now, the entire source code of `RegisterInvoiceAction.java` looks like this:

```
package articles.invoices.actions;
import org.jbpm.graph.def.ActionHandler;
import org.jbpm.graph.exe.ExecutionContext;
public class RegisterInvoiceAction implements ActionHandler {
    public void execute(ExecutionContext executionContext)
    throws Exception {
        //extract the invoice information
        String author_name = String.valueOf (executionContext.
        getContextInstance().getVariable("author_name"));
String author_email = String.valueOf (executionContext.
getContextInstance().getVariable("author_email"));
        String article_name = String.valueOf (executionContext.
        getContextInstance().getVariable("article_name"));
        String article_url = String.valueOf (executionContext.
        getContextInstance().getVariable("article_url"));
        String article_fee = String.valueOf (executionContext.
        getContextInstance().getVariable("article_fee"));
        //check to see if the information were correctly extracted
        System.out.println("Author name:"+author_name);
        System.out.println("Author e-mail:"+author_email);
        System.out.println("Article name:"+article_name);
        System.out.println("Article URL:"+article_url);
        System.out.println("Article fee:"+article_fee);
        //PUT HERE MORE CODE TO PROCESS THE INVOICE INFORMATION
        //store the invoice information into a database, XML file, text
        //file, etc.
        //leave this node
        executionContext.leaveNode("leave register");
    }
}
```

Our first action is ready!

Next, follow the above logic to implement an action that is making the payment to the author (this action is for the pay the author node). We named that action `PayInvoiceAction.java` and its final code looks like this (place it in the `articles.invocies.actions` package):

```
package articles.invoices.actions;
import org.jbpm.graph.def.ActionHandler;
import org.jbpm.graph.exe.ExecutionContext;
public class PayInvoiceAction implements ActionHandler {
    public void execute(ExecutionContext executionContext)
    throws Exception {
```

```
//display a start log message
System.out.println("SEND PAYMENT STARTED!");
//PUT HERE MORE CODE TO ACCESS AN ONLINE PAYMENT SYSTEM
//per example, use the ECHOPay for Java
//display an end  log message
System.out.println("SEND PAYMENT ENDED!");
//leave this node
executionContext.leaveNode("leave payment");
    }
}
```

At this moment, we have two actions corresponding to our nodes, but jBPM doesn't know that. Therefore, it is time to associate nodes with their actions, and for this we can follow these steps:

1. Select the `register invoice` node from the graph.
2. In the **Properties** view, switch to the **Action** tab.
3. Check the **Configure Action** checkbox.
4. In the embedded tabbed form, **General** tab, type **register invoice action** in the **Name** field. Note that if you want to refer to this action from another location, where actions can be specified, you can check the **Reference** checkbox. By default, this facility is not active.
5. Switch to **Details** tab and from the drop-down list, select the **Handler** type.
6. In the **Class Name** field, type **articles.invoices.actions. RegisterInvoiceAction** (or use the **Search** button). This is shown in the following screenshot.
7. In the **Config Type** drop-down list, select **Field** (this is the default configuration type). More details about configuration types can be found in the jBPM jPDL manual.
8. Leave everything else as default and save the project.

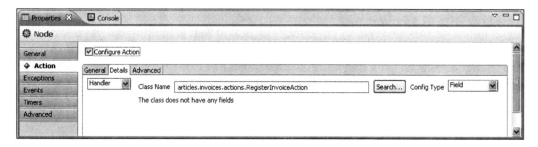

9. Repeat steps 1-8 for associating the `pay the author` node with the `articles.invoices.actions.PayInvoiceAction` action class.

Now, the actions are set and they are ready to be executed by the jBPM process engine. When the process engine encounters a node in the process definition that has an action associated with it, all related action handlers are invoked.

Configuring Mail node

In this section, we will discuss configuring the mail-node. When the financial controller rejects an invoice, the execution path will follow the reject invoice transition. The destination of this transition is the invoice rejected e-mail node, which is meant to send an email to the author who has submitted the invoice. The email address should be picked from the invoice field (author_email **variable**). To configure this node, follow these steps:

1. Select the invoice rejected e-mail node from the graph.
2. In the **Properties** view, switch to the **General** tab.
3. In the **Name** field of the **General** tab, type **send email** (this is just a name).
4. Switch to the **Mail Info** tab.
5. From the **Destination** drop-down list, select the **To** item.
6. Next to the **Destination** drop-down list, in the text field, type #{author_ email}. This is an expression written in jPDL language that will capture the value of the **author_email** variable.
7. In the **Subject** field, type the email subject. Per example, type there **Your invoice was rejected**.
8. In the **Body** field type, the email content comes in. Per example, type there a message as shown in the following screenshot:

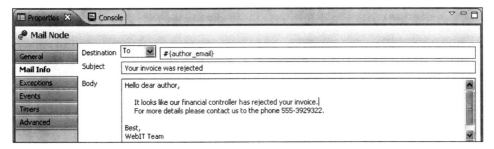

9. Save the project.

Now, our process definition is ready!

 By default, when sending an email, jBPM will try to connect to a server mail on localhost port 25, protocol SMTP. Obviously, to test this case, you will need such a server running on your machine!

Source view

This view contains the source code of the XML document that was generated for the `article-invoice-pd` process definition. From this view, we can manually manipulate this XML by adding/modifying/removing elements or/and attributes. Anyway, this is not just a simple editor, because the code assist facility is also active.

Design view

This view reveals the generated XML of the process definition as a table with two columns. First column (left-hand side) contains the process structure elements/attributes, and the second column (right-hand side) contains their values. From this view, we can manage these elements/attributes by right-clicking inside of it and selecting the desired operation from the contextual menu.

Deployment view

This view contains the main settings that are involved in the deployment stage. As you can see (screenshot given below), these settings have their default values that can be adjusted accordingly to our needs.

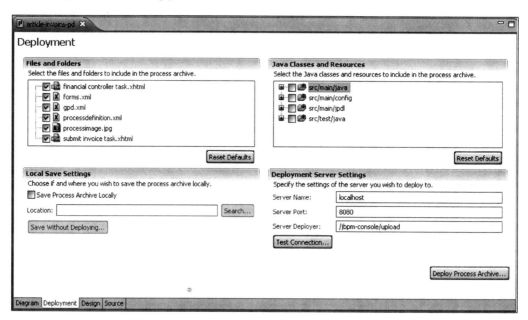

Per example, we have made the following changes to the default settings:

- We saved the process archive locally, for this focus on the **Local Save Settings** section. Here, select the **Save Process Archive Locally** checkbox and after that use the **Search** button to navigate to the location where you want to save the process archive (per example, we saved it in `C:\jBPMinvoices`—note that `jBPMinvoices` is a file not a folder).

- We selected to include in the process archive all the resources, for this focus on the **Java Classes and Resources** section. Here, select the four node's checkboxes. Note that you have the possibility to expand these four nodes and to make a finest selection of the resources that will go into the final process archive.

- We select to deploy the process in the default server configuration, this is `localhost:8080`, **folder** `/jbpm-console/upload`.

Now, the settings are reflected in the following screenshot:

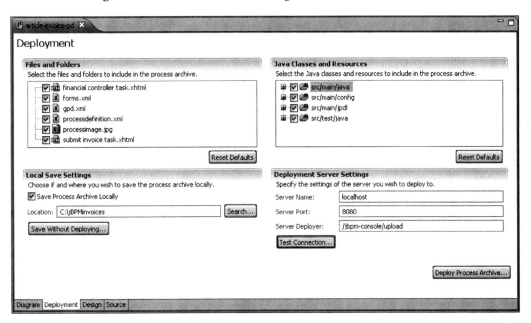

Now that the settings correspond to our desires, we can try to test the connection to the server. This test is not mandatory, but it is a good possibility to see if the server works propertly, without actually deploying something. For this, start the JBoss jBPM Server and click on the **Test Connection** button. If you received a message such as **The server connection was successfully tested**. then we are ready to deploy the process archive. In case of an error, follow the error's details and try to fix the settings that generate it (if you want to come back to the default settings, then use the **Reset Defaults** buttons). When no more errors are reported, you can deploy the process archive by clicking on the **Deploy Process Archive** button. If you received a message of type **The process archive deployed successfully**. then it is obvious what just happened.

 If the JBoss jBPM Server is displaying a message like **Not binding factory to JNDI, no JNDI name configured** then don't worry about it. This in not an error! this is just an INFO message for Hibernate. The server was successfully started and it is ready to be used.

Running a process on JBoss jBPM server

At this moment, the process is deployed and it is ready to be tested. For this, open your favorite browser and open the `http://localhost:8080/jbpm-console` link. You should see something resembling that in the following screenshot:

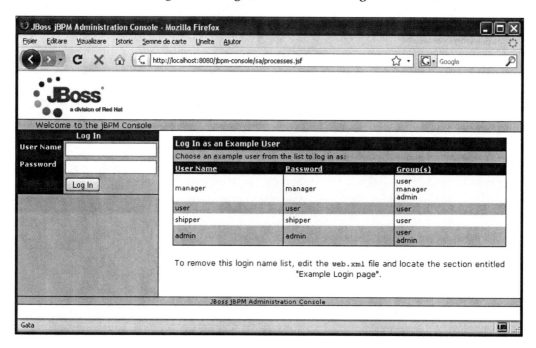

Before seeing the available processes, you have to log in. For this, use the **admin** username and **admin** password, and click the **Log In** button. The processes list should be displayed, and the **INVOICE-PD** name should be in the list (the rest of the processes are examples that came with jBPM). The screenshot given below is an example of this list:

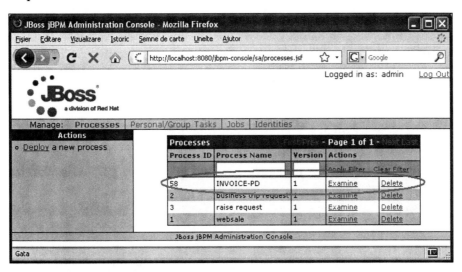

If you see the **INVOICE-PD** process, just click on the **Examine** link. After that start the process by clicking the **Start** link (screenshot given below):

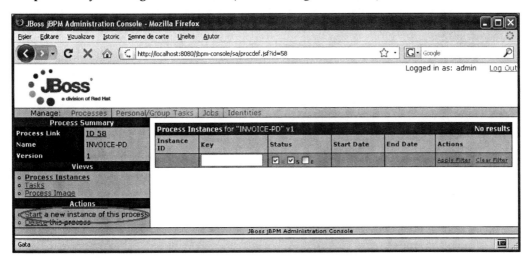

From this point forward, the process is started and ready to be tested. Don't forget to start the email server for testing the case when the financial controller rejects an invoice.

Creating a JUnit test for a jBPM process

A good technique when working with jBPM processes is to write JUnit tests that can reveal the possible errors. In this section you will see how to develop a simple JUnit test case for our process.

First, notice that when we have created our process, the wizard has already put in place all the library requirements that we need to start writing unit tests. You can see them in **Project Explorer** view, under the **jBPM Library** node.

Next, we can create a unit test by following these steps:

1. In **Project Explorer** view, right-click on the **src/test/java** node.

2. Select **New | Package** from the contextual menu and create a new package named com.junit.tests.

3. Right-click on the new package name and select **New | Other** option from the contextual menu.

4. In the **New** window, select the **Java | JUnit | JUnit Test Case** node and click on the **Next** button.

5. At this step, just type a name for the JUnit test case in the **Name** field. Per example, type here **ArticleInvoiceTest**. Leave everything else as default and click on the **Finish** button.

Now, the test stub is ready and it looks like this:

```
package com.junit.tests;

import junit.framework.TestCase;

public class ArticleInvoiceTest extends TestCase {

}
```

Next, we will use this empty test case to build a simple test that will follow the next scenario:

1. Extract a process definition from the processdefinition.xml file.

2. Check that the extracted process definition is not null.

3. Create an instance of the process definition.

4. Check if the process execution is in the start-state (submit article invoice node).

5. Set a demo invoice fields.

6. Leave the start-state and go further.

7. Test if the execution is in `financial controller` state.

8. Check whether the demo invoice fields are null or not.

9. Leave the `financial controller` node and go further using the `accept invoice` transition.

10. Test if the process ended successfully.

All the above steps can be found in the next source code delimited by identical comments:

```
package com.junit.tests;

import org.jbpm.graph.def.ProcessDefinition;
import org.jbpm.graph.exe.ProcessInstance;

import junit.framework.TestCase;

public class ArticleInvoiceTest extends TestCase {
    public void testProcess() throws Exception {
    // Extract a process definition from
    //the processdefinition.xml file.
    ProcessDefinition processDefinition =
      ProcessDefinition.parseXmlResource("article-invoice-
      pd/processdefinition.xml");

     //test if the process definition is null
     assertNotNull("Definition should not be null",
         processDefinition);

     // Create an instance of the process definition.
        ProcessInstance instance = new
        ProcessInstance(processDefinition);

     // Test if the execution is in start state.
     assertEquals("Instance is in start-state",
     instance.getRootToken().getNode().getName(),"submit article
     invoice");

     // Set the invoice fields.
     instance.getContextInstance().
      setVariable("author_name","Anghel");

     instance.getContextInstance().
     setVariable("author_email","leoprivacy@yahoo.com");

     instance.getContextInstance().
     setVariable("article_name","Writing JUnit test cases for jBPM
```

```
process");

instance.getContextInstance().
setVariable("article_url","http://devx/...");

instance.getContextInstance().
setVariable("article_fee","300$");

  // Leave the start-state and go further.
  instance.signal();

  // Test if the exection is in financial controller state.
  assertEquals("Instance is in financial controler
    state",instance.getRootToken().getNode().getName(),
    "financial controller");

  // Test if the invoice fields are null or not.
  assertNotNull("Check the author
   name!",instance.getContextInstance().
   getVariable("author_name"));
  assertNotNull("Check the author
   email!",instance.getContextInstance().
   getVariable("author_email"));
  assertNotNull("Check the article
   name!",instance.getContextInstance().
   getVariable("article_name"));
  assertNotNull("Check the article
   url!",instance.getContextInstance().
   getVariable("article_url"));
  assertNotNull("Check the article
   fee!",instance.getContextInstance().
   getVariable("article_fee"));

  // Leave the financial controller node and go further using the
   //"accept invoice" transition.
  instance.signal("accept invoice");

  // Test if the process ended successfully.
  assertEquals("Instance is in end-
    state",instance.getRootToken().
    getNode().getName(),"the end");

  }
}
```

Finally, it is now time to run our JUnit test, and for this right-click on its class name (in **Package Explorer** view) and select the **Run As | JUnit Test** option from the contextual menu. After the test runs you should get a green light which proves that the test was a total success (screenshot given below):

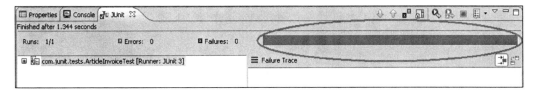

Also, you may want to check the **Console** view for more details about the test flow.

Summary

This chapter tried to get you familiar with the jBPM Tools. You have learnt how to create a jBPM graph and how to populate it with the main components of a jBPM process (nodes, task-nodes, start-state, end-state, fork-join, transitions, etc.). Also, you saw how to prepare a jBPM process for the deployment stage and how to deploy and run it on the JBoss jBPM Server. Finally, you have seen how to build a JUnit test case for a jBPM process.

Using this knowledge, you are now ready to start developing your own jBPM processes. Anyway, for more advanced features of jBPM, you can try to access the jBPM manual at `http://docs.jboss.org/jbpm/v3/userguide/`.

9
ESB Tools

In this chapter, we will discuss the JBossESB and ESB tools. If you have worked with products like Cape Clear Server and PolarLake Jintegrator, then it is not news for you that **ESB** (**Enterprise Service Bus**, also known as **message broker**) represents an extension of **EAI** (**Enterprise Application Integration**) strongly related to the **SOA** (**Service Oriented Architecture**) paradigm. ESB is another form of middleware that enables SOA by providing support for increasing the availability of a set of reusable business services. In other words, we are talking about a set of rules that provide a powerful method of preserving the data integrity while it is passed to and from their destinations. Therefore, enterprise applications can interact via standardized rules (like XML, web services interfaces) without altering the information.

For more details about ESB and JBossESB, you may want to access the `http://www.jboss.org/jbossesb/docs/index.html` address.

In the following sections, our goal is to develop a HelloWorld JBossESB Service capable of processing ESB/JMS Messages. We will use the ESB Tools support to develop the main configuration file of the Service, named `jboss-esb.xml`, and we will also use the general Eclipse features to develop the other components of an ESBJBoss Service.

In our scenario, the Service will contain two ESB Listeners (one ESB Aware and the other one, ESB Unaware), two ESB Buses based on two JMS Queues, and two ESB Actions (a Pipeline Action with a pre-defined Action and with a user-defined Action). Also, we will use a Service Registry based on JAXR API using Scout as its implementation, jUDDI as the registry, and RMI as the transport protocol.

Before putting our scenario on stage, we must configure our system to support JBossESB Services. We start by downloading and installing the JBossESB Server.

Downloading and installing the JBossESB Server

In principle, there are three ways of running JBossESB. They are as follows:

- Deploy it on JBoss AS or JBossESB Server
- Deploy it on Apache Tomcat
- Run it standalone

Most commonly the JBossESB components are deployed on a JBossESB Server. "Why?", you may ask. Because, it offers the best support for JBossESB functionalities, it has a great boot time, no additional installations are required, and the deployment is straightforward. The biggest disadvantage of JBossESB Server is that it doesn't support EAR deployment (only WAR and SAR) and doesn't offer EJB3 support. If you want to use these kinds of facilities, then you need the JBoss AS with JBoss ESB 4.4 GA distribution. In conclusion, choosing between these two is subjective, related directly to and dependent on our projects needs. We suggest that you use the JBossESB Server in this chapter.

The JBossESB Server can be downloaded from `http://www.jboss.org/jbossesb/downloads/`. At this address, there are three distributions of JBoss ESB 4.4 GA available. They are as follows: the `jbossesb-[version]-src` (this is the JBossESB 4.4 GA source code), the `jbossesb-[version]` (this is the JBossESB 4.4 GA binary distribution—needed for JBoss AS server), and the `jbossesb-server-[version]` (this is the JBossESB 4.4 GA Server). Obviously, we need to download the `jbossesb-server-[version]` (screenshot given below):

Name	Description	Size	Released	License	Downloads		
jbossesb-4.4.GA-src.zip	The JBossESB 4.4 GA Source	184 MB	Wed Aug 06 09:20:08 EDT 2008	LGPL	2227	Download	Notes
jbossesb-server-4.4.GA.zip	The JBossESB 4.4 GA Binary server	138 MB	Wed Aug 06 09:20:08 EDT 2008	LGPL	4347	Download	Notes
jbossesb-4.4.GA.zip	The JBossESB 4.4 GA Binary	116 MB	Wed Aug 06 09:20:08 EDT 2008	LGPL	2912	Download	Notes

 Besides JBossESB Server, you will also need JDK (version 5 is recommended) and Ant (version 1.6.5 is recommended).

Now, installing the JBossESB Server is a simple task that consists of extracting the ZIP archive into your favorite location. For example, we extract it in `C:\Packt\jbossesb-server-4.4.GA` folder).

It's time to configure the JBossESB Server and the JBossESB Runtime under Eclipse IDE. Configuring the JBossESB Server is a goal that can be accomplished by following the example from the *Adding a WTP Runtime in Eclipse* and *Adding a WTP Server in Eclipse* sections from the second chapter (*JBoss AS Tools*). Anyway, here are some clues that you may find useful during this job (adjust the paths and names according to your settings):

- Select a **JBoss 4.2 Runtime** from the available runtimes
- Use the name "*JBoss ESB 4.4*" for the **JBoss 4.2 Runtime**
- The home directory of **JBoss 4.2 Runtime** is `C:\Packt\ jbossesb-server-4.4.GA`
- The recommended JRE is version 5.0
- Use the name "*JBoss ESB 4.4 Server*" for the JBossESB Server
- The deploy directory of JBossESB Server is `C:\Packt\ jbossesb-server-4.4.GA\server\default\deploy`

If you have correctly configured the JBossESB Server in Eclipse, then the **JBoss Server** view should display the new server, as shown in the screenshot given below:

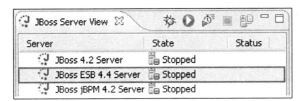

Now, let's focus on how to configure a standalone JBoss ESB Runtime in Eclipse. Without this runtime the Eclispe IDE will not recognize the JBossESB classes, so here are the steps for configuring it:

1. Launch the Eclipse IDE.
2. Open the Eclipse **Window** main menu and select the **Preferences** option.
3. In the **Preferences** window, expand the **JBoss Tools** node (left panel) and select the **JBoss ESB Runtimes** leaf.

4. In the same window, right panel, click on the **Add** button to open the **New JBoss ESB Runtime** window. In this window, start by typing a name for this runtime instance. Continue by selecting the runtime version, which in our case is 4.4, and finish by using the **Browse** button to navigate to the folder where you have the JBoss ESB Runtime distribution. In our case this is the folder where you have extracted the ZIP archive containing the JBossESB Server (this server supplies in its root directory a JBoss ESB Runtime distribution). This is shown in the following screenshot. Note that you also have the possibility to customize the runtime by manually indicating the desired JARs, but since we are not interested in this aspect so just click on the **Finish** button.

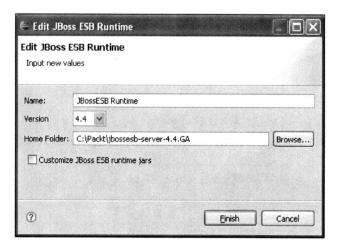

Note that the new runtime is added in the **Preferences** window, right panel. Click on the **OK** button to validate the new runtime.

 There is a peculiarity here that you should be aware of. In case of JBossESB Server, we can skip configuring a standalone JBoss ESB Runtime and use the server supplied JBoss ESB Runtime instead. However, this aspect will not be applicable for other servers, like Tomcat for example, so it is a good thing to know how to configure a standalone JBoss ESB Runtime.

Creating a JBossESB stub project

Since we want to develop a JBossESB application named ESBJMSApp, we begin by creating a stub project with this name. The advantages of using an ESB Tools generated stub, instead of a manually created stub, is that we will obtain a classic JBossESB project structure in a short time and we can use the **JBoss ESB Editor** for managing the jboss-esb.xml configuration file.

Now, the steps for creating a JBossESB stub project are:

1. From the Eclipse **File** main menu, select the **New | Other** item.

2. In the **New** window, expand the **ESB** node and select the **ESB Project** leaf. Click on the **Next** button.

3. Now, you have to indicate the project name (type **ESBJMSApp**), the server target runtime (select **JBoss ESB 4.4** from the available runtimes), and the JBoss ESB version (select **4.4** from the available versions). The screenshot is given below. Click on the **Next** button.

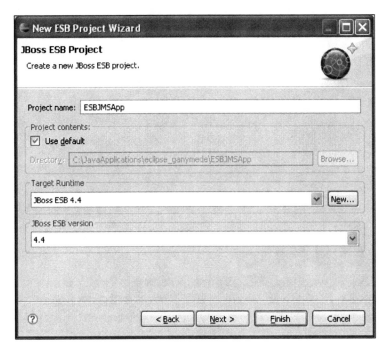

4. At this step we can indicate custom names for project folders. By default, these folders are named **esbcontent** (this folder will contain the configuration files, like `jboss-esb.xml` and `deployment.xml`) and **src** (this folder will contain the project Java classes). Note that, at this step, we can also choose between a standalone JBoss ESB Runtime and a server supplied JBoss ESB Runtime. Since earlier we have configured a standalone JBoss ESB Runtime and a JBossESB Server, which is a complete JBossESB solution, we can choose any of these two runtimes. But, because we don't want to leave our standalone JBoss ESB Runtime "unused", we will select it to be the **JBoss ESB Runtime** for our project (as shown in the following screenshot). Keep in mind that the settings in this step will affect the project structure and classpath. Click on the **Finish** button.

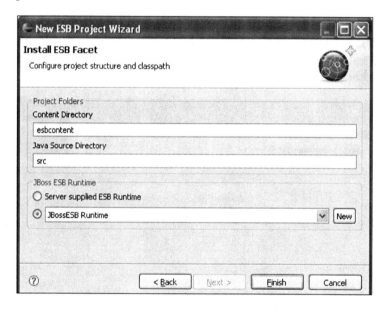

JBoss ESB Editor

As you probably know, a JBossESB application is typically based on a set of XML configuration files. The most important of them is the document that contains the Service configurations, like Listeners, Actions, and Providers. Its name is `jboss-esb.xml` and, by default, its location is in the `META-INF` directory of the Service.

When you have created the `ESBJMSApp` stub project, an empty `jboss-esb.xml` file was placed in the `ESBJMSApp/esbcontent/META-INF` directory and it was automatically opened in the **JBoss ESB Editor**. This editor will help us populate the `jboss-esb.xml` document conforming to our Service.

The JBoss ESB Editor consists of two views, **Tree** view and **Source** view. Next, we will present to you the **Tree** view, which is a visual representation of the `jboss-esb.xml` document.

Defining a Service skeleton in JBossESB

If we dissect a JBossESB project (especially from an SOA perspective), then we can resume everything in two words: Services and Messages. Services are responsible for business logic and Messages deal with the communication layer between servers and clients. Every JBossESB project will contain Services and Messages of different types.

Now, resuming to Services, you should know that in the `jboss-esb.xml` document, a Service is characterized by the `<service>` element. This element should contain three attributes, as follows: `category`, `name`, and `description`. The `category` and `name` attributes are used to register the Service Endpoints (Listeners) in the Service Registry. (From an SOA angle, a registry provides to applications and businesses a common place for storing information about their services. In JBossESB, the Service Registry is a JAXR Registry implementation, typically based on RMI communications.)

In our example, we will develop a single Service that will be able to print to the console the content of an ESB message and a JMS message. Let's start by creating our Service skeleton by following these steps:

1. Open the **JBoss ESB Editor** and switch to the **Tree** view.

2. In the tree representation (left panel), select the **Services** node.

3. In Services list (right panel), click on the **Add** button.

4. Now, it is mandatory to provide values for the `category`, `name`, and `description` attributes. Per example, fill these fields like in the screenshot shown below and click on the **Finish** button:

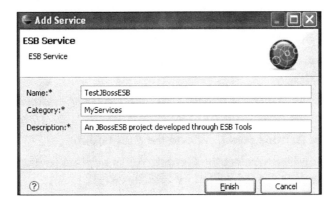

Now, if you take a look in the **Source** view, you should see that the following code was added:

```
<service category="MyServices" description="A JBossESB project
developed through ESB Tools" name="TestJBossESB"/>
```

Defining the Action Pipeline

In JBossESB, the ESB Messages are processed by Action classes. These are the pre-defined Java classes (like, `org.jboss.soa.esb.actions.SystemPrintln`) or user-defined classes. A Service can contain one or more Actions that are traversed in sequential manner by every ESB Message. When the Service contains a set of Actions, we say that we have an Action Pipeline. In XML format, every Action is represented by an `<action>` element and three attributes: `name`, `class`, and `process`. These attributes represent:

- `name` — a unique name for the current Action (required)
- `class` — the qualified name of the Action class (required)
- `process` — the name of the method from the Action class that will process the ESB Message (typically, this attribute is present for user-defined Action classes)

Before exploring the ESB Tools in this direction, you should know that JBossESB client and servers can communicate through one-way and request/response Messages. To ensure the loose coupling of services and to develop SOA applications, it is recommended to use one-way Messages. In case of request/response Messages, you should know that these are independent Messages, related only by the application logic.

For example, if we want to add to our Service an Action that simply prints out a one-way ESB Message content, then we can follow these steps:

1. Open the **JBoss ESB Editor** and switch to the **Tree** view.
2. In the tree representation (left panel), expand the **Services | TestJBossESB | Actions** node.
3. In the **Actions List** (right panel), select the **OneWay** option from the **MEP** drop-down list.
4. Next, in the **Actions** panel, click on the **Add** button.
5. In the popup menu, select the **Generic Action** option (notice how many kinds of Actions are supported by ESB Services!).

6. In the **Add Action** window, it is mandatory to specify the Action's attributes like in the following screenshot:

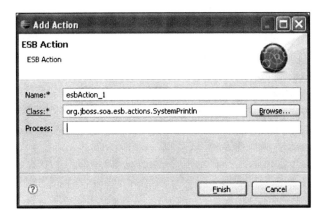

7. Click on the **Finish** button.

Next, let's create a user-defined Action. Our Action will print out the ESB Message in a personalized way, as you can see below:

```
-------------------
--- ESB Message ---
-------------------
```

We named this class esb.actions.MySystemPrintln and its source code is listed below (note that we spread our code with some explanatory comments, but more details about ESB API and how to write ESB Actions can be found in the Programmer's Guide for ESB developers). Put this class under the src folder in the proper package:

```
package esb.actions;

import org.jboss.soa.esb.actions.AbstractActionLifecycle;
import org.jboss.soa.esb.helpers.ConfigTree;
import org.jboss.soa.esb.message.Message;

//The org.jboss.soa.esb.actions.AbstractActionLifecycle is an //
abstract class for lifecycle methods. This class implements the //
ActionLifecycle interface that should be implemented by all Actions //
that want to participate in the application lifecycle and should //not
contain any state specific to a particular message instance.
public class MySystemPrintln extends AbstractActionLifecycle
{
    //The ConfigTree class is used for run time configuration of ESB
    //components.
```

```
    protected ConfigTree configTree;

    public MySystemPrintln(ConfigTree configTree)
    {
        this.configTree = configTree;
    }

    //The Message class encapsulates a ESB message, which is made of
    //the following components: Header, Context, Body, Fault,
    //Attachment and Properties.
    public Message printlnMessage(Message message) throws Exception{

     System.out.println("------------------------------------------");
     //get the body component of the message
     System.out.println("---" + message.getBody().get() + "---");
     System.out.println("------------------------------------------");
     return message;
     }
}
```

We now have to configure this Action for our Service. For this, repeat the above steps to add the **MySystemPrintln** Action like in the screenshot given below:

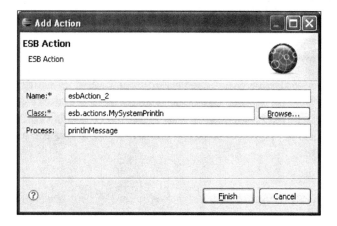

Now, if you take a look in the **Source** view, you will notice that the following code was added (these two Actions will be sequentially processed):

```
<action class="org.jboss.soa.esb.actions.SystemPrintln"
name="esbAction_1"/>
<action class="esb.actions.MySystemPrintln" name="esbAction_2" process
="printlnMessage"/>
```

Defining a list of Listeners

A Service can define a list of Listeners, which are used to redirect Messages to the Action Pipeline. By default, every Service has an InVM Listener, which is used by the `ServiceInvoker` for locally deployed Services (the `ServiceInvoker` class acts as an invoker for managing asynchronous/synchronous Message delivery to a specified Service). Actually, even when there are other Listeners defined, the `ServiceInvoker` will prefer to use the InVM Listener instead. There are two main kinds of Listeners:

- **Gateway Listeners** — a Gateway Listener is a bridge between the ESB Aware and Unaware Messages and Endpoints. This kind of listener is the gateway to the ESB from Endpoints outside the domain of the ESB. It will convert a Message into an ESB Message before it goes further into the Action Pipeline (the Gateway's goal is to adapt messages by making them an ESB Aware Message for consumption by an ESB Aware Endpoint). The Endpoint addresses made available to the `ServiceInvoker` will depend on the list of available Listeners (FTP, JMS, SQL, FS, HTTP, etc.). In our example, we will use a JMS Gateway Listener.

- **ESB Aware Listeners** — this is an ESB Aware Endpoint, which means that they are used to exchange ESB Messages on the bus. In our case, you will see how to configure an ESB Aware Listener that listens for ESB Messages on a JMS queue.

In XML format, a Listener is represented depending on its type. For example, a JMS Gateway Listener is represented by a `<jms-listener>` element and the `name`, `busidref`, and `is-gateway` attributes. These attributes indicate:

- `name` — a unique Listener name.

- `busidref` — a reference to the corresponding JMS Provider (soon, you will see how to configure a JMS Provider).

- `is-gateway` — if the Listener is a Gateway, then this attribute value is `true`.

Therefore, the steps for defining a JMS Gateway Listener are:

1. Open the **JBoss ESB Editor** and switch to the **Tree** view.

2. In the tree representation (left panel), expand the **Services | TestJBossESB | Listeners** node.

3. In the Listeners list (right panel), click on the **Add** button.

4. From the popup menu, select the **JMS Listener** option (notice how many kinds of Listeners are supported by ESB Services!).

5. In the **Add JMS Listener** window, type the values for the **Name** and busidref attributes like in the following screenshot:

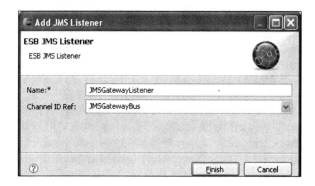

6. Click on the **Finish** button.

Now, for making our Listener a Gateway, you have to set the `is-gateway` attribute to `true`. Do this from the **Is Gateway** field as in the screenshot given below:

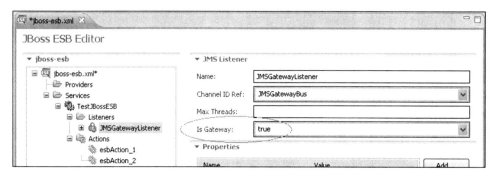

If you take a look in the **Source** code, you can notice our JMS Gateway Listeners like this:

```
<jms-listener busidref="JMSGatewayBus" is-gateway="true" name="JMSGate
wayListener"/>
```

As you have seen earlier, we have specified a reference to a JMS Provider by setting the `busidref` attribute's value to **JMSGatewayBus**. In JBossESB terminology, a Provider is a mechanism responsible for the transport level details of Endpoints. For example, in our case, we will need a JMS Provider, `<jms-provider>`, which will define a JMS Bus, `<jms-bus>`, for a JMS Queue, `<jms-message-filter>`. The name of this JMS Provider will be **JBossMQ** and the unique identifier of the JMS Bus will be **JMSGatewayBus**. The steps for configuring a JMS Provider are:

1. Open the **JBoss ESB Editor** and switch to the **Tree** view.
2. In the tree representation (left panel), select the **Providers** node.
3. In the **Providers** list (right panel), click on the **Add** button.
4. From the popup menu, select the **JMS Provider** option.
5. In the **Add JMS Provider** window, type the values for the **Name** and the **Connection-Factory** attributes, like in the screenshot given below:

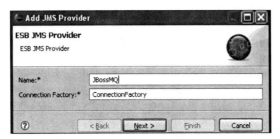

6. Click on the **Next** button.
7. It is now mandatory to set the unique identifier of the JMS Bus. Type here **JMSGatewayBus** and click on the **Finish** button (screenshot given below).

The last thing we have to configure for our JMS Bus is the JMS Queue. For this, follow these steps:

1. In the left panel of **Tree** view expand the **Providers | JBossMQ | JMSGatewayBus | Filter** node.
2. In the right panel, type **queue/ESBJMSApp_queue_gateway** in the **Destination Name** field and select the **QUEUE** option from the **Destination Type** drop-down list (screenshot given below).

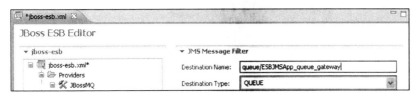

3. Save the project.

Now, in the **Source** view, you can see this JMS Provider like this:

```
<jms-provider connection-factory="ConnectionFactory" name="JBossMQ">
   <jms-bus busid="JMSGatewayBus">
    <jms-message-filter dest-name="queue/ESBJMSApp_queue_gateway"
                        dest-type="QUEUE"/>
   </jms-bus>
</jms-provider>
```

At this moment, the ESBJMSApp is invocable via two Endpoints—the InVM Endpoint and the JMS Gateway Endpoint. The best way of proving how the JMS Gateway is working consists in configuring an ESB Aware Listener able to process the ESB Message obtained from a JMS Message. A minor configuration detail will make the difference between these two Listeners; we are talking about the value of the is-gateway attribute, which will be false for the ESB Aware Listener.

Use what you have learnt in the previous sections and try to reproduce the following Listener and JMS Bus:

```
<jms-listener busidref="ESBAwareBus" is-gateway="false" name="ESBAwar
eListener"/>

<jms-bus busid="ESBAwareBus">
    <jms-message-filter dest-name="queue/ESBJMSApp_queue_not_gateway"
                        dest-type="QUEUE"/>
</jms-bus>
```

The Service should now be successfully configured and the jboss-esb.xml should look like this:

```
<?xml version="1.0"?>
<jbossesb parameterReloadSecs="5"
 xmlns="http://anonsvn.labs.jboss.com/labs/jbossesb/trunk/product/etc/
schemas/xml/jbossesb-1.0.1.xsd"
 xmlns:xsi="http://www.w3.org/2001/XMLSchema-instance" xsi:
schemaLocation="http://anonsvn.labs.jboss.com/labs/jbossesb/trunk/
product/etc/schemas/xml/jbossesb-1.0.1.xsd http://anonsvn.labs.jboss.
com/labs/jbossesb/trunk/product/etc/schemas/xml/jbossesb-1.0.1.xsd">
 <providers>
  <jms-provider connection-factory="ConnectionFactory"
                name="JBossMQ">
   <jms-bus busid="JMSGatewayBus">
    <jms-message-filter dest-name="queue/ESBJMSApp_queue_gateway"
                dest-type="QUEUE"/>
   </jms-bus>
   <jms-bus busid="ESBAwareBus">
    <jms-message-filter dest-name="queue/ESBJMSApp_queue_not_gateway"
                dest-type="QUEUE"/>
```

```
    </jms-bus>
   </jms-provider>
  </providers>
  <services>
   <service category="MyServices"
    description="An JBossESB project developed through ESB Tools"
                name="TestJBossESB">
    <listeners>
     <jms-listener busidref="JMSGatewayBus" is-gateway="true"
                name="JMSGatewayListener"/>
     <jms-listener busidref="ESBAwareBus" is-gateway="false"
                name="ESBAwareListener"/>
    </listeners>
    <actions mep="OneWay">
     <action class="org.jboss.soa.esb.actions.SystemPrintln"
                name="esbAction_1">
      <property name="message"/>
     </action>
     <action class="esb.actions.MySystemPrintln" name="esbAction_2"
                process="printlnMessage"/>
    </actions>
   </service>
  </services>
</jbossesb>
```

Configuring message queues in JBossESB Server

Since our Service is using the JMS technology, it is our goal to configure the JMS support for JBossESB Server (queues/topics are known as administered objects and in JBoss, they can be deployed through XML files). As you probably know, JBoss servers activate JMS queues based on an XML document typically named {arbitrary_name}-queue-service.xml. In our case, this document will look like this (note how we specify our two queues):

```
<?xml version="1.0" encoding="UTF-8"?>
<server>
   <mbean code="org.jboss.jms.server.destination.QueueService"
     name="jboss.esb.esbjmsapp.destination:service=Queue,
     name=ESBJMSApp_queue_not_gateway"
     xmbean-dd="xmdesc/Queue-xmbean.xml">
   <depends optional-attribute-name=
        "ServerPeer">jboss.messaging:service=ServerPeer</depends>
   <depends>jboss.messaging:service=PostOffice</depends>
```

```
    </mbean>
    <mbean code="org.jboss.jms.server.destination.QueueService"
      name="jboss.esb.esbjmsapp.destination:service=Queue,
      name=ESBJMSApp_queue_gateway"
      xmbean-dd="xmdesc/Queue-xmbean.xml">
      <depends optional-attribute-name=
          "ServerPeer">jboss.messaging:service=ServerPeer</depends>
      <depends>jboss.messaging:service=PostOffice</depends>
    </mbean>
  </server>
```

Name this file ESBJMSApp-queue-service.xml and save it under the esbcontent directory (the name must end with -service.xml or JBoss AS will not recognize it).

If you are not familiar with JMS and how JMS and JBoss interact, then try to read a dedicated tutorial like those available at http://java.sun.com/developer/ technicalArticles/Ecommerce/jms/ and http://www.outwardmotion.com/ outwardmotion/jmsjboss1.php. Note that explaining these technologies is beyond the scope of this book.

This document can be developed under Eclipse, but don't expect anything from the ESB Tools, because it won't help you very much. This is normal since JMS is a totally different technology and is not related by default to ESB.

Indicating the classes loading order

As we know, one of the main conditions that sustain the success of our Service is the presence of our two queues, ESBJMSApp_queue_not_gateway and ESBJMSApp_queue_gateway. If in the above section we have configured these queues, it is the perfect time now to indicate that these queues should be activated before the Service is loaded. This order is very important; the Service will not run properly if the queues are not present when it is loaded by the JBossESB Server. To accomplish this task we create an XML file named deployment.xml. The content of this file is pretty intuitive as you can see below (it just creates a dependency between the Service and JMS queues):

```
<jbossesb-deployment>
  <depends>jboss.esb.esbjmsapp.destination:service=Queue,
          name=ESBJMSApp_queue_not_gateway</depends>
  <depends>jboss.esb.esbjmsapp.destination:service=Queue,
          name=ESBJMSApp_queue_gateway</depends>
</jbossesb-deployment>
```

Save this file under the esbcontent/META-INF folder.

 Again ESB Tools will not help you much.

Sending an ESB Message through the ServiceInvoker

Finally, our Service is ready to process ESB and JMS Messages. The ESB Messages will go into the ESBJMSApp_queue_not_gateway queue and be processed by the ESB Aware Listener, while the JMS Messages will go into the ESBJMSApp_queue_gateway queue and be processed by the JMS Gateway, which will transform them into ESB Messages and put them in the ESBJMSApp_queue_not_gateway queue for the ESB Aware Listener. We can send an ESB Message by using a ServiceInvoker instance, which is a class that acts as an invoker for managing asynchronous/synchronous Message delivery to a specified Service. For example, we can access our Service and send an ESB Message like this:

```
ServiceInvoker serviceInvoker = new
        ServiceInvoker("MyServices", "TestJBossESB");
message.getBody().add
        ("Hello! I am an ESB Message ... who are you ?");
serviceInvoker.deliverAsync(message);
```

As you can see, the ServiceInvoker gets the Service category and name. This information is used to look up in the Service Registry for all the endpoint addresses that correspond to the MyServices:TestJBossESB Service. Also, behind the scene, ServiceInvoker is responsible to respect and monitor the transport between Client and Service Endpoints.

The entire source code is listed below (save this class under the src folder in the esb.send.message package):

```
package esb.send.message;
import org.jboss.soa.esb.client.ServiceInvoker;
import org.jboss.soa.esb.message.Message;
import org.jboss.soa.esb.message.format.MessageFactory;
public class ESB
{
    public static void main(String args[]) throws Exception
    {
        //Setting the ConnectionFactory such that it will use scout
```

```
System.setProperty("javax.xml.registry.ConnectionFactoryClass",
"org.apache.ws.scout.registry.ConnectionFactoryImpl");
//access the TestJBossESB Service
ServiceInvoker serviceInvoker = new
 ServiceInvoker("MyServices", "TestJBossESB");
//Get a Message instance
Message message = MessageFactory.getInstance().getMessage();
//Prepare the Message body
message.getBody().add
  ("Hello! I am an ESB Message ... who are you ?");
//Deliver the message in asynchronous manner
serviceInvoker.deliverAsync(message);
}
}
```

Sending a JMS Message in a classical manner

In this section we will write a JMS Client that will send a message into the ESBJMSApp_queue_gateway queue. This will be a classical JMS Client, so there is no need for details. Anyway, if you are not familiar with JMS technology then, before proceeding further, it is a good idea to read a JMS tutorial like the one found at http://java.sun.com/developer/technicalArticles/Ecommerce/jms/.

Save the class below under the src folder into the jms.send.message package:

```
package jms.send.message;
import javax.jms.ObjectMessage;
import javax.jms.Queue;
import javax.jms.QueueConnection;
import javax.jms.QueueConnectionFactory;
import javax.jms.QueueSender;
import javax.naming.Context;
import javax.naming.InitialContext;
import javax.jms.QueueSession;
import java.util.Properties;
import javax.jms.JMSException;
import javax.naming.NamingException;
public class JMS {

    QueueConnection queueConnection;
    QueueSession queueSession;
    Queue queue;

    public void init() throws JMSException, NamingException
```

```
{
//you can put these properties in a jndi.properties file if don't
//want them here
    Properties prop = new Properties();
    prop.put(Context.INITIAL_CONTEXT_FACTORY,
    "org.jnp.interfaces.NamingContextFactory");
    prop.put(Context.URL_PKG_PREFIXES,
    "org.jboss.naming:org.jnp.interfaces");
    prop.put(Context.PROVIDER_URL, "jnp://127.0.0.1:1099");
     InitialContext iniContext = new InitialContext(prop);

     Object object = iniContext.lookup("ConnectionFactory");
     QueueConnectionFactory queueConnectionFactory =
      (QueueConnectionFactory) object;
     queueConnection =
      queueConnectionFactory.createQueueConnection();
     queue = (Queue)
      iniContext.lookup("queue/ESBJMSApp_queue_gateway");
     queueSession = queueConnection.createQueueSession(false,
      queueSession.AUTO_ACKNOWLEDGE);

     queueConnection.start();
     System.out.println("Connection Started Successfully !");
}
public void sendJMSMessage(String my_msg) throws JMSException {
    QueueSender queueSender = queueSession.createSender(queue);
    ObjectMessage objectMessage =
     queueSession.createObjectMessage(my_msg);

    queueSender.send(objectMessage);
    queueSender.close();
}
public void endAndClean() throws JMSException
{
    queueConnection.stop();
    queueSession.close();
    queueConnection.close();
}
public static void main(String args[]) throws Exception
{
   JMS jms = new JMS();
   jms.init();
   jms.sendJMSMessage
    ("Hello! I am an JMS Message ... who are you ?");
   jms.endAndClean();
}
}
```

Service Registry configuration

We mentioned earlier that the Service Endpoints are registered in the Service Registry, and that a `ServiceInvoker` will use the Service's category and name to locate the corresponding entry in the Registry. You should know that this is a common way to publish/discover Services, and it is especially used when SOA is involved. Therefore, JBossESB doesn't make an exception. So, it is important to know how to configure a Service Registry for our Service. By default (out of the box), the JBossESB is configured to expose a Service Registry based on the JAXR API using Scout as its implementation and jUDDI as the registry (in the screenshot given below, you can see the architecture of our Service Registry).

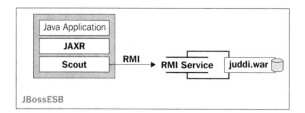

The JBossESB comes with a WAR named `juddi.war` (located at `{JBossESB Server HOME}/default/deploy/juddi-service.sar` folder) that brings up the regular web services and also an RMI service. Along with the `juddi.war`, you need to deploy a data source that points to your jUDDI database (this is also provided by default by the JBossESB). When you start the JBossESB Server, this WAR is automatically deployed, and thus should be ready to use without other preparations.

 A `juddi.war` is also located in the `{JBossESB Server HOME}/default/deploy/jbossesb.sar` folder. Also, in this folder, under `juddi-sql` sub-folder, you can find the SQL statements to create a jUDDI database. There is a folder for each supported RDBMS.

Next, we will write the XML configuration file that will provide the settings for our Service. It will contain two main entries, *core* (base settings) and *registry* (Service Registry settings), and a set of sub-entries explained through inline comments. More details about the content of this file and how to write it are in the Programmer's Guide and Service Guide, which are located in the `{JBossESB Server HOME}/docs` folder. Name this file `jbossesb-properties.xml` and save it under the `ESBJMSApp` root:

```xml
<?xml version="1.0" encoding="ISO-8859-1"?>
<!-- The jbossesb-properties.xml that provides settings for ESBJMSApp
application-->
<esbxmlns:xsi="http://www.w3.org/2001/XMLSchema-instance"
```

```
        xsi:noNamespaceSchemaLocation="jbossesb-1_0.xsd">
          <!-- core settings -->
        <properties name="core">
              <!--  Indicate server type and URL -->
          <property name="org.jboss.soa.esb.jndi.server.type"
                    value="jboss"/>
          <property name="org.jboss.soa.esb.jndi.server.url"
                    value="localhost"/>
          </properties>

          <!-- Service Registry settings. We use JARX+Scout+jUDDI-RMI. -->
          <properties name="registry">

          <!-- By default we use the JAXR API. -->
          <property name="org.jboss.soa.esb.registry.implementationClass"
            value=
          "org.jboss.internal.soa.esb.services.registry.JAXRRegistryImpl"/>

          <!-- Pick the class that will provide JAXR implementation to be
          used. By default, this is Scout, therefore we indicate the scout
          factory -->
          <property name="org.jboss.soa.esb.registry.factoryClass"
          value="org.apache.ws.scout.registry.ConnectionFactoryImpl"/>

          <!-- Tell the JAXR implementation the location of the registry or
          repository for querying and updating -->
          <property name="org.jboss.soa.esb.registry.queryManagerURI"
    value=
    "jnp://localhost:1099/InquiryService?org.apache.juddi.registry.rmi.
    Inquiry#inquire"/>
          <property name="org.jboss.soa.esb.registry.lifeCycleManagerURI"
    value=
    "jnp://localhost:1099/PublishService?org.apache.juddi.registry.rmi.
    Publish#publish" />

          <!-- Indicate username and password for the UDDI -->
          <property name="org.jboss.soa.esb.registry.user"
                    value="jbossesb"/>
            <property name="org.jboss.soa.esb.registry.password"
                    value="password"/>

          <!-- Indicate the transport class that should be used for
        communication between Scout and jUDDI. We choosed RMI, but SOAP,
        SAAJ and embedded Java are also available -->
            <property name="org.jboss.soa.esb.scout.proxy.transportClass"
              value="org.apache.ws.scout.transport.RMITransport"/>
        </properties>
        </esb>
```

This file will not be included in the deployable archive, but it will be used when we send ESB/JMS messages.

Importing the "endorsed" libraries

It seems that when Eclipse has imported the project necessary libraries (see the **JBoss ESB Runtime** and **JBoss 4.2 Runtime [JBoss ESB 4.4]** nodes in **Package Explorer** view), it "forgot" to import the libraries from the {*JBossESB Server HOME*}/ `lib/endorsed` folder. Well, without these three libraries the application will not run properly, because it needs these libraries for processing the XML documents involved in our Service. Note that these libraries are actually the Apache Serializer, Xalan, and Xerces implementations, especially used in operations that require XML documents processing.

The idea is to import these libraries in the `ESBJMSApp` project. You can do this in many ways, but a simple solution is to right-click on the **JBoss ESB Runtime** node in **Package Explorer** view, select the **Build Path | Configure Build Path** option from the contextual menu, and use the **Add External JARs** button to add these libraries to our project. A new node, named **Referenced Libraries**, is added in the **Package Explorer** view.

Preparing and deploying a Service on JBossESB Server

There is one more step to accomplish before we can test our Service. We have to deploy the Service on JBossESB Server (in the `deploy` directory), and for this you need to be familiar with a few things about the procedure of deploying ESB Services. First of all, you have to know that an ESB Service is deployed as an ESB archive containing the Service classes and configuration files. These kinds of archives are actually simple ZIP archives with the `.esb` extension. Typically, an ESB archive will have the structure as shown in the following figure:

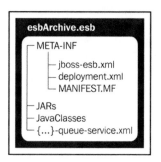

The archive's components represent:

- `jboss-esb.xml` — contains Service's configuration (Actions, Providers, and Listeners), and is mandatory
- `deployment.xml` — contains the classes loading order (optional)
- `JARs` — contains additional archives for Actions (optional)
- `JavaClasses` — contains user-defined Actions classes (optional)
- `{...}-service.xml` — contains deployment information for queues/topics (optional)

For obtaining an `.esb` archive for our Service, you can use different approaches. Per example, we have used an Ant script, being the most popular approach. Note that explaining Ant technology is beyond the scope of our book, so if you are not familiar with Ant then try a different solution (like creating the `.esb` archive manually) or read an Ant tutorial or manual like the one at `http://ant.apache.org/manual/`.

In principle our Ant script will create the `.esb` archive exactly in the way of creating a WAR archive. Save the following script under `ESBJMSApp` root and name it `build.xml`:

```xml
<project name="Create ESB Archive" default="esb" basedir=".">
<target name="esb">
  <jar destfile="${basedir}/ESBJMSApp.esb">
    <fileset dir="${basedir}/esbcontent" excludes="lib" />
    <fileset dir="${basedir}/build/classes" />
  </jar>
</target>
</project>
```

Run this script as follows:

1. Save the project and be sure that the Java classes were successfully compiled. They should be placed in the `ESBJMSApp/build/classes` folder, but if you are using a different folder, then adjust the Ant script according to your paths.
2. In **Package Explorer** view, select the **build.xml** node file.
3. Right-click on it and select the **Run As | Ant Build** option from the contextual menu.

Note that the building status is displayed in the **Console** view. If everything worked fine then the ESBJMSApp.esb archive should be displayed in the **Package Explorer** view (try a refresh (*F5*), if it doesn't appear) and it should contain the following folders and files (screenshot given below):

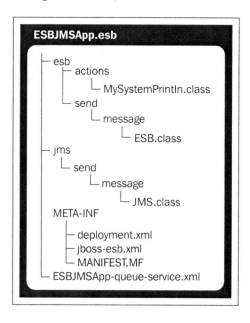

Finally, we are ready to deploy our .esb archive on JBossESB Server. This is a very simple step that can be accomplished by right-clicking on the ESBJSMApp.esb archive (in **Package Explorer** view) and selecting the **Make Deployable** option from the contextual menu (you will be prompted only to select the desired server, which is obviously the JBossESB Server). The reverse process consists in selecting the **Make Undeployable** option from the same contextual menu. Note that the archive will be deployed/undeployed even if the JBossESB Server is not running.

Testing the ESB Service

After all this work it is time for some fun! In this section, we will test our service by running the ESB and JMS classes. For this, follow these steps:

1. Be sure that the ESBJMSApp.esb archive is deployed in {*JBossESB Server HOME*}/server/default/deploy folder.

2. Start the **JBoss ESB 4.4 Server** from the **JBoss Server** view.

3. In the **Package Explorer** view, expand the **ESBJMSApp | src | esb.send. message** node.

4. Right click on the **ESB.java** node and select **Run As | Java Application** option from the contextual menu. The result should look as shown in the following screenshot.

```
INFO   [STDOUT] [Hello! I am an ESB Message ... who are you ?].        ◄─────── esbAction_1
INFO   [STDOUT] ------------------------------------------------
INFO   [STDOUT] ---Hello! I am an ESB Message ... who are you ?--- ◄─────── esbAction_2
INFO   [STDOUT] ------------------------------------------------
```

5. In the **Package Explorer** view, expand the **ESBJMSApp | src | jms.send. message** node.

6. Right-click on the **JMS.java** node and select **Run As | Java Application** option from the contextual menu. The result should look like as shown in the following screenshot.

```
INFO   [STDOUT] [Hello! I am an JMS Message ... who are you ?].        ◄─────── esbAction_1
INFO   [STDOUT] ------------------------------------------------
INFO   [STDOUT] ---Hello! I am an JMS Message ... who are you ?--- ◄─────── esbAction_2
INFO   [STDOUT] ------------------------------------------------
```

What just happened?

Apparently, everything is straightforward and simple as our first HelloWorld Java application. But, if we take a closer look, we will see that the above application is quite "crooked" and the application flow is far away from being straightforward, especially for the JMS Message case. For example, in the following screenshot, you can see the flow of steps when we use the JMS.class to send a JMS Message:

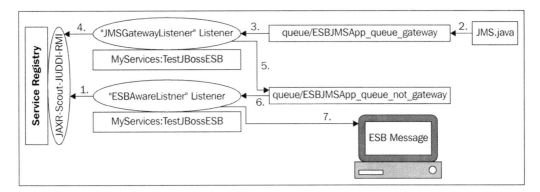

Steps 1-7 encapsulate the following details:

1. Before any Message is sent, the `MyServices:TestJBossESB` Service is registered with Service Registry.

2. The JMS Client (`JMS.java`) puts an ESB Unaware Message into the JMS Queue, `queue/ESBJMSApp_queue_gateway`.

3. The `JMSGatewayListener` receives the ESB Unaware Message.

4. The `JMSGatewayListener` looks up the Endpoint Reference (EPR) for `MyServices:TestJBossESB` Service, which is the JMS Queue `queue/ESBJMSApp_queue_not_gateway`.

5. The `JMSGatewayListener` "converts" the ESB Unaware Message into an ESB Aware Message and places it in the `queue/ESBJMSApp_queue_not_gateway`. Now, the Message can be consumed by the `ESBAwareListener`.

6. The `ESBAwareListener` now receives the ESB Aware Message.

7. Finally, the `MyServices:TestJBossESB` Service prints the Message in the console.

In case of an ESB Message (`ESB.class`), the flow is much simpler because the Message is already an ESB Aware Message and it goes directly in the `queue/ESBJMSApp_queue_not_gateway` queue. The `ServiceInvoker` will work hard to process every Message that arrives in this queue (even from other Services) and to send them in the Action Pipeline.

Summary

In this chapter you have learnt the basic concepts of JBossESB Services, and you have seen how to use ESB Tools to develop such a Service. Currently, ESB Tools is sustaining only the development of the `jboss-esb.xml` configuration file, but I'm sure that in the further releases of JBoss Tools this tool will increase its features and will became a stronger "partner" for the developers of ESB Services.

10
Web Services Tools—JBossWS

By JBossWS, we understand a web service framework based on JAX-WS (Java API for XML Web Services) specifications and dedicated to developing J2EE compatible web services (Java EE 5). JBossWS has reached version 3.0.4, and it is developed as a part of JBoss Application Server (JBossAS-5.0 and JBossAS-4.2), using JBoss AS as its target container.

Starting with JBoss Tools 3.0, we can exploit the Web Services Tools, which is a set of source and graphical editors, wizards, and built-in applications dedicated to simplifying the web services development process. It offers important features, like developing **WSDL (Web Services Description Language)** documents, generating web services and clients from WSDL documents, generating web services from Java bean, testing web services for standards compliance, and more. In addition, it also provides support for three web services runtime, those being, Apache Axis, Apache Axis2, and JBossWS runtime. Obviously, we are interested in JBossWS runtime, and thus we will ignore the Apache Axis runtimes here.

Before exploring JBossWS and Web Services Tools, you should get familiar with web services technology and at least "scratch" the JAX-WS approach. The basic idea of web services and JAX-WS can be extracted from the next section, but you can get more information by accessing `http://java.sun.com/webservices/` (for web services) and `https://jax-ws.dev.java.net/` (for JAX-WS) links.

After we download and install JBossWS, we will use the features of Web Services Tools to put in practice four main steps as follows:

- First scenario: we will develop from scratch a WSDL document, named `converterTemp.wsdl`. This WSDL will model a temperature converter, and it will map two operations named `toCelsius` (converts Fahrenheit to Celsius) and `toFahrenheit` (converts Celsius to Fahrenheit). In addition, the WSDL will map a SOAP address for the service, indicating that SOAP will be the supported protocol.

- Second scenario: this will show you how to generate a web service, named `TempWs`, from the `converterTemp.wsdl` document. We will pass the WSDL document in a Web Services Tools wizard, and we will wait for it to "bake" a complete and functional web service, without human intervention. In addition to this, we will generate a simple Java client for `TempWs` web service, and we will test the web service through this client and through the Web Services Explorer (WSE) facility. It is needless to say that you will see how to deploy a web service on JBoss AS, and how to verify whether the web service was successfully deployed or not.

- Third scenario: Next, we will write a Java bean and we will ask the Web Services Tools to generate the main web service artifacts from it. This Java bean
will model the same temperature converter; therefore, it will be very easy to understand.

- Fourth scenario: The final act will cover another important feature of Web Services Tools. We will publish the `TempWs` web service through jUDDI and the Web Services Explorer facility.

Well…stop talking, let's start working!

Overview of Web Services

Following are some of the basic definitions for complex technologies. Therefore, don't expect to become a web services expert after reading this section. These are just definitions for the uninitiated and their scope is to profile the web service paradigm:

Web service: A web service is a generic description of a software system designed to serve the clients/machines of a network. The offered services can cover many tasks, and the implementation may vary, but the basic idea of a typical web service presumes the following:

- It's seen as a server that can be interrogated based on a set of operations.
- It publishes its operations using an XML document, known as the WSDL (Web Services Description Language) document. Normally, this document is generated and parsed (interpreted) by machine.
- The entities that access the web services are known as web service clients.
- SOAP is used as the communications protocol between clients and servers.

SOAP (Simple Object Access Protocol): This is an XML-based request/response messaging protocol. One important characteristic of SOAP is that it is independent of any transport protocol (HTTP is the most frequently used, but you can use SMTP, MIME, and so on), operating system, or programming language. This makes it very flexible over different software architectures—and also very easy to use.

JAX-WS: The Java API for XML Web Services (JAX-WS) is a Java programming language API for creating web services. It is part of the Java EE platform and it is available at `https://jax-ws.dev.java.net/`.

Downloading and installing JBossWS Native

Currently, JBossWS has reached version 3.0.4 and it is available for JBoss AS 4.2 and 5.0 distributions with the following three web service stacks:

- Native—this is the native web service stack recommended by JBoss (more details at `http://www.jboss.org/jbossws/`).
- Metro—this is a high-performance, extensible, easy-to-use web service stack (more details at `https://metro.dev.java.net/`).
- Apache CXF—this is an open source services framework from Apache (more details at `http://cxf.apache.org/`).

Depending on which web service stack you decide to use, you can download the corresponding binary distribution from `http://www.jboss.org/jbossws/ downloads/`. We decided to download and test the JBossWS Native web service stack, version 3.0.4, and thus we have downloaded the `jbossws-native-3.0.4.GA` archive (screenshot given below):

JBoss Web Services Downloads

JBoss Web Services > Downloads

Files:

Name	Description	Size	Released	License	Downloads			
jbossws-native-3.0.4.GA	Binaries, Docs, Samples	14 MB	Tue Oct 21 10:12:55 EDT 2008	LGPL	3638	Download	Release Notes	Installation instructions
jbossws-native-3.0.4.GA-src	JBossWS Native Sources	7 MB	Tue Oct 21 10:12:55 EDT 2008	LGPL	407	Download		
jbossws-metro-3.0.4.GA	Binaries, Docs, Samples	12 MB	Tue Oct 21 10:12:55 EDT 2008	LGPL	466	Download	Release Notes	Installation instructions
jbossws-metro-3.0.4.GA-src	JBossWS Metro Sources	1 MB	Tue Oct 21 10:12:55 EDT 2008	LGPL	136	Download		
jbossws-cxf-3.0.4.GA	Binaries, Docs, Samples	10 MB	Tue Oct 21 10:12:55 EDT 2008	LGPL	281	Download	Release Notes	Installation instructions

Next, you have to install the JBossWS under JBoss AS (details at: `http://www. jboss.org/file-access/default/members/jbossws/downloads/Install- jbossws-native-3.0.4.GA.txt`). For this, extract the ZIP archive in your favorite location (by default, the archive is extracted in a folder named `jbossws-native- bin-dist`) and follow these steps:

1. Make a copy of the `{JBossWS_HOME}/ant.properties.example` file and name it `ant.properties`.

2. Edit the `ant.properties` according to your configuration. If you have followed this book from the start and you have installed the JBoss AS 4.2.2.GA in the same location as we did, then the modifications are highlighted below:

```
#
# A sample ant properties file
#

# Optional JBoss Home
jboss422.home= C:/Packt/jboss-4.2.2.GA
jboss423.home=/dati/jboss-4.2.3.GA
jboss424.home=/dati/jboss-4.2.4.GA
jboss500.home=/dati/jboss-5.0.0.CR2
jboss501.home=/dati/jboss-5.0.0.GA
```

```
# The JBoss server under test. This can be [jboss422|jboss423|jbos
s424|jboss500|jboss501]
jbossws.integration.target= jboss422

# The JBoss settings
jboss.server.instance=all
jboss.bind.address=localhost

# JBoss Repository
#jboss.repository=file:/home/tdiesler/svn/jboss.local.repository
jboss.repository=http://repository.jboss.org

# JBoss JMX invoker authentication
#jmx.authentication.username=admin
#jmx.authentication.password=admin

# Java Compiler options
javac.debug=yes
javac.deprecation=no
javac.fail.onerror=yes
javac.verbose=no
```

3. Point a command prompt to the folder where you have extracted the
    JBossWS archive, {*JBOSSWS_HOME*}, and execute one of the following (replace
    x by a supported minor version; for JBossAS 4.2.2.GA, replace the x with 2):

    ```
    ant deploy-jboss42x

    ant deploy-jboss50x
    ```

 In case you had a JBossWS distribution already installed (which is
very possible, since JBoss AS comes by default with a JBossWS Native
distribution), then it will be updated by the new one.

Regarding the used JDK, it is something you should know and accomplish next:

For JDK 6 and JbossWS Native, copy the `jaxb-api.jar`, `jbossws-native-jaxrpc.`
`jar`, `jbossws-native-jaxws.jar`, `jbossws-native-jaxws-ext.jar`, `jbossws-`
`native-saaj.jar` from {*JBOSSWS_HOME*}/`deploy/lib` folder to {*JBOSS_HOME*}/
`lib/endorsed` folder. More details can be found at `http://jbossws.jboss.org/`
`mediawiki/index.php?title=Installation`.

If you are using JDK 5 and JbossWS Native, like us, then you have to keep in mind
this issue: if you ever get an error containing a message like *JAXB 2.0 API is being*
loaded from the bootstrap classloader, but this RI needs 2.1 API. Use the endorsed directory
mechanism to place jaxb-api.jar in the bootstrap classloader., then you have to copy the
`jaxb-api.jar` from {*JBOSSWS_HOME*}/`deploy.lib` folder to the {*JBOSS_HOME*}/
`lib/endorsed` folder. This is a just-in-case modification, so don't do it now!

If everything worked smoothly, then in the {`JBOSS_HOME`}\server\all\deploy folder, you will find the `jboossws.sar` and `juddi-service.sar` folders. Start the JBoss AS (you can start it manually or from Eclipse using **JBoss Server View**) and access JBossWS at `http://localhost:8080/jbossws`. In case you see something like in the following screenshot, you have a valid JBossWS distribution:

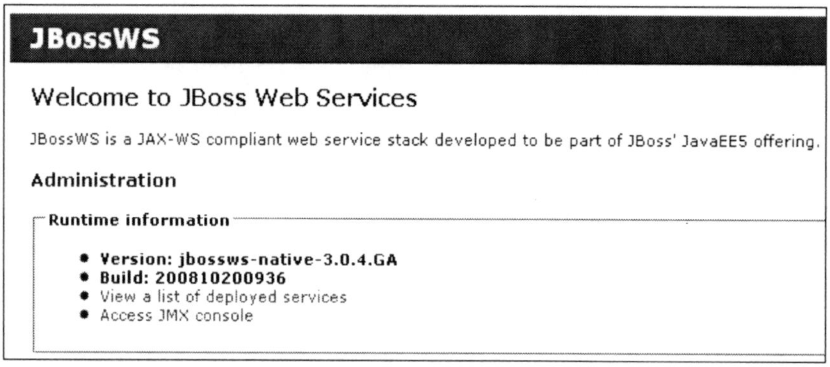

JBossWS

Welcome to JBoss Web Services

JBossWS is a JAX-WS compliant web service stack developed to be part of JBoss' JavaEE5 offering.

Administration

Runtime information

- **Version: jbossws-native-3.0.4.GA**
- **Build: 200810200936**
- View a list of deployed services
- Access JMX console

Now, JBossWS is ready to serve you! Warm it up by running a suite of JUnit tests provided by JBossWS. For this, point a command prompt to {`JBOSSWS_HOME`} and run the following Ant command (note that you will need Ant 1.7):

`ant tests`

A detailed report of tests results can be found at {`JBOSSWS_HOME`}\output\ test-reports\html\index.html.

Configuring JBossWS under Eclispe IDE

Since we want to take advantage of JBossWS, we need to configure the JBossWS environment in Eclispe IDE. First, we need to set a JBossWS runtime and second, we need to select the default server and runtime. Setting the JBossWS runtime can be done like this:

1. From the Eclipse **Window** main menu, select the **Preferences** option.

2. In the **Preferences** window, expand the **Web Services** node and select the **JBossWS Preferences** leaf.

3. In the right panel, you should see a table with the available runtimes. Click the **Add** button to open the **New JBossWS Runtime** window.

4. Indicate the name, version, and home folder of the JBossWS runtime, like in the screenshot given below (since we have installed JBossWS under JBoss AS 4.2.2.GA server, you can indicate the home folder of the JBoss AS server as the home folder for JBossWS). This wizard also provides the possibility to specify a custom set of runtime JARs. This will allow you to add or remove JARs from the default runtime distribution.

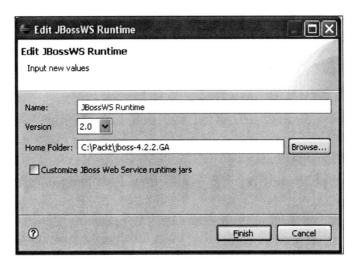

5. Click on the **Finish** button.

6. Next, you have to set the current server and runtime. This task can be accomplished from the **Preferences** window like below:

7. Expand the **Web Services** node and select the **Server and Runtime** leaf.

8. In the right panel, you should see two combo boxes that contain a set of servers, respectively, and a set of runtimes. From the **Server** combo box, select **JBoss AS 4.2** option, and from the **Web service runtime**, select the **JBossWS** option (screenshot given below).

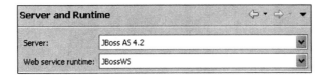

9. Click on the **Apply** button and close the **Preferences** window.

10. At last, after all this work, it's time to pick up the fruits. We are ready to start creating our first web service developed with the help of Web Services Tools, and hosted by JBossWS Native and JBoss AS.

Creating a web service using Web Services Tools

Let's start to materialize our first scenario, which assumes that we want to develop a temperature converter web service starting from a WSDL document. Before creating a web service, we should have a **Dynamic Web Project** created (this is not a special treatment for our web service, it is just a general requirement). This project will encapsulate the web service and it will be deployed on JBoss AS as an EAR archive. Therefore, we start by developing a **Dynamic Web Project** stub in the classical approach:

1. From the Eclipse **File** menu, select **New | Other** option.

2. In the **New** window, expand the **Web** node and select the **Dynamic Web Project** leaf.

3. Click on the **Next** button.

4. In the **New Dynamic Web Project** window, type **TempWs** as the project name.

5. Next, focus on the **Target Runtime** field. In principle, conforming to our configuration, we can choose the **JBoss 4.2** server (which contains the JBossWS), or **<None>**. We arbitrarily decide to select **<None>**, and later, when we shall configure the JBoss web service facet, we will also indicate the target runtime.

6. Continue by selecting the dynamic web module version (we selected version **2.4**) and the configuration (we selected **Default Configuration**).

7. Finally, check the **Add project to an EAR** checkbox and click on the **Next** button. Remember that we want to deploy our web service in an EAR archive (deploying it as a WAR is also a solution, since this is a POJO-based web service). In the following screenshot, you can see our settings:

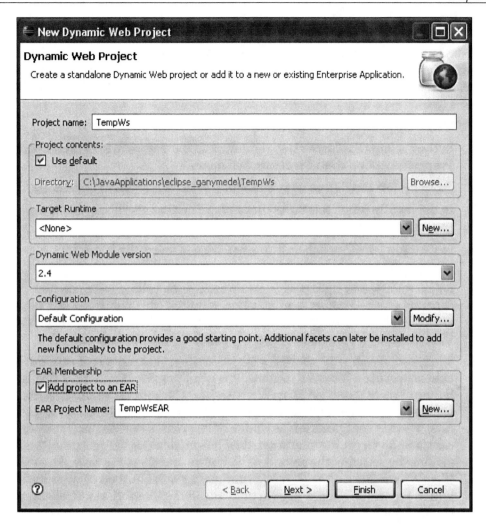

8. Now you have to configure web module values. Normally, the default values will satisfy our needs, and therefore, we won't modify them. Click on the **Finish** button.

In just a few seconds, the **Package Explorer** view will be populated with the TempWs and TempWsEAR folders.

Adding the JBoss Web Service facet

Until now, our `TempWs` project is just a usual **Dynamic Web Project**, and it is not aware of our intentions of developing a web service under its wing. For making it aware, we have to add the JBoss web service facet (in addition, we will exploit this moment to indicate a target runtime to our web service). The steps to accomplish this task are:

1. In the **Package Explorer** view, right-click in the **TempWs** node and select the **Properties** option from the contextual menu.

2. From the left panel (tree representation), select the **Project Facets** node.

3. In the middle panel, select the **JBoss Web Services** checkbox (this is the JBoss web service facet).

4. In the right panel, switch to **Runtimes** tab and select the **JBoss 4.2** target runtime.

5. Below middle and right panels, you should see a yellow rectangle that contains a link — **Further configuration required** (this link is marked by an error-bubble, indicating that it is mandatory to go there and fix some things). Click on that link to open the **Modify Faceted Project** window.

6. Since we have already selected a target runtime, and our target runtime is able to provide a JBossWS runtime, it is good practice to select the first radio button, **Server Supplied JBossWS Runtime**. Click on the **OK** button and notice that the error-bubble has become an info-bubble and the message is now, **Further configuration available**. If our case is not the same as your case, and no target runtime is set, then it is mandatory to indicate a JBossWS runtime by selecting the second radio button and choosing from the available JBossWS runtimes. If no JBossWS runtime is available, then click on the **New** button for creating a new one (in our case, in the JBossWS runtimes list, we should have a single runtime named **JBossWS Runtime**, which is actually the same runtime as the server supplied one).

7. Click on the **Apply** and the **OK** buttons (as shown in the following screenshot).

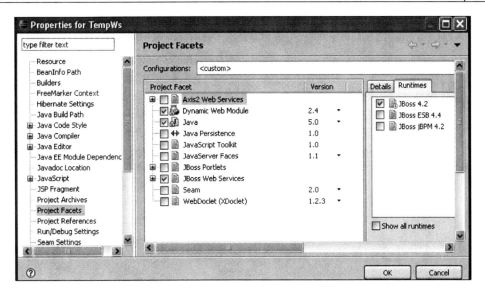

Now, the JBoss web service facet has been added and it is time to go further and see how to write a WSDL document.

Writing a WSDL document using the WSDL wizard

Using a WSDL document, a client can locate the corresponding web service and invoke any of its publicly available functions. Based on this affirmation and conforming to our first step we need a WSDL document that will be the starting point for developing our web service. In real life, WSDL documents are rarely written by hand; they are created by machines for machines, not for humans (most commonly, they are generated by different tools, resources, processes, and so on). Nevertheless, you should have at least a minimum amount of knowledge about WSDL content, in case you have to interact with the code lines of a WSDL document. Speaking of minimum knowledge, you should know that a WSDL document describes a web service using these major elements:

- `<types>`—maps the data types used by the web service. For cross-platform portability, the data types are defined in XML Schema syntax (XML Schema must be supported by any of the vendors of WSDL products).

- `<message>`—maps the data elements of an operation (there are four types of supported operations, as follows: `one-way`, `request-response`, `solicit-response`, and `notification`). Messages may contain one or more parts, which can be compared to the parameters of a function call in a traditional programming language.

- `<portType>` — describes the web service, the available operations, and messages. This is the "epicenter" of the WSDL document.

- `<binding>` — maps the communication protocols used by the web service (in other words, it describes the concrete specifics of how the service will be implemented on the wire).

- `<service>` — maps the ports supported by the web service and defines the address for invoking the specified service (most commonly, this includes a URL invoking the SOAP service). For each of the supported protocols, there is one `<port>` element. The binding attribute of the `<port>` element associates the address of the service with a `<binding>` element defined in the web service.

 The official WSDL specification can be accessed at http://www.w3.org/TR/wsdl.

Based on this minimum knowledge, our WSDL document may look like this (remember that our WSDL should map a temperature converter — converts Celsius to Fahrenheit and vice versa):

```xml
<?xml version="1.0" encoding="UTF-8" standalone="no"?>
<wsdl:definitions xmlns:soap="http://schemas.xmlsoap.org/wsdl/soap/"
xmlns:tns="http://temperature.ws.com" xmlns:wsdl="http://schemas.
xmlsoap.org/wsdl/" xmlns:xsd="http://www.w3.org/2001/XMLSchema"
name="converterTemp" targetNamespace="http://temperature.ws.com">
  <wsdl:types>
    <xsd:schema targetNamespace="http://temperature.ws.com">
      <xsd:element name="toCelsius">
        <xsd:complexType>
          <xsd:sequence>
            <xsd:element name="fahrenheit" type="xsd:float"/>
          </xsd:sequence>
        </xsd:complexType>
      </xsd:element>
      <xsd:element name="toCelsiusResponse">
        <xsd:complexType>
          <xsd:sequence>
            <xsd:element name="returnFahrenheit" type="xsd:float"/>
          </xsd:sequence>
        </xsd:complexType>
      </xsd:element>
      <xsd:element name="toFahrenheit">
        <xsd:complexType>
          <xsd:sequence>
```

```
                <xsd:element name="celsius"
                    type="xsd:float"></xsd:element>
            </xsd:sequence>
        </xsd:complexType>
    </xsd:element>
    <xsd:element name="toFahrenheitResponse">
        <xsd:complexType>
            <xsd:sequence>
                <xsd:element name="returnCelsius"
                    type="xsd:float"></xsd:element>
            </xsd:sequence>
        </xsd:complexType>
    </xsd:element>
    </xsd:schema>
</wsdl:types>

<wsdl:message name="toCelsiusRequest">
    <wsdl:part element="tns:toCelsius" name="parameters"/>
</wsdl:message>
<wsdl:message name="toCelsiusResponse">
    <wsdl:part element="tns:toCelsiusResponse" name="parameters"/>
</wsdl:message>
<wsdl:message name="toFahrenheitRequest">
    <wsdl:part name="parameters" element="tns:toFahrenheit"></wsdl:
part>
</wsdl:message>
<wsdl:message name="toFahrenheitResponse">
    <wsdl:part name="parameters" element="tns:
toFahrenheitResponse"></wsdl:part>
</wsdl:message>

<wsdl:portType name="TempWs">
    <wsdl:operation name="toCelsius">
        <wsdl:input message="tns:toCelsiusRequest"/>
        <wsdl:output message="tns:toCelsiusResponse"/>
    </wsdl:operation>
    <wsdl:operation name="toFahrenheit">
        <wsdl:input message="tns:toFahrenheitRequest"></wsdl:input>
        <wsdl:output message="tns:toFahrenheitResponse"></wsdl:output>
    </wsdl:operation>
</wsdl:portType>
<wsdl:binding name="TempWsSOAP" type="tns:TempWs">

    <soap:binding style="document"
        transport="http://schemas.xmlsoap.org/soap/http" />
    <wsdl:operation name="toCelsius">
```

```
        <soap:operation
          soapAction="http://temperature.ws.com/toCelsius" />
        <wsdl:input>
          <soap:body use="literal" />
        </wsdl:input>
        <wsdl:output>
          <soap:body use="literal" />
        </wsdl:output>
      </wsdl:operation>
      <wsdl:operation name="toFahrenheit">
        <soap:operation
          soapAction="http://temperature.ws.com/toFahrenheit" />
        <wsdl:input>
          <soap:body use="literal" />
        </wsdl:input>
        <wsdl:output>
          <soap:body use="literal" />
        </wsdl:output>
      </wsdl:operation>
    </wsdl:binding>
    <wsdl:service name="TempWsService">
      <wsdl:port binding="tns:TempWsSOAP" name="converterTempSOAP">
        <soap:address location="http://127.0.0.1:8080/TempWs/TempWs"/>
      </wsdl:port>
    </wsdl:service>
</wsdl:definitions>
```

Here are some clues about our WSDL structure:

- Our service target namespace is `http://temperature.ws.com`.

- Our `<service>` name is `TempWsService`.

- Our `<portType>` name is `TempWs`.

- Our `<binding>` name is `TempWsSOAP`.

- Our operations are request-response type and they are named `toCelsius` and `toFahrenheit`.

- The `toCelsius` operation has an input message called `tns:toCelsiusRequest` and an output message called `tns:toCelsiusResponse`.

- The `toFahrenheit` operation has an input message called `tns:toFahrenheitRequest` and an output message called `tns:toFahrenheitResponse`.

- The used protocol is SOAP.

- The SOAP address is `http://127.0.0.1:8080/TempWs/TempWs` (this is also known as the **service endpoint**).

Now is the time for Web Services Tools to get involved in the equation. It will provide a powerful wizard for creating the above WSDL, but for starting, we need to create a skeleton WSDL document. Begin by creating an empty `wsdl` folder under the `TempWs` folder. Thereafter, open the Eclipse **File** menu and select the **New | Other** option. Continue by expanding the **Web Services** node, select the **WSDL** leaf, and click on the **Next** button. Name the new WSDL `converterTemp.wsdl`, and save it under the `wsdl` folder. Again, click on the **Next** button and configure the new WSDL attributes like in the screenshot given below (all the settings are extracted from the above WSDL listing). Afterwards, click on the **Finish** button.

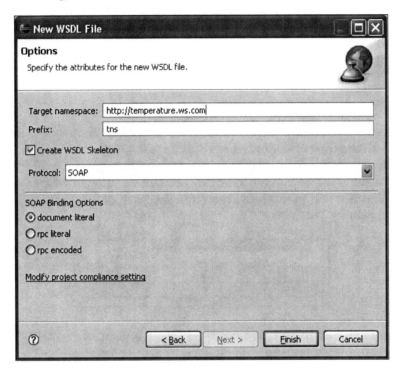

A new WSDL skeleton is created and is automatically opened in the **WSDL Editor**. Next, we will explore the **Design** view of **WSDL Editor**. From this view, we can manage the WSDL document components through an intuitive graphical diagram. This feature of WS Tools will allow us to populate the above WSDL skeleton without "touching" its source code, which by the way is available in the **Source** view (it is recommended that you take a look at this code before modifying it).

The following screenshot is corresponding to our WSDL skeleton (numbered with 1 is the sub-diagram representing the `<service>` element; numbered with 2 is the sub-diagram representing the `<binding>` element; and numbered with 3 is the sub-diagram representing the `<portType>` element):

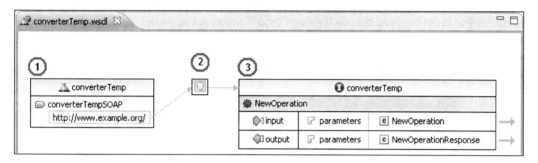

Phase 1: Focus on `<portType>` element.

> **Phase 1.1**: First thing that we want to accomplish is creating two new request-response operations, named `toCelsius` and `toFahrenheit` (they represent the methods that our web service will expose to its clients). The first one can be easily created by using the default existing **NewOperation** option. Just double-click on the **NewOperation** field and type **toCelsius** (screenshot given below). That's it!

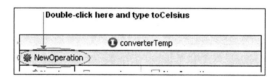

Next, right-click on the **converterTemp** field, and select the **Add Operation** option from the contextual menu. After that, type **toFahrenheit** as the operation name (as shown in the following screenshot).

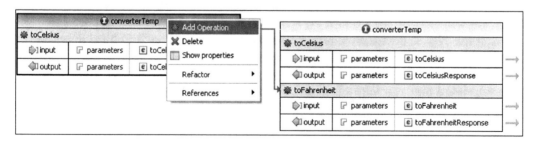

Phase 1.2: Next, we will specify the operation's input/output messages (in traditional programming, these are like function's input/return parameters). Every new request-response operation contains an input message and an output message. The corresponding `<message>` elements define the parts of each message and the associated data types. In this case, our operations take an input message, which maps a single parameter representing the temperature to be converted, and returns an output message that maps the conversion result. By default, every new operation generated by JbossWS Tool is a request-response operation, and the input message maps an element named of type `xs:string` (corresponds to `String` type in Java) and the output message maps an element named of type `xs:string`. This is very convenient for us as we can modify these default input/output messages (we will modify their names and types) to obtain ours.

For example, let's indicate that the input message of the `toCelsius` operation maps an element named `fahrenheit` of type is `xs:float` (corresponds to `float` type in Java). Start by clicking on the arrow shown in the following screenshot, left view. This action will open the **Inline Schema of converterTemp.wsdl** tab, and will expose a diagram containing the elements of the input message for the `toCelsius` operation (middle view of the following screenshot). Continue by double-clicking inside this diagram, on the **in** text, and type **fahrenheit** instead of this text. Go a little bit to the right and double-click on the **string** text. A combo box is activated, and you can select **float** as the element type. Now, you should have something like in the screenshot given below, right view.

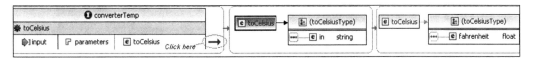

Repeat the above technique for the output message of the `toCelsius` operation and the input/output messages for the `toFahrenheit` operation. You can get the corresponding elements from the WSDL listing.

If you need to add more elements then right-click on the diagram and select **Add Element** from the contextual menu (as shown in the following screenshot).

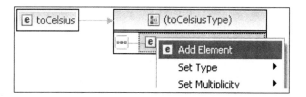

Phase 1.3: Rename the <portType> as TempWs. By default, the name attribute of <portType> will reflect the name of the WSDL document. For providing another name, just double-click on **converterTemp** field and type **TempWs** instead (screenshot given below).

Phase 2: Focus on <service> element.

Phase 2.1: Since we deal with a SOAP service, we will use the <soap:address...> element, and we will specify the local host address through the location attribute. For this, double-click on the field of the <service> element sub-diagram and type the new address, **http://127.0.0.1:8080/TempWs/TempWs** (screenshot given below). By default, JBossWS will fill up this address with the web service target namespace.

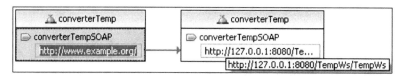

Phase 2.2: Rename the <service> as TempWsService. By default, the name attribute of <service> will reflect the name of the WSDL document. For providing another name, just double-click on **converterTemp** field and type **TempWsService** instead (screenshot given below).

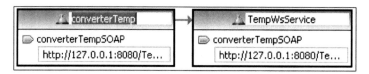

Phase 3: Focus on `<binding>` element.

> **Phase 3.1**: Rename the `<binding>` as `TempWsSOAP`. By default, the name attribute of `<binding>` will reflect the name of the WSDL document + `SOAP` ending. For providing another name, just right-click on the `<binding>` sub-diagram and select the **Refactor | Rename** option from the contextual menu. In the **Rename** wizard window, type the **TempWsSOAP** name and click on the **OK** button.
>
> **Phase 3.2**: Update the content of the `<binding>` element. Before going further, it is good practice to re-generate the `<binding>` element content. We are especially interested in this aspect because the `toFahrenheit` operation wasn't configured in the `<binding>` element (it seems that when a new operation is created, it is not automatically added in the `<binding>` element, until the `<binding>` is re-generated). To accomplish this task, right-click on the `<binding>` sub-diagram and select the **Generate Binding Content** option from the contextual menu. In the **Binding Wizard** window, select the **Overwrite existing binding information** checkbox and click on the **Finish** button.

Finally, save the WSDL and the first step is accomplished. Now, our WSDL is complete, and it is ready to serve us for generating the web service and sample client (you can see it in the **Source** view).

> Note that we have explored just a small part of the **WSDL Editor**, but enough to put you on tracks. In principle, using your intuition and the contextual menus, you can control the entire WSDL without manually editing the WSDL source. In addition, the **WSDL Editor** is accompanied by the Eclipse **WSDL Editor** menu, the **Outline** view (a tree representation of the current WSDL), and **Properties** view (list of detailed properties about current WSDL). Both views can be displayed from the **Show View** window, which is opened from the Eclipse **Window** menu | **Show view** | **Other** option.

Generating the web service from a WSDL document

Generating web services from WSDL documents is a common practice among the developers of web services. Any professional web service tool offers the possibility to generate web service artifacts from a WSDL document. Besides the gained time, the developer can focus more on web service business logic, and he/she doesn't have to worry about the redundant process of writing the web service and their client. Since this is the task of our second step, let's see how to do this with WS Tools.

WS Tools can generate web services (including sample clients) and provides a great wizard that offers to the developer a fine control over the entire process. Returning to our WSDL, we can assume that WS Tools should generate a web service that will expose to its clients two methods, named `toCelsius` and `toFahrenheit`. Both of them should be call-able through SOAP request at `http://127.0.0.1:8080/TempWs/TempWs` and should respond through SOAP responses. Obviously, there is only one way to check out our assumption. Therefore, here are the steps that should be followed:

1. In the **Package Explorer**, right-click on the **TempWs** node and select the **New | Other** option from the contextual menu.

2. In the **New** window, expand the **Web Services** node and select the **Web Service** leaf. Click on the **Next** button.

3. The **Web Service** wizard is displayed. Here, we will configure the main settings used by JBossWS to generate our web service.

4. Select the web service type—WS Tools can generate a web service's artifacts starting from a WSDL document or from a Java bean. Since we want to provide our WSDL as the starting point, we should select the **Top down Java bean Web Service** option from the **Web service type** list. The other option from this list refers to a Java bean as the starting point.

5. Select a service implementation—next, we have to indicate the WSDL location. For this, click on the **Browse** button, next to the **Service implementation** field. In the **Select Service Definition** window, click on the **Browse** button, and select the `converterTemp.wsdl` document from the **Resource browser** window. Returning to the **Select Service Definition** window, observe that WS Tools has accepted the `converterTemp.wsdl` document as a valid one. The success of validation is marked by the message *WSDL validation completes with no warning or error.*, while any errors/ warnings are listed in the WSDL validation messages table (as shown in the following screenshot). Click on the **OK** button.

If the WSDL validation facility is not active, then you can activate it like this: select the **Preferences** option from the Eclipse **Window** menu; in the **Preferences** window, left panel, select the **Web Services | Wizard Validation** leaf; in the right panel, select the **Wizard WSDL validation for all WSDL files** radio button; click on the **Apply** and **OK** buttons.

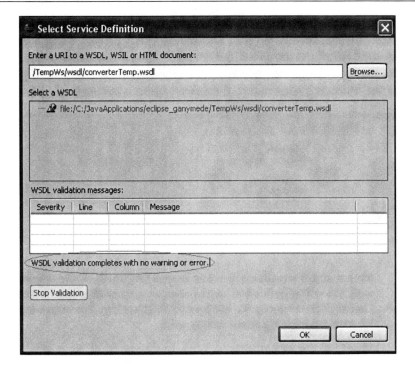

6. Set the server generation level — the service slidebar allows us to control the level of service generation. From bottom to top, we have the following levels:

    - **Develop service** – this level will develop the service's artifacts.

    - **Assemble service** – this level will assemble the service in an EAR.

    - **Deploy service** – this level will generate the deployment code for the service.

    - **Install service** – this level will install and configure the web module and EARs on the target server.

    - **Start service** – this level will start the target server.

    - **Test service** – this level will provide various options for testing the service, such as using the **Web Service Explorer** or sample JSPs.

7. The most convenient for us is to set the slider on **Install service** level (as shown in the following screenshot). There is no reason to set it below this level, since we want to let WS Tools work for us, but there is also no reason to go further and start the service, since we don't have a client yet and the service business logic is not implemented.

8. **Configuration**—from this section, we can modify the target server, web service runtime, service project, and service EAR project. Most commonly these configurations are pre-filled correctly, but if you need to modify one of them, then just follow the corresponding link. If you see the configurations from the following screenshot, then everything is set according to our needs.

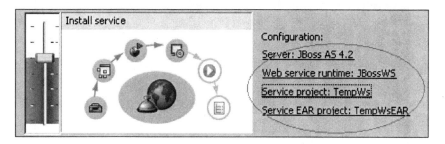

 Note that this wizard can be used to generate a web service client as well. We will skip this feature here as it is discussed in detail in the *Generate the web service's client from a WSDL* section. For now, we are keen on talking only about web service.

9. Optionally, you may want to publish the web service to a UDDI Registry or monitor the SOAP traffic over this service. Note that these features may require additional configurations over the target server; therefore, it is a better idea to leave them unchecked this time. About how to monitor SOAP requests-responses and how to use UDDI Registry, we will talk later in this chapter.

10. Finally, before clicking on the **Next** button, take a final look at the following screenshot to see if your settings match ours.

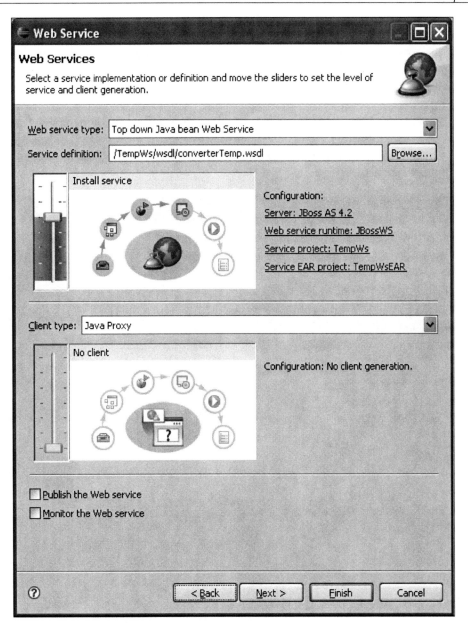

11. In this window, you can specify a new package name (by default, the provided package reflects the WSDL namespace) and JAX-WS specification (for JBossWS Native runtime, JAX-WS version should be **2.0**). In addition, you can specify a catalog file and the binding files if you have them. If you want the wizard to generate empty implementation classes for the web service, check the **Generate default Web Service implementation classes** checkbox. If you want to update the default web.xml file with the web service servlets configured, check the **Update the default web.xml** checkbox (as shown in the following screenshot) and then click on the **Finish** button to generate code.

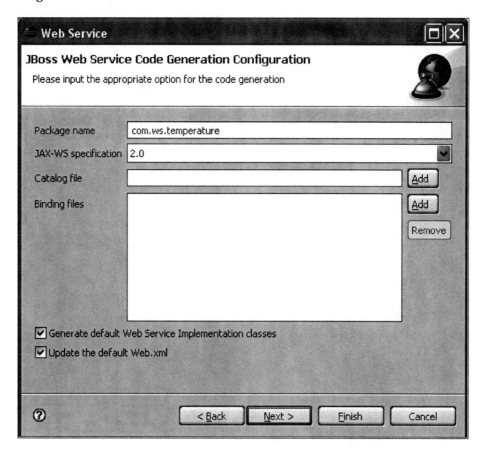

- After a few seconds, the artifacts are generated. In **Package Explorer**, src folder, you should see the com.ws.temperature package and the classes corresponding to our service. Take your time, and explore every source code to better understand how JBossWS works.

Providing service business logic

The server-side of our web service is almost ready. At this moment, our web service knows how to expose the toCelsius and toFahrenheit methods to its potential clients, but it doesn't know what they should actually do. In other words, calling these methods will not reveal the desired functionality because WS Tools has generated only the skeleton of these methods in TempWsImpl.java. Implementing their business logic is our job, therefore open the TempWSImpl.java and locate the toCelsius method, like below:

```
public float toCelsius(float fahrenheit) {
       return 0;
   }
```

Since this method should convert Fahreinheit degrees to Celsius, we can implement its business logic like this:

```
public float toCelsius(float fahrenheit) {
       return (fahrenheit - 32) * 5/9;
   }
```

Following the same logic, the toFahreinheit method should look like this:

```
public float toFahrenheit(float celsius) {
       return (celsius * 9/5) + 32;
   }
```

Apply the modification by saving the TempWsImpl.java file.

Generating the web service's client from a WSDL

XE "web service, creating:web service client, generating from WSDL" Based on the same WSDL document, we can ask WS Tools to generate a Java client for our web service. Because JBossWS uses a Java class to test web service, the WS Tools will generate a standalone Java client sample class that can be executed as a Java application to call a web service. From a simple perspective, the client is our service requestor, responsible for locating our web service, calling the two exposed methods, and displaying the received responses. The communication between the client and server will be mapped by the SOAP request-response paradigm.

The steps for generating a web service client from a WSDL document are:

1. In the **Package Explorer**, right-click on the **TempWs** node and select the **New | Other** option from the contextual menu.

2. In the **New** window, expand the **Web Services** node and select the **Web Service Client** leaf. Click on the **Next** button.

3. Next, select the `converterTemp.wsdl` document in the **Service definition** field. The procedure for locating the WSDL document should be familiar to you by now.

4. In this version, the only supported client type is the **Java Proxy** type. Therefore, select **Java Proxy** in the **Client type** field.

5. Drag the slidebar to **Install client** generation level (these generation levels are similar to the web service ones, but this time they refer to the client).

6. Everything else should be left as default (as shown in the following screenshot). Click on the **Next** button.

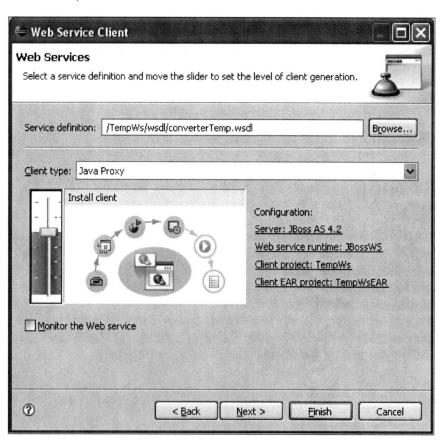

7. This page is similar to the one from generating a web service section, as shown in the screenshot on page 23, and therefore no extra information is needed. Click on the **Finish** button.

After a few seconds, the client is generated and you can see it in **Package Explorer** view, `com.ws.teperature.clientsample` package, under the name `ClientSample.java`.

Providing client business logic

When WS Tools generates a web service client, it usually adds a line of code for calling each web service method. By default, the generated client will require command-line arguments through the `args[]` `String` array, and will pass these arguments to the corresponding web service methods. In our case, these lines are:

```
System.out.println("Server said: " + port1.toCelsius(args[0]));
System.out.println("Server said: " + port1.toFahrenheit(args[0]));
```

There are two things that we are not conveying to these lines: first, we don't want to provide command-line arguments, and second our arguments are of type `float`, not `String`. Therefore, we have adjusted these calls according to our needs, and we have obtained the following web service client:

```
package com.ws.temperature.clientsample;

import com.ws.temperature.*;

public class ClientSample {

    public static void main(String[] args) {
        System.out.println("************************");
        System.out.println("Create Web Service Client...");
        TempWsService service1 = new TempWsService();
        System.out.println("Create Web Service...");
        TempWs port1 = service1.getConverterTempSOAP();
        System.out.println("Call Web Service Operation...");
        System.out.println("Server said: 150 Fahrenheit = "+port1.
toCelsius(150)+" Celsius");
        System.out.println("Server said: 65.55 Celsius = "+port1.
toFahrenheit(65.55f)+ " Fahrenheit");
        System.out.println("**********************");
        System.out.println("Call Over!");
    }
}
```

Deploying and testing a web service

Deploying and testing the `TempWs` web service are the final tasks. Since the step of web service generation included the **Install service** step, we can say that the first task is already solved. When we start the JBoss 4.2 Server from **JBoss Server View**, the web service should be there and should wait for us to call its methods. We can check the web service's presence by accessing the `http://localhost:8080/jbossws/` link. Continue by following the **View a list of deployed services** link from the **Runtime information** section. The `TempWs` web service should appear like in the following screenshot:

JBossWS/Services

Registered Service Endpoints

| Endpoint Name | jboss.ws:context=TempWs,endpoint=TempWs |
| Endpoint Address | http://localhost:8080/TempWs/TempWs?wsdl |

StartTime	StopTime	
Tue Dec 23 22:45:11 PST 2008		
RequestCount	ResponseCount	FaultCount
0	0	0
MinProcessingTime	MaxProcessingTime	AvgProcessingTime
0	0	0

 If you want to manually deploy an EAR containing a web service, then start the JBoss AS server and follow these three simple steps: in the **JBoss Server View**, right-click on the **JBoss 4.2 Server** and select **Add and Remove Projects** option from the contextual menu; in the **Add and Remove Projects** wizard, select the desired web service project from the **Available projects** panel and click the **Add >** button; click on the **Finish** button and monitor the **Console** view to see how the web service is configured on JBoss AS.

Testing the web service is even simpler than deploying it. Our web service's client is a Java standalone application that can be executed from the **Package Explorer** view by right-clicking on the **ClientSample.java** node and selecting the **Run As | Java Application** option from the contextual menu. The result of communication with web service should look as shown in the following screenshot:

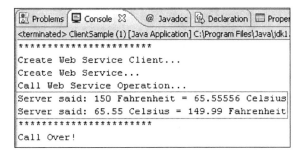

There are two known problems that may appear when you try to run your web service's clients (keep in mind that this is not a particularity of our example; it may appear for any web service).

If, instead of the expected output, you get an error like *Two classes have the same XML type name "address". Use @XmlType.name and @XmlType.namespace to assign different names to them.*, then you have to delete the `jaxws-rt.jar` and `jaxws-tools.jar` JARs from the `{JBOSS_HOME}/client` folder.

In addition, if you get an error like *Exception in thread "main" java.lang. NoClassDefFoundError: org/apache/xerces/xs/XSModel*, then you have to import in your classpath the `xercesImpl.jar`. This library can be found in the `{JBOSS_HOME}/lib/ endorsed` folder.

Testing a web service through Web Services Explorer

If the Java client, `ClientSample.java`, generated by WS Tools doesn't satisfy your needs, and you still want to test the web service operations, then you can use the Web Services Explorer feature. The WSE is a web service client based on JSP technology that may run in the Eclipse Web Browser or on an Internet browser, like Mozilla. From the WSE's GUI, we can call the web service's operations, monitor SOAP request-response messages, and see web service details.

This section shows how to use the Web Service Explorer to test a web service via native WSDL and SOAP. In particular, it demonstrates how to use the Web Services Explorer to invoke `toCelsius` and `toFahrenheit` operations of `TempWs` web service.

Bring in front the Web Services Explorer like this:

1. Start the JBoss 4.2 Server from **JBoss Server View**.

2. In the **Package Explorer**, right-click on the WSDL document (**TestWs | wsdl | converterTemp.wsdl** leaf). From the contextual menu, select the **Web Services | Test with Web Service Explorer** option.

3. The WSE is opened in the Eclipse **Web Browser**, and the `TempWs` web service is available through its `converterTemp.wsdl` document. Click on the **toCelsius** link and follow the indications (as shown in the screenshot below):

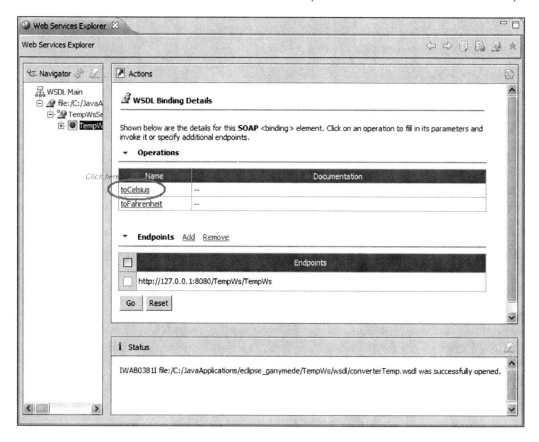

Creating a Web service from a Java bean

Conforming to our third step, we now want to generate the temperature converter web service starting from a Java bean instead of the WSDL document. Actually, among web service artifacts, we will ask WS Tools to generate from scratch the corresponding WSDL document.

Based on Java bean capabilities, we have developed the following classical code. There isn't much to say, it is just a simple Java class in which we have marked its name with the `@WebService` annotation, and then marked the `toCelsius` and `toFahrenheit` methods with the `@WebMethod`, `@WebResult`, `@RequestWrapper`, and `@ResponseWrapper` annotations.

```java
package com.ws.temperature.bean;

import javax.jws.WebMethod;
import javax.jws.WebParam;
import javax.jws.WebResult;
import javax.jws.WebService;
import javax.xml.ws.RequestWrapper;
import javax.xml.ws.ResponseWrapper;

@WebService(name = "TempWsBean", targetNamespace = "http://
temperature.ws.bean.com")
public class TempWsBean {

    @WebMethod(action = "http://temperature.ws.bean.com/toCelsius")
    @WebResult(name = "returnFahrenheit", targetNamespace = "")
    @RequestWrapper(localName = "toCelsius", targetNamespace =
"http://temperature.ws.bean.com", className = "com.ws.temperature.
bean.ToCelsius")
    @ResponseWrapper(localName = "toCelsiusResponse", targetNamespace
= "http://temperature.ws.bean.com", className = "com.ws.temperature.
bean.ToCelsiusResponse")
    public float toCelsius(
        @WebParam(name = "fahrenheit", targetNamespace = "")
        float fahrenheit){
      return (fahrenheit - 32) * 5/9;
    }

    @WebMethod(action = "http://temperature.ws.bean.com/toFahrenheit")
    @WebResult(name = "returnCelsius", targetNamespace = "")
    @RequestWrapper(localName = "toFahrenheit", targetNamespace =
"http://temperature.ws.bean.com", className = "com.ws.temperature.
bean.ToFahrenheit")
    @ResponseWrapper(localName = "toFahrenheitResponse",
targetNamespace = "http://temperature.ws.bean.com", className = "com.
ws.temperature.bean.ToFahrenheitResponse")
    public float toFahrenheit(
        @WebParam(name = "celsius", targetNamespace = "")
        float celsius){
      return (celsius * 9/5) + 32;
    }

}
```

Now, having the Java bean as the generation starting point, we can put WS Tools at work. Begin by creating a new **Dynamic Web Project** and add the JBoss web service facet to it, respecting the following particularities (unspecified settings are the same as in our first step):

- The **Dynamic Web Project** name will be TestWsBean.
- The project's EAR is named TestWsBeanEAR.

Next, create/import the TempWsBean bean under the project's src folder, in a package named com.ws.temperature.bean. Continue by launching the **Web Service** wizard and take a look at the following screenshot. As you can see from this figure, this time you should select the **Bottom up Java bean Web Service** option from the Web service type combo box, and navigate to TempWsBean bean using the **Browse** button. In addition, drag the generation level slider on **Install service** level and click on the **Next** button.

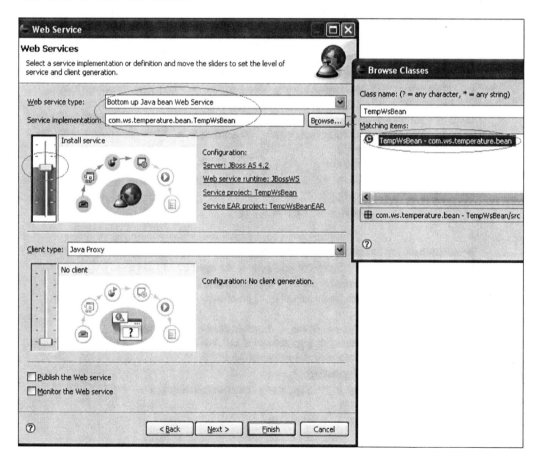

In the next page, you should allow WS Tools to generate the WSDL document and to update the project's web.xml configuration file. Click on the **Finish** button.

When the generation process ends, take a look in the **Package Explorer** view, **TempWsBean | src | com.ws.temperature.bean** leaf. You should see the web service's artifacts that map the corresponding input/output messages. In addition, under **TempWsBean | WebContent | wsdl** node, you should have the generated WSDL, TempWsBeanService.wsdl (you can use this WSDL to generate a client). In conclusion, the web service's artifacts were successfully generated!

If you open the WSDL document in the **WSDL Editor**, you may notice that the SOAP address is not practically specified, being set as REPLACE_ WITH_ACTUAL_URL. You can replace the text between quotes with the desired SOAP address, like http://localhost:8080/TempWsBean/ TempWsBean URL per example (obviously, machine name and port value may vary, depending on your server configuration).

The third scenario is complete!

Publishing web services and business entities

"Why do I need to publish a web service?" The answer is simple and it sounds like this: because your organization wants to be a part of a web services exchange program between it and other business partnerships; you should allow those organizations to discover and use your organization's web services without involving technical experts (remember that they can originate in a business field, and they are not software developers). In order for a service requestor to discover a service, a service provider must first publish a business entity, at least one business service, and a service interface in a UDDI registry. This is what we are going to do next!

Conforming to our fourth step, we will publish our TempWs web service through UDDI mechanism. Since UDDI is the main point of interest in this section, we start with a brief UDDI introduction meant to provide you with sufficient knowledge to understand how to accomplish our goal.

A brief introduction to UDDI

For a start, you should know that UDDI is the acronym for Universal Description, Discovery, and Integration, and it represents a standard mechanism for publishing and discovering information about web services. Practically, UDDI is an XML-based registry that stores information about business and web services and allows companies to find one another on the Web, for putting their systems in an inter-operable environment. A deeper look at UDDI will reveal the following structure:

- **business entity** — contains general information about a business (organization), like business name, address, contact information, and unique identifiers such as D-U-N-S numbers or tax IDs. This information allows others to discover the web service based upon the business identification.

- **business service** — contains a list of services provided by the business entity. Every single entry contains a service description, a classifications list describing the service, and a binding templates list that points the service technical information.

- **binding template** — as we just said above, every business service entry has an associated binding templates list. This is responsible for providing useful information to discover the service. Per example, a binding template may contain the service implementation access point and a pointer to the corresponding WSDL document.

- **service type** — a generic representation of a registered service. A **tModel** is a data structure representing a service type and consists of a name (identifies the service), a description (more information), and a UUID (Universal Unique Identifier). The UUID is known as a **tModelKey** and consists of a set of alphanumeric characters (for example, a valid tModelKey may be: A035A07C-F362-44DD-8F95-E2B134BF43B4).

Commonly, a UDDI has two types of users: business analysts and software developers. For a business analyst, UDDI is like Google, used to discover services, while for a developer, it is more like an interface for publishing new business entities and services. When a business analyst finds a service they can receive the corresponding WSDL document; therefore, it has the information needed to develop a SOAP client for the service. Obviously, when a software developer publishes a web service, he/she has to provide at least the minimum amount of information that makes the service discoverable.

Speaking of programming UDDI aspects, you should know that two APIs are described by the UDDI specification: the Inquiry API and the Publish API. The first one locates information about a business, the business's services, the service's specifications, and failure situation information. Any read operation from a UDDI registry uses one of the inquiry API's messages. Normally, the inquiry API does not require authentication and is accessed using HTTP protocol. The second one is used to create, store, and/or update information located in a UDDI registry. Since we are able to modify the content of the UDDI registries, it is obvious that all functions of this API require authenticated access. In addition, this API is commonly accessed through HTTPS.

In principle, these are the fundamentals of UDDI mechanism, especially when we refer to UDDI and web services. Nevertheless, we have talked so much about UDDI and web services that you probably get the idea that UDDI is only about registering and discovering web services, which is not true. UDDI can be used to register any type of services, not just web services. Therefore, when you think of UDDI, don't automatically think of it as the "Yellow Pages" for web services lookup and discovery, think of it more as a versatile repository for publishing and discovering services. Thinking this way will make things clear!

 We know that this UDDI introduction is not much, but it is better than nothing. If you are still confused regarding UDDI mechanism, then before going further it is recommended that you take a look at the UDDI official specification at `http://uddi.xml.org/uddi-org` and `http://www.uddi.org/pubs/uddi_v3.htm`. Anyway, if you are not interested in the deeper aspects of UDDI, and simply wish to learn how to use it, then just keep reading further.

JBoss AS 4.2 and jUDDI

Rewinding to our goals, we must say that JBoss AS 4.2 integrates jUDDI (pronounced "Judy"), which is an open source Java implementation of the UDDI specification for Web Services. As you will see, jUDDI is based on three main components: a servlet, a set of tables, and a properties file. The core of jUDDI is located in the `{JBOSS_HOME}/server/{all | default}/deploy` folder under `juddi-service.sar` name (this was updated when you installed JBossWS distribution).

The built-in jUDDI will allow us to easily perform certain UDDI-related tasks, such as defining a data source, creating DDLs for UDDI database, binding data source to UDDI database, writing configuration files, and so on. Basically, the jUDDI will work on these default settings:

- The jUDDI servlet, representing the jUDDI Registry, is named `JUDDIServlet` and is located in the `{JBOSS_HOME}`/server`{all | default}`/deploy/ `juddi-service.sar/juddi.war/WEB-INF/classes` folder.

- The jUDDI database is named `localDB` and is a Hypersonic database accessed through `java:/DefaultDS` JNDI name. It is physically located in the `{JBOSS_HOME}`/`{all | default}`/data/hypersonic folder and its JDBC driver is named `org.hsqldb.jdbcDriver` (available in the `{JBOSS_HOME}`/server/`{all | default}`|/lib/hsqldb.jar library). More details about this database configuration are in the `{JBOSS_HOME}`/server/`{all | default}`/deploy/juddi-service.sar/juddi.war/WEB-INF/jboss-web. xml file and the `{JBOSS_HOME}`/server`{all | default}`/deploy/hsqldb- ds.xml file. The `java:/DefaultDS` data source is indicated in the `{JBOSS_HOME}`/server`{all | default}`/deploy/juddi-service.sar/juddi.war/ WEB-INF/juddi.properties file.

- The DDLs to model the corresponding jUDDI database tables are located in the `{JBOSS_HOME}`/server/`{all | default}`/deploy/juddi-service. sar/META-INF/ddl folder, `juddi_create_db.ddl` (SQL statements for creating tables), `juddi_drop_db.dll` (SQL statements for dropping tables), and `juddi_data.ddl` (SQL statements for populating tables with minimum information).

- The `{JBOSS_HOME}`/server/`{all | default}`/deploy/juddi-service. sar/META-INF/jboss-service.xml file allows us to configure the jUDDI service.

- Inquiry and publishing access point URLs are `http://localhost:8080/ juddi/inquiry`, and respectively `http://localhost:8080/juddi/ publish`. More details are in the `juddi.properties` file.

- To access the jUDDI home page, start JBoss AS 4.2 and navigate to `http://localhost:8080/juddi` link. You should see something like in the following screenshot:

Preparing the jUDDI database

Now that we are aware of jUDDI implementation, and we know where and what to look in JBoss AS 4.2, it is time to make a few changes to the default jUDDI configuration. These changes will help us a lot in our attempt of publishing the `TempWs` web service in jUDDI Registry. First, let's take a look in `jboss-service.xml`, and note that the jUDDI tables are managed through three attributes, highlighted below:

```
<!-- Should all tables be created on Start-->
<attribute name="CreateOnStart">false</attribute>
    <!-- Should all tables be dropped on Stop-->
<attribute name="DropOnStop">true</attribute>
    <!-- Should all tables be dropped on Start-->
<attribute name="DropOnStart">false</attribute>
```

Conforming to these attributes' values, when JBoss AS 4.2 starts, it will not create the jUDDI necessary tables, but it will try to drop these tables when it stops. Obviously this means that when we start JBoss AS 4.2, the jUDDI tables are not present in the `localDB` database, which will take us to an inevitable error while we try to publish the web service. In principle, the `localDB` will contain only the tables shown in the following screenshot:

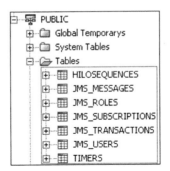

Adding the jUDDI dedicated tables on resuming is achieved by modifying the above lines, like this (the highlighted values were modified):

```
<!-- Should all tables be created on Start-->
<attribute name="CreateOnStart">true</attribute>
    <!-- Should all tables be dropped on Stop-->
<attribute name="DropOnStop">false</attribute>
    <!-- Should all tables be dropped on Start-->
<attribute name="DropOnStart">false</attribute>
```

Later, when you start JBoss AS 4.2 server, the tables from `juddi_create_db.ddl` will be added to the `localDB`. Afterwards, the tables are populated with a set of default information, provided by the `INSERT` statements from the `juddi_data.ddl` file.

By default, only two users may have access to publish in jUDDI. Both of them have administrator roles and they are listed at the end of the `juddi_data.ddl` file, as you can see below (the `PUBLISHER` table stores the users that can modify the jUDDI content):

```
INSERT INTO PUBLISHER (PUBLISHER_ID,PUBLISHER_NAME,EMAIL_
ADDRESS,IS_ENABLED,IS_ADMIN) VALUES ('jboss','JBoss User','jboss@
xxx','true','true');
INSERT INTO PUBLISHER (PUBLISHER_ID,PUBLISHER_NAME,EMAIL_ADDRESS,IS_
ENABLED,IS_ADMIN) VALUES ('jbosscts','JBoss User','jboss@
xxx','true','true');
```

Obviously, adding a new user is a simple task that can be accomplished in many ways. But, for simplicity, just add a new `INSERT` line in the `juddi_data.ddl` file. For example, let's add a user with id, `TCAdmin`, and email, `tca@yahoo.com`.

```
INSERT INTO PUBLISHER (PUBLISHER_ID,PUBLISHER_NAME,EMAIL_ADDRESS,IS_
ENABLED,IS_ADMIN) VALUES ('TCAdmin','Temperature Converter User','tca@
yahoo.com','true','true');
```

Now, jUDDI has its corresponding tables available, and we have a user who can modify jUDDI content. This means that we are ready to try to publish and discover services hosted by our registries.

Using Web Services Explorer as a UDDI Browser

Publishing and discovering web services through UDDI is a job normally handled by a UDDI Browser, like those available at `http://www.soapclient.com/UDDISearch.html` (this is an online UDDI Browser), `http://sourceforge.net/projects/uddibrowser/`, or `http://www.uddibrowser.org/`.

Remember that in the section *Test a web service through Web Services Explorer*, we said that Web Services Explorer is a web service client based on JSP technology? Actually, WSE is much more than that, because it supports the publication, discovery, and maintenance of business entities, business services, and service interfaces, exactly like a UDDI Browser. Since WSE is already available in Web Services Tools, there is no need to download and install another UDDI Browser.

At this moment, we have everything that we need to publish our `TempWs` web service. Start the JBoss AS 4.2 from **JBoss Server View** and launch the Web Services Explorer. (In **JavaEE** perspective, select the **Launch the Web Service Explorer** option from the Eclipse **Run** main menu.)

> If you want to open the Web Services Explorer in an Internet browser, then you have to keep in mind that the port is randomly selected each time WSE is launched. Therefore, one way or another, you have to know the port that should be replaced in the link `http://localhost:{random_port}/wse/wsexplorer/wsexplorer.jsp`. When you launch WSE in Eclipse, the entire URL, including generated port number, is visible in the Eclipse window title.

Adding a Registry to the Web Services Explorer

Before we can publish anything, we need to have a registry in WSE. By default, WSE doesn't expose a registry, and therefore we have to start by creating one from scratch. The steps are simple and straightforward:

1. In the **Navigator** panel, click on the **UDDI Main** node.

2. In the **Actions** panel, type a name for the new registry in **Registry Name** field (for example, type **TemperatureRegistry**).

3. In the **Inquiry URL**, type `http://localhost:8080/juddi/inquiry`.

4. Click on the **Go** button (as shown in the following screenshot).

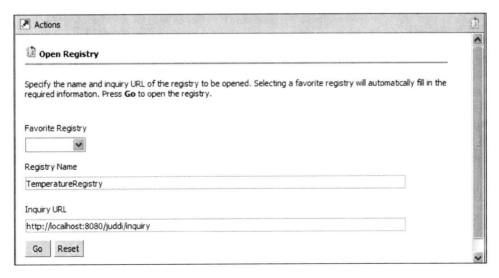

5. The `TemperatureRegistry` registry is added and opened like in the following screenshot (on the **Actions** toolbar, click on the **Add to Favorites** icon—the favorites page of the Web Services Explorer allows you to store the location of UDDI registries, business entities, Web services, service interfaces, as well as WSIL and WSDL documents).

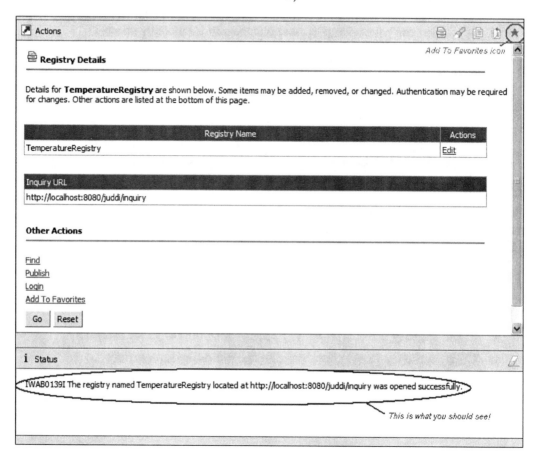

Note that after you click on the **Add to Favorites** icon, the registry details will disappear from the **Actions** panel. You can restore the previous page by clicking on the **Registry Details** icon on the **Actions** panel toolbar (this is the first icon from left to right).

In the future, to view the favorites content, just click on the **Favorites** icon from Web Services Explorer toolbar, and you should see something like in the following screenshot (in **Navigator** panel, expand **Favorite UDDI Registries** node, select **TemperatureRegistry** leaf, and follow the **Add to UDDI page** link in **Actions** panel).

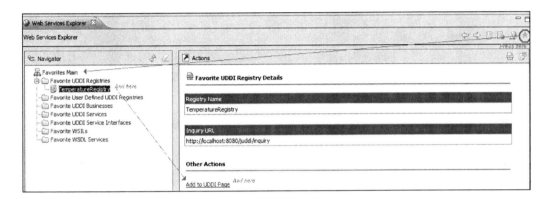

Publishing a business entity

Next, we can publish a business entity in `TemperatureRegistry` registry, like this (we continue from the previous window, therefore don't close WSE):

1. In the **Actions** panel, **Other Actions** section, click on the **Publish** link.

2. In the **Publish** section, select **Business** option from the **Publish** combo box.

3. Check the **Simple** radio button as the publication format (in **Advanced** publication format you can enter more information about your business entity, and you can specify multiple names and descriptions for multi-lingual support).

4. Type **http://localhost:8080/juddi/publish** as the publish URL.

5. Next, enter the userID and password that we have inserted earlier in the `PUBLISHER` table (type userID: **TCAdmin**, and password: **tca@yahoo.com**).

6. Provide a business name and a description in the **Name** and **Description** text fields and click on the **Go** button (as shown in the following screenshot).

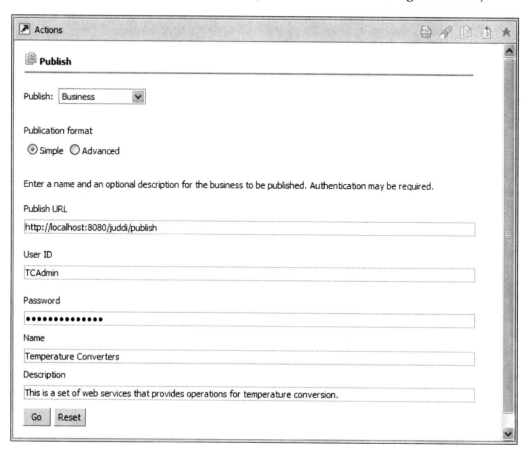

The business is published and you should see something like in the following screenshot (on the **Actions** toolbar, click on the **Add to Favorites** icon). Restore the page by clicking on the **Registry Details** icon on the **Actions** panel toolbar.

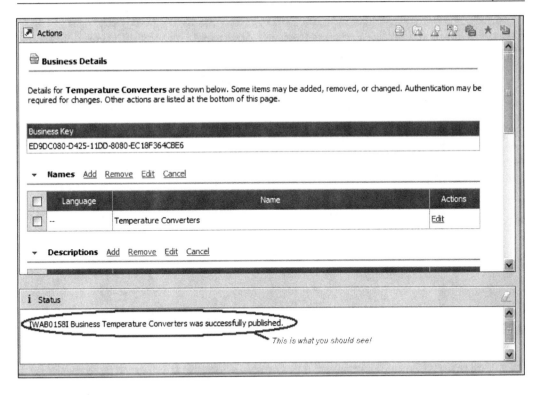

Publishing a web service

Now that we have a business entity, we are ready to publish a business service (we continue from the previous window, therefore don't close WSE). The steps to accomplish this goal are:

1. In the **Other Actions** section, follow the **Publish Service** link (scroll down to the bottom of the page).

2. Check the **Simple** radio button as the publication format (in **Advanced** publication format you can enter more parameters about your web service).

3. Next, you have to provide the WSDL URL. Use the **Browse** button to navigate to the `converterTemp.wsdl` document (screenshot given below).

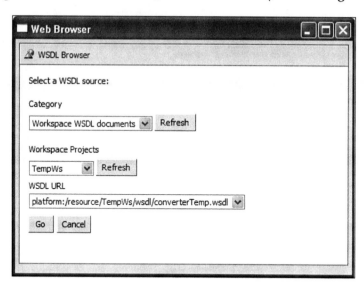

4. Provide a web service name and a description in the **Name** and **Description** text fields and click on the **Go** button (as shown in the following screenshot).

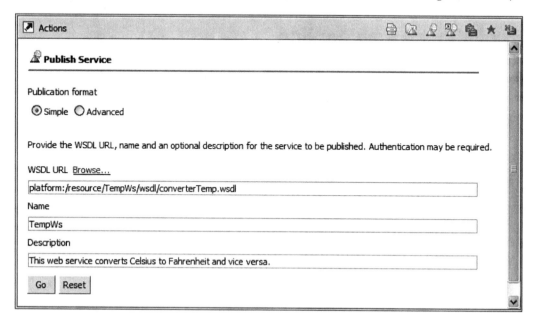

The web service is published and you should see something like in the screenshot given below (on the **Actions** toolbar, click on the **Add to Favorites** icon). Now, our job is done! You may close WSE.

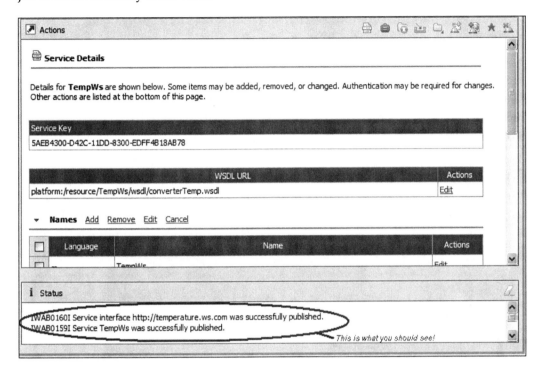

Discovering our own web service through WSE

In this section, we will use WSE to discover our web service. Obviously we know that the service is there, but let's assume that we don't know that. Let's assume that we know only the registry name, `TemperatureRegistry`, and the business entity name, `Temperature Converters`.

Launch WSE again and follow the next steps:

1. In the **Navigator** panel, click on the **UDDI Main** node.
2. In the **Actions** panel, select **TemperatureRegistry** registry from the **Favorite Registry** combo box.
3. Click on the **Go** button.
4. Locate the **Other Actions** section and follow the **Find** link.
5. Select **Business** from **Search for** combo box.
6. Check the **Simple** radio button for the type of search.

7. Type **Temperature Converters** as business name.

8. Click on the **Go** button (you should see another page containing business details).

9. Locate the **Other Actions** section and follow the **Get Services** link.

10. The TempWs service should be displayed in a new page (the service was discovered!). Note that in the **Status** window you received a message indicating that this business contains a single web service.

Further, you can call the web service operations by following the **Add to WSDL Page** link from the **Other Actions** section. This link will open the page (from page 28), which should be familiar to you by now.

Discovering "external" web service through WSE

This section demonstrates how to use the Web Services Explorer to invoke operations on a Web service named Temperature Converter as available from XMethods on the Internet (http://www.xmethods.net/ve2/index.po). The only prerequisite is that you be connected to the Internet, therefore we don't use JBoss AS or jUDDI.

 If you have a firewall activated, then it is recommended to disconnect it.

Start WSE and follow these steps:

1. On WSE toolbar, click on the **WSDL Page** icon (second icon from right to left).

2. In the **Navigator** panel, click on the **WSDL Main** node.

3. In the **Actions** panel, type **http://coeservice.en.kku.ac.th:8080/ TemperatureConvertor/TemperatureConvertorService?WSDL** for the WSDL URL.

4. Click on the **Go** button (screenshot given below).

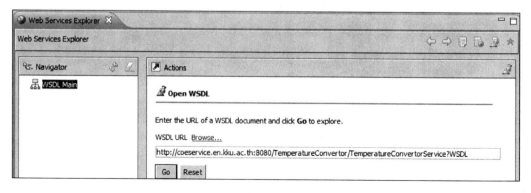

After a few seconds, the service's operations are displayed as in the screenshot given below. Take your time and explore them in the same manner that you did with the `TempWs` operations.

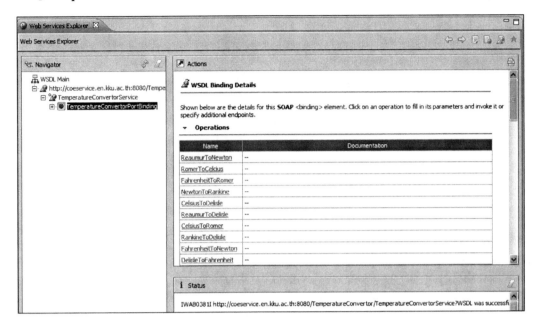

 More details about WSE and publishing/discovering web services through UDDI are available at `http://help.eclipse.org/stable/index.jsp?topic=/org.eclipse.jst.ws.consumption.ui.doc.user/tasks/tuddiexp.html`.

WSDL to WSIL, WSIL in WSE

Released in 2001 by IBM and Microsoft, WSIL (Web Service Inspection Language) is an XML document format similar in scope to the UDDI. Nevertheless, WSIL is much simpler and the flexible, and it tries to provide solutions for the criticisms brought to UDDI. It is beyond our scope to go into detail on WSIL, but you can read more about WSIL at `http://download.boulder.ibm.com/ibmdl/pub/software/dw/specs/ws-wsilspec/ws-wsilspec.pdf`.

Anyway, it is our duty to let you know that Web Services Tools does support WSIL, and in the next two sections we will show you how to do it.

Convert WSDL to WSIL

First, you should know that Web Services Tools allow us to generate WSIL documents from WSDL documents. For example, if we want to obtain a WSIL document from the `converterTemp.wsdl` document, you can proceed like this:

1. In the **Package Explorer**, expand the **TempWs | wsdl** node and select the **converterTemp.wsdl** leaf.

2. Right-click on this leaf and select the **Web Services | Generate WSIL** option from the contextual menu.

3. In the WSIL wizard, click on the **Finish** button (the WSLI and WSDL URL fields were automatically populated with `/TempWs/wsdl/converterTemp.wsil`, and `/TempWs/wsdl/converterTemp.wsdl` respectively).

4. Next, refresh the **Package Explorer** view content (press *F5*) and take a look in the `wsdl` folder. The `converterTemp.wsil` should be there.

WSIL and WSE

In addition to UDDI and WSDL, WSE also provides support for WSIL. We may say that WSE is a JSP web service client, a UDDI WSDL, and a WSIL Browser. For example, let's add the `converterTemp.wsil` WSIL document in WSE, and let's inspect the available WSDL services through it:

1. Start JBoss AS (if is not already running) and launch WSE.

2. Click on the **WSIL Page** icon on WSE toolbar.

3. In the **Navigator** panel, select the **WSIL Main** node.

4. Provide (type) the WSIL URL, which should be **platform:/resource/TempWs/wsdl/converterTemp.wsil** in our case.

5. Choose **WSDL Services** as the type of objects to inspect (note that you may also inspect WSIL details, UDDI services and business, and WSIL links).

6. Click on the **Go** button. A list of WSDL services should appear, like in the screenshot given below (obviously, we have a single WSDL service—if you want to call its operations then select it and click on the **Add To WSDL Page** button):

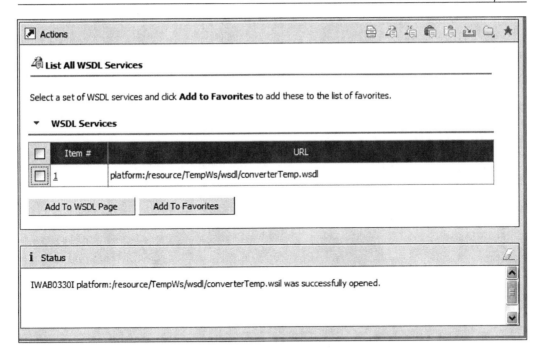

More details about WSE and publishing/discovering web services
through WSIL are available at `http://help.eclipse.org/stable/`
`index.jsp?topic=/org.eclipse.jst.ws.consumption.`
`ui.doc.user/tasks/tuddiexp.html`.

Summary

In this chapter, you saw how to use JbossWS and WS Tools to reproduce four
common steps related to the web services development. Among other things, we
have created from scratch a WSDL document using WSDL Editor; we have generated
a complete web service from a WSDL document and from a Java bean using WS
Tools wizards; and we have published a web service using jUDDI and Web Services
Explorer. In addition, you have seen how to generate a web service's client; how to
test a web service through Web Services Explorer; how to convert WSDL documents
to WSIL documents; and how to inspect WSDL web services through WSIL and WSE.

Now, you should have had sufficient practice to be able to develop, deploy, and
publish your own web services in just a few minutes. Good luck!

11
JBoss Portal Tools

In this chapter, we will talk about JBoss Portal Tools. This feature is available starting from JBoss Tools 3, and it supports the JSR-168 Portlet Specification (Portlet 1.0), JSR-286 Portlet Specification (Portlet 2.0), and works with Portlet Bridge for supporting Portlets in JSF/Seam applications. The portlets developed under JBoss Portal Tools guidance will be tested on the JBoss Portal, which is currently developed by JBoss Enterprise Middleware developers and community contributors. This provides a standards-based environment for hosting and serving a portal's web interface. The JBoss Portal framework contains the portal container, and supports a variety of features, such as standard portlets, single sign-on, clustering, and internationalization. Practically, every component of JBoss Portal is configurable and customizable according to the JBoss Portal Reference Guide available at `http://www.jboss.org/ jbossportal/docs/index.html`.

In the following sections our goal is to install the JBoss Portal bundle and the JBoss Portlet Bridge and to develop four portlets. They are as follows:

- A Java portlet—this will be a simple Java portlet. It will introduce you to the portlet architecture and will familiarize you with the main wizards of the JBoss Portal Tools. In addition, we will also talk about the structure of Java portlets and their specific descriptors.

- A JSP portlet—this portlet will add JSP capabilities to a Java portlet. You will see how to provide an implementation for the **VIEW**, **EDIT**, and **HELP** portlet modes for developing a temperature converter portlet. You will see how to interact with this portlet and how to set the portlet preferences.

- A JSF portlet—this will be a JSF portlet stub. You will see how to transform an empty **Dynamic Web Project** into a JSF portlet.

- A Seam portlet—this will be a Seam portlet stub. You will see how to transform an empty **Dynamic Web Project** into a Seam portlet.

Before developing a portlet, let's see a brief overview of portals and portlet technologies. This overview is more for the uninitiated, so don't expect to become a portlet expert as soon as you read it.

Overview of Portals and Portlets

Portal and Portlet technologies require learning a lot of new concepts, and it won't be possible for us to cover everything in this chapter, but we can provide a few basic definitions and notions that will help you in the following sections. We will start by defining the portal and portlet concepts:

Portal — According to the Portlet Specification, "*a portal is a web application that commonly provides personalization, single sign on, content aggregation from different sources, and hosts the presentation layer of information systems. Aggregation is the act of integrating content from different sources within a web page.*" Typically, a portal page looks as shown in the figure below (as you can see, a portal page is made up of more portlets windows, and every portlet window is made up of two parts: a **Decorations and Controls** bar and a **Portlet Fragment**, which is the part contributed by the portlet application).

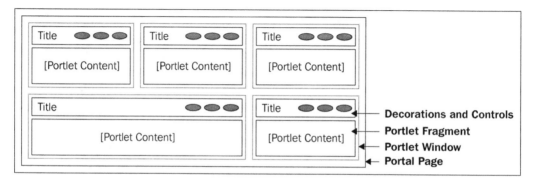

We can divide the portal functionality as follows:

- **Portlet container** — similar to a servlet container, a portlet container manages the portlet's life cycle, including initialization and destroy.

- **Content aggregator** — they aggregate content generated by various portlet applications.

- **Common services** — a set of common services provided by the portal (not part of the portlet specification, but a common marketing approach).

Portlet — According to the Portlet Specification, "*Portlets are web components — like servlets — specifically designed to be aggregated in the context of a composite page. Usually, many portlets are invoked in the single request of a portal page. Each portlet produces a fragment of markup that is combined with the markup of other portlets, all within the portal page markup.*" A portlet can contain anything from a simple web page to a personalized view of various data in multiple systems. Portlets are deployed as WARs inside a portlet container and they implement the **javax.portlet.Portlet** interface.

We can divide portlets functionality as follows:

- **Storage for user preferences** — portlets have the capability to store the user's preferences (configuration data) in a persistent data store. This job is accomplished by an object named **javax.portlet.PortletPreferences**. Therefore, the users can customize their preferences once, and take advantage of them in the future, even if the server is restarted.

- **Request processing** — portlets can handle different kinds of requests generated when users take actions on them (known as the action phase).

- **Portlet modes** — they describe what the user is doing (known as mode). For example, **VIEW** mode is a default mode commonly associated with functionalities like reading, viewing, composing, sending, checking, and so on, while **EDIT** view will take care of the functionalities that allow the user to configure the behavior of the application. **HELP** mode is also a default portlet mode responsible for providing help information about the portlet. The possible modes that a portlet can assume are available in the **javax.portlet.PortletMode** class. Besides the default modes, additional portlet modes may be defined by calling the constructor of this class.

- **Window state** — describe how much space should be given to content generated by a portlet on a portal page. The portlet can use this information to decide how much information to render. The three window states for each portlet are:
  - **normal** — a portlet shares this page with other portlets.
  - **minimized** — a portlet may show very little information, or none at all.
  - **maximized** — a portlet may be the only portlet displayed on this page.

- **User information** — provides access to the user attributes (name, surname, email, phone, zip, etc.). This is known as the user attributes concept, and the attributes are used to provide a personalized content to the user who initiates a request.

- **Portlet Instance** — a portlet instance can be placed on multiple pages and will show the same state.

Our "journey" in portal and portlets specifications ends here, but for a complete specification you can access http://www.jcp.org/en/jsr/detail?id=168 (version 1.0 of the Java portlet specification), http://www.jcp.org/en/jsr/detail?id=286 (version 2.0 of the Java portlet specification), http://en.wikipedia.org/wiki/JSR_168#JSR_168, and http://java.sys-con.com/node/131819. In principle, the notions presented in this brief introduction have covered the aspects discussed next about JBoss Portal.

Downloading and installing JBoss Portal + JBoss AS

JBoss Portal 2.7.0 is available for download as a binary distribution or as a bundle. The JBoss Portal bundle contains everything needed to execute JBoss Portal with the exception of the Java distribution itself. This is the easiest and fastest way to get JBoss Portal installed and running. The JBoss Portal bundle contains JBoss AS, JBoss Portal, and the embedded Hypersonic SQL database. Therefore, it is more preferable to download and install the bundle distribution instead of the binary. Once you have Java installed (JDK 1.6, 1.5, or 1.4), you are ready to download the JBoss Portal bundle from the `http://www.jboss.org/jbossportal/download/index.html` link (screenshot given below).

JBoss Portal Community Downloads

Package	Version	Category	Released	License	Notes	Download
JBoss Portal Source Code	2.7.0	Community Final Release	2008-10-30	LGPL	Notes	Download
JBoss Portal Binary	2.7.0	Community Final Release	2008-10-30	LGPL	Notes	Download
JBoss Portal + JBoss AS 4.2.3	2.7.0	Community Final Release	2008-10-30	LGPL	Notes	Download
JBoss Portal Binary (Clustered)	2.7.0	Community Final Release	2008-10-30	LGPL	Notes	Download

Now, installing the JBoss Portal bundle is a simple task that consists of extracting the ZIP archive in your favorite location. For example, we extract it in `C:\Packt\jboss-portal-2.7.0.GA` folder.

> If you choose to download the JBoss Portal binary distribution, then after you extract the ZIP archive, the installation instructions are in the `${JBOSS_PORTAL_BINARY_HOME}/docs/referenceGuide/html/installation.html` file.

Configuring the JBoss Portal bundle under Eclipse IDE

It's time to configure the JBoss Portal bundle under Eclipse IDE. Configuring the JBoss Portal bundle is a goal that can be accomplished by following the example from the *Adding a WTP Runtime in Eclipse* and *Adding a WTP Server in Eclipse* sections in *JBoss AS Tools*, that is, Chapter 2. Nevertheless, here are some clues that you may find useful during this job (adjust the following paths and names according to your favorites):

- Select a **JBoss 4.2 Runtime** from the available runtimes.

- Use the name **JBoss Portal 4.2** for the **JBoss 4.2 Runtime**.

- The home directory of **JBoss 4.2 Runtime** is C:\Packt\jboss-portal-2.7.0.GA.

- The recommended JRE is version 5.0 (4.0 and 6.0 are also supported).

- The selected configuration should be default (the JBoss Portal, represented by the jboss-portal.sar archive, is placed in the ${JBOSS_PORTAL_BUNDLE_HOME}/server/default/deploy folder).

- Use the name **JBoss Portal 4.2 Server** for the JBoss Portal bundle.

- The deploy directory of JBoss Portal bundle is C:\Packt\jboss-portal-2.7.0.GA\server\default\deploy.

If you have followed our clues and have correctly configured the JBoss Portal bundle in Eclipse, then the **JBoss Server View** should display the new server as shown in the following screenshot:

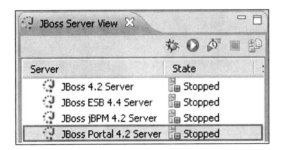

Starting JBoss Portal

The default page of JBoss Portal is available right after you start the **JBoss Portal 4.2 Server**.

When the **JBoss Portal 4.2 Server** starts for the first time, a set of SQL errors will be reported in **Console** view — that the initial tables have not been created yet. You don't have to worry about them, just ignore any **ERROR** message. These are not "real" errors.

After the JBoss Portal server has successfully started, bring up your web browser and go to the following URL: `http://localhost:8080/portal`. You should see the default page for JBoss Portal (screenshot given below—notice that we have identified with red the portal components from the first screenshot given in this chapter).

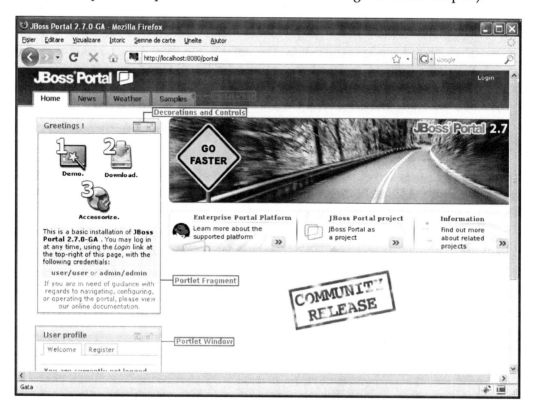

The default portal has four portal pages (**Home**, **News**, **Weather**, and **Samples**), and the default portal page has four portlets on it (**Greetings!**, **User profile**, **Current users**, and **content view**). In addition, each portlet window is made up of decorations/controls and a portlet fragment (the content view does not have any decoration/controls). Each portlet can represent a fragment of information that you want to make available to the portlet's users.

For exploring JBoss Portal, it is recommended that you use the JBoss Portal Reference Guide available at `http://www.jboss.org/jbossportal/docs/index.html`.

Adding a Java portlet in JBoss Portal

To get started with JBoss Portal and JBoss Portal Tools, you should first have a **Dynamic Web Project** pointed to the JBoss Portal runtime. Therefore, we start by developing a **Dynamic Web Project** stub in the classical approach:

1. From the Eclipse **File** menu, select **New | Other** option.
2. In the **New** window, expand the **Web** node, and select the **Dynamic Web Project** leaf. Click on the **Next** button.
3. In the **New Dynamic Web Project** window, type **myJavaPortlets** as the project name.
4. Next, focus on the **Target Runtime** field. Conforming to our configuration, we select **JBoss Portal 4.2** runtime (we can also select **<None>** and postpone this selection for later when we add the JBoss Portlets facet). If you don't have a JBoss Portal runtime, then click on the **New** button and follow the wizard dedicated to runtimes creation.
5. Continue by selecting the dynamic web module version (we selected version **2.5**) and the configuration (we selected **Default Configuration for JBoss Portal 4.2**).
6. In the following screenshot, you can see our settings (click on the **Next** button).
7. The last wizard page is for configuring web modules. Here, all the values are set, so you can leave everything as it is. Click on the **Finish** button.

In just a few seconds, the **Package Explorer** view will be populated with the `myJavaPortlets` folder.

Adding JBoss Portlets Facet

So far, **myJavaPortlets** project is just a usual **Dynamic Web Project**, and is not aware of our intentions of developing a Java portlet in it. In other words, at this moment our project can nest different kinds of projects, depending on the added facets. Since we want to develop a Java portlet, we add the JBoss Portlets facet. The steps to accomplish this task are:

> In some cases, it is possible to first go to Windows | Preferences | JBoss Tools | JBoss Portlets, and uncheck the Check Runtimes for Portlet Components checkbox, before following these five steps.

1. In the **Package Explorer** view, right-click on the **myJavaPortlets** node and select the **Properties** option from the contextual menu.
2. From the left panel (tree representation), select the **Project Facets** node.
3. In the middle panel, expand the **JBoss Portlets** node and select the **JBoss Core Portlet** checkbox (**JSF Portlet** and **JBoss Seam Portlet** chechboxes remain deselected, because they are useless in our Java portlet).
4. In the right panel, switch to the **Runtimes** tab and verify that **JBoss Portal 4.2** runtime is selected (screenshot given below).
5. Click on the **Apply** button and then the **OK** button.

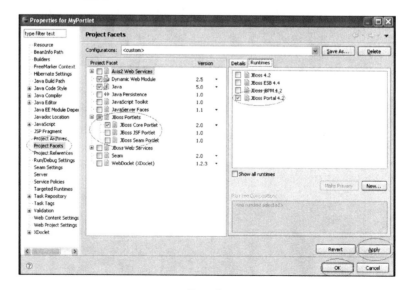

Now, let's look at the structure of the `myJavaPortlets` project. Fully expand the **myJavaPortlets** node in **Package Explorer** and note that JBoss Tools has added the JBoss Portlet facet to the project, created an empty `portlet.xml` file, and added the portlet library to the project classpath.

Creating a Java Portlet

According to JBoss Portal Tools 3.0, there are two kinds of wizards dedicated to portlets creation: the **Java Portlet** wizard and the **JSF/Seam Portlet** wizard. In this section we will explore the **Java Portlet** wizard, and we will create a simple portlet for JBoss Portal. We start with this kind of portlet because we want to familiarize you with the wizard's capabilities and application descriptors (JBoss Portal needs certain descriptors to be present in a portlet WAR file. A number of them are required in conformity with the Portlet Specification, and others are specific to JBoss Portal).

Now, using `myJavaPortlets` project as a Java portlets nest, we can launch and use the **Java Portlet** wizard like below:

1. From the Eclipse **File** menu, select **New | Other** option.
2. In the **New** window, expand **JBoss Tools Web | Portlet** node, select **Java Portlet** leaf, and click on the **Next** button.
3. The **Java Portlet** wizard is launched and it fills in the web project (`myJavaPortlets`) and source folder fields for you (`\myJavaPortlets\src`). Then, you need to specify the class Java package (for example, type **java. portlet**) and the class name (per example, type, **HelloWorldPortlet**), like in the screenshot given below. There is no trick here, so click on the **Next** button.

4. On the next screen you can define which methods from GenericPortlet you want to override. Since we just want to display a message to the portlet's user, the doView method is called when the portlet is in **VIEW** mode — it is all that we need to select. Click on the **Next** button.

5. Now, you will be able to set the display name of the portlet, a title, a description, the supported modes, and the init parameters. Leave everything as default and click on the **Next** button.

6. The last page lets you build JBoss Portal-specific descriptors to create an instance during the deployment phase and place it directly on the JBoss Portal. Note that if you uncheck the **Create Portlet Instance** checkbox, then JBoss Tools will not generate the deployment elements in the portlet-instances. xml and default-object.xml files. Leave everything as default and click on the **Finish** button.

Shortly, the portlet's artifacts are generated and you can explore them in the **Package Explorer** view. First, in the src folder, you can see the HelloWorldPortlet.java, which looks like this:

```
1: package java.portlet;
2: import java.io.IOException;
3: import java.io.PrintWriter;
4: import javax.portlet.GenericPortlet;
5: import javax.portlet.PortletException;
6: import javax.portlet.RenderRequest;
7: import javax.portlet.RenderResponse;
8: import javax.portlet.UnavailableException;
9:
10: public class HelloWorldPortlet extends GenericPortlet {
11:
12:    /* (non-Javadoc)
13:     * @see javax.portlet.GenericPortlet#doView
14: * (javax.portlet.RenderRequest,javax.portlet.RenderResponse)
15:     */
16:    @Override
17:    protected void doView(RenderRequest request,
18:       RenderResponse response) throws PortletException,
19:       IOException, UnavailableException {
20:       response.setContentType("text/html");
21:       PrintWriter writer = response.getWriter();
22:       writer.write("Hello World!");
23:        writer.close();
24:    }
25: }
```

A quick look at the above code:

- Line 10: The portlet extends the `GenericPortlet` class. This is an implementation of the `javax.portlet.Portlet` interface. Instead of an explicit implementation of this interface, we can extend the `GenericPortlet` class, which comes with a default and useful implementation.

- Lines 17-24: Since we are interested only in the **VIEW** mode, we have to provide an implementation only for the `doView` method. This is a simple implementation: we use the `RenderResponse` object to obtain a writer, we write the markup, and we close the writer. Later you will see how to work with `doEdit` and `doHelp`.

Getting deeper, in the `WebContent/WEB-INF` folder, we find the application descriptors. The following code is the `portlet.xml` descriptor.

```
 1: <?xml version="1.0" encoding="UTF-8"?>
 2: <portlet-app
 3:     xmlns="http://java.sun.com/xml/ns/portlet/portlet-app_2_0.xsd"
 4:     xmlns:xsi="http://www.w3.org/2001/XMLSchema-instance"
 5:     xsi:schemaLocation=
 6:      "http://java.sun.com/xml/ns/portlet/portlet-app_2_0.xsd
 7:          http://java.sun.com/xml/ns/portlet/portlet-app_2_0.xsd"
 8:     version="2.0">
 9:
10:     <portlet>
11:       <portlet-name>HelloWorldPortlet</portlet-name>
12:       <display-name>HelloWorldPortlet</display-name>
13:       <portlet-class>java.portlet.HelloWorldPortlet</portlet-class>
14:       <supports>
15:          <mime-type>text/html</mime-type>
16:          <portlet-mode>VIEW</portlet-mode>
17:       </supports>
18:       <portlet-info>
19:          <title>HelloWorldPortlet</title>
20:       </portlet-info>
21:     </portlet>
22: </portlet-app>
```

In this descriptor, you define portlets conforming to JSR-286 Portlet Specification. For starting, you have to provide the portlet name (line 11), continue with the portlet class fully qualified name (line 13), declare all of the markup types that the portlet supports in the `render` method (lines 14-17), and finish with the portlet title displayable at the portlet window header (line 19).

The next application descriptor is named `portlet-instances.xml`, and this is a JBoss Portal-specific descriptor:

```
1: <?xml version="1.0" encoding="UTF-8"?>
2: <!DOCTYPE deployments PUBLIC
3: "-//JBoss Portal//DTD Portlet Instances 2.6//EN"
4: "http://www.jboss.org/portal/dtd/portlet-instances_2_6.dtd">
5: <deployments>
6:    <deployment>
7:       <instance>
8:          <instance-id>HelloWorldPortletInstance</instance-id>
9:          <portlet-ref>HelloWorldPortlet</portlet-ref>
10:       </instance>
11:    </deployment>
12: </deployments>
```

This descriptor allows you to create portlet instances. An instance is mapped in the `<instance>` element, lines 7-10, by the `<portlet-ref>` element (its value must match the portlet name from `portlet.xml`) and by the `<instance-id>` element (its value can be anything that matches the `<instance-ref>` value from the `*-object.xml` descriptor).

Going further, we list another JBoss Portal specific descriptor, named `default-object.xml`:

```
1: <?xml version="1.0" encoding="UTF-8"?>
2: <!DOCTYPE deployments PUBLIC
3: "-//JBoss Portal//DTD Portal Object 2.6//EN"
4: "http://www.jboss.org/portal/dtd/portal-object_2_6.dtd">
5: <deployments>
6:    <deployment>
7:       <parent-ref>default.default</parent-ref>
8:       <if-exists>overwrite</if-exists>
9:       <window>
10:          <window-name>HelloWorldPortletWindow</window-name>
11:          <instance-ref>HelloWorldPortletInstance</instance-ref>
12:          <region>center</region>
13:          <height>1</height>
14:          <initial-window-state>maximized</initial-window-state>
15:       </window>
16:    </deployment>
17: </deployments>
```

This descriptor is used to define the structure of your portal instances, and create and configure your windows and pages. In our example, we start by telling the portal where this portlet appears—line 7. The `default.default` specifies that the portlet appears in the portal instance named `default`, and on the page named `default`. Next, we are telling the portal to overwrite this object if it already exists, line 8 (if you want to keep it, then replace the `overwrite` value with `keep` value—creates a new one if it does not exist). Further, between lines 9 and 15, we are creating a new window (`<window>` element). The new window is configured between lines 10-14.

In the JBoss Portal Reference Guide, you can see a figure that illustrates the relationship between the `portlet.xml`, `portlet-instances.xml`, and `default-object.xml` descriptors. The screenshot given below is a reproduction of that figure, adjusted to our example:

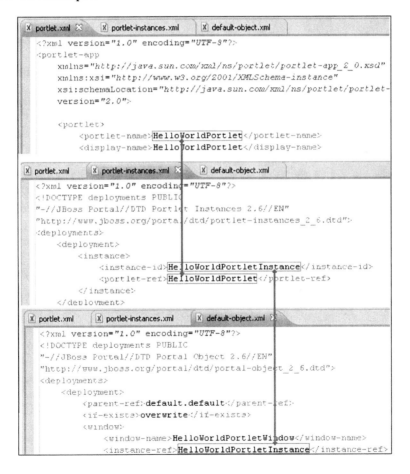

Well, now that you know what a Java portlet generated by JBoss Portal Tools looks like, let's deploy and run it on JBoss Portal.

Deploying and running a portlet

Deploying and running a portlet is a straightforward process made up of two simple steps (these steps are applicable to any portlet type):

1. In **Package Explorer**, right-click on the project that contains the portlet, and select the **Run As | Run on Server** option from the context menu (this action has the unfortunate side effect of opening a browser tab in Eclipse, and that tab contains a 404 error because Eclipse does not know anything about portals and thinks this is a web project, thus using the wrong URL. Close that tab). Deploying a portlet is as simple as copying/moving the corresponding WAR to the server deploy directory. Doing this on a running instance of the portal and application server will trigger a hot-deploy.

2. Open your favorite browser and access `http://localhost:8080/portal`.

Now, you should see the portlet as a new portal page or as an "inline" portlet, depending on its settings. For example, if you apply the above two steps to the `MyJavaPortlets` project, you should get the portlet from the screenshot shown below:

Adding a JSP portlet in JBoss Portal

In this section, we will develop a JSP portlet that will act as a temperature converter. It will convert from Celsius degrees to Fahrenheit and vice versa. Among the facilities, it will contain a view, an edit and a help page, it will allow users to customize the default conversion, and it will provide a data vaildator. In the following screenshot, you can see what we will obtain at the end of this section:

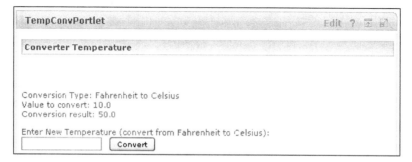

Before developing our JSP portlet, create a **Dynamic Web Project** stub and name it `myJSPPortlets`. Also, add the JBoss Portlet facet to it. You should be able to successfully accomplish these two tasks based on previous sections.

Creating a JSP Portlet

Practically, a JSP portlet is a Java portlet with JSP capabilities. This means that we can generate the JSP portlet's artifacts by following the same scenario used to generate the `HelloWorldPortlet` portlet. Nevertheless, this time we will seriously alter the default settings of the Java Portlet wizard, as you can see in the following steps:

1. From the Eclipse **File** menu, select **New | Other** option.

2. In the **New** window, expand the **JBoss Tools Web | Portlet** node, select **Java Portlet** leaf, and click on the **Next** button.

3. The **Java Portlet** wizard is launched and it fills in the web project (myJSPPortlets) and source folder fields for you (\myJSPPortlets\src). Then, you need to specify the Java package (for example, type *jsp.portlet*) and the class name (for example, type *TempConvPortlet*). Click on the **Next** button.

4. On the next screen, you can define which methods from GenericPortlet you want to override. We will need to override the init, doView, doEdit, doHelp, and processAction methods; so select them accordingly and click on the **Next** button (as shown in the following screenshot).

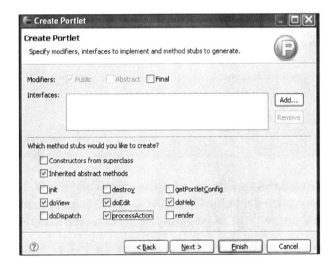

5. This page is used to provide information for the portlet deployment descriptor. Leave portlet name, display name, and title as default, and focus on the **Portlet Modes** section. Since we have previously selected the doView, doEdit, and doHelp methods, it is obvious that we are interested in the **VIEW**, **EDIT**, and **HELP** modes. Therefore, select the corresponding checkboxes (as shown in the following screenshot). Click on the **Next** button.

It is not our case, but if you need any global initialization parameters (like the servlets parameters defined in deployment descriptor through the `<init-param>` element), then focus on the Initialization Parameters section. Using the Add button, you can easily store in the portlet deployment descriptor as many parameters as you want.

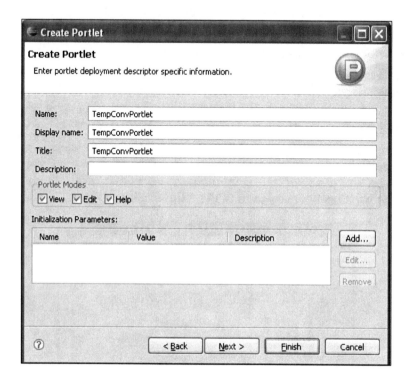

6. The last page allows us to customize the portlet window (at a closer look, you may recognize the values from the `default-object.xml` descriptor). Customize these settings as you want, and click on the **Finish** button.

Now that we have a portlet stub, it's time to implement its functionality by implementing the `init`, `doView`, `doEdit`, `doHelp`, and `processAction` methods, by creating the JSP pages and by writing the auxiliary classes.

Implementing the init method

The first method of the portlet that is called is the init method. The init method is called to initialize the portlet before the portal sends any request to it. We can use the init method for initialization of some terms; these terms enter in temperature conversion formulae. The init method is listed below (save this class in the myJSPPortlets/src folder, jsp.portlet package, under the name TempConvPortlet.java):

```java
package jsp.portlet;

import java.io.IOException;

import javax.portlet.ActionRequest;
import javax.portlet.ActionResponse;
import javax.portlet.GenericPortlet;
import javax.portlet.PortletException;
import javax.portlet.PortletMode;
import javax.portlet.PortletPreferences;
import javax.portlet.PortletRequestDispatcher;
import javax.portlet.PortletSecurityException;
import javax.portlet.RenderRequest;
import javax.portlet.RenderResponse;
import javax.portlet.UnavailableException;
import javax.portlet.ValidatorException;

public class TempConvPortlet extends GenericPortlet {

    double c_1;
    double c_2;
    double c_3;

    /* (non-Javadoc)
     * @see javax.portlet.Portlet#init()
     */
    @Override
    public void init() throws PortletException {
        super.init();

        c_1 = 32.0d;
        c_2 = (5.0d/9.0d);
        c_3 = (9.0d/5.0d);
    }

...
```

 You may use the init method for many other things, like initializing a web service connection, managing sockets, obtaining database connections, and so on. Practically, you can accomplish here the same initializations goals as in the init method of servlets.

Implementing the doView method

Assuming the portlet initializes successfully, when users go to the portal the `doView` method is invoked to render the content of the portlet (this method is called when the portlet is in **VIEW** mode). The source code of the `doView` method is as follows:

```
...
/* (non-Javadoc)
 * @see javax.portlet.GenericPortlet#doView(javax.portlet.
RenderRequest, javax.portlet.RenderResponse)
 */
@Override
protected void doView(RenderRequest request, RenderResponse response)
        throws PortletException, IOException, UnavailableException {
    //Sets the content type for the response.
    response.setContentType("text/html");

    //Gets the supplied temperature.
    String tempVal = request.getParameter("temp_val");

    //Clean up.
    Double tempNrVal = 0.0;
    request.setAttribute("errorAttr", "");

    //Validate the supplied temperature as a number.
    if (tempVal == null) { tempVal = "0.0";    }

    try {
        tempNrVal = Double.valueOf(tempVal);
        } catch (Exception e) {
        tempNrVal = 0.0;
        tempVal = "0.0";
        request.setAttribute("errorAttr","<font color=\"red\
"><b>ERROR:</b> The inserted value is not a number!</font></error>");
        }

    //Check the PortletPreferences to get the conversion type.
    PortletPreferences portletPreferences =
                            request.getPreferences();

    String fromWhat = portletPreferences.getValue("fromWhat", "C");
    String toWhat = portletPreferences.getValue("toWhat", "F");
    //Apply the conversion formula,depending on conversion type.
    double result = 0.0;
    if (fromWhat.equals("C") && (toWhat.equals("F"))) {
        result = (tempNrVal - c_1) * c_2;
    } else {
        result = (tempNrVal * c_3) + c_1;
```

```
    }
    if (fromWhat.equals("C")) {
        request.setAttribute("fromWhatAttr", "Celsius");
        request.setAttribute("toWhatAttr", "Fahrenheit");
    } else {
        request.setAttribute("fromWhatAttr", "Fahrenheit");
        request.setAttribute("toWhatAttr", "Celsius");
    }
    request.setAttribute("tempValAttr", tempNrVal);
    request.setAttribute("convValAttr", result);

    //Dispatch to view.jsp.
    response.setProperty("expiration-cache","0");
    PortletRequestDispatcher portletRequestDispatcher =
getPortletContext().getRequestDispatcher("/WEB-INF/view.jsp");
    portletRequestDispatcher.include(request, response);
}
...
```

First, the `doView` method sets the content type for the response. After that, the supplied temperature should be validated as a number (if the supplied temperature is not a number, then it is set as 0.0). Continue by checking the portlet preferences to obtain the desired type of conversion (Celsius to Fahrenheit, which is the default type or Fahrenheit to Celsius). Once we have the supplied temperature value and the conversion type, we can apply the proper conversion formula (in real life, these formulae can be provided by a web service). The `doView` method ends its job by requesting a set of attributes (supplied temperature, result of conversion, and the conversion type) and dispatches the portlet flow to the `view.jsp` page. If something goes wrong, the portlet renders an error message through the request dispatcher. Before invoking the dispatch, the cache is set to 0 (no cache) to ensure that, upon the next render request, the portlet will not use the cached state.

Implementing the view.jsp page

The `view.jsp` code is listed below (save it in the `myJSPPortlets/WebContent/ WEB-INF` folder):

```
<%@ taglib uri="http://java.sun.com/portlet" prefix="portlet" %>

<h3>Converter Temperature</h3>
<br />
<%=request.getAttribute("errorAttr")%>
<br />
<p>
```

```
Conversion Type: <%= request.getAttribute("fromWhatAttr") %> to
<%= request.getAttribute("toWhatAttr") %><br />
Value to convert: <%= request.getAttribute("tempValAttr") %><br />
Conversion result: <%= request.getAttribute("convValAttr") %><br />

<form method="post" action="<portlet:actionURL/>">
Enter New Temperature (convert from <%= request.getAttribute("fromWhat
Attr") %> to <%= request.getAttribute("toWhatAttr") %>):<br />

<input type="text" name="temp_val" value="">
<input type="submit" name="submit" value="Convert">

</form>
<p>
```

First, the `view.jsp` defines the portlet tag library (the `portlet.tld` library enables
direct access to portlet-specific elements, like `RenderRequest`, `RenderResponse`,
and creation of portlet URLs). Then, using the JSP native tag library, it displays the
temperature conversion information. At the end, it creates a form that allows users
to enter a new temperature to be converted. This form uses the `actionURL` tag from
the portlet tag library. Portlets must use the `actionURL` portlet tag (or the `renderURL`
portlet tag) to create links targeted to them. This is required because portlets are not
bound to a URL, rather they are invoked through the portal.

> If Eclipse doesn't recognize the `portlet.tld` library, then you should
> add in the project build path the `portal-portlet-lib.jar` library,
> from the `${JBOSS_PORTAL_BUNDLE_HOME}/server/default/`
> `deploy/jboss-portal.sar/lib` folder.

Implementing the doEdit method

In JBoss Portal, the EDIT mode is available only for the registered users (the simplest
and quickest way is to use the *admin* user and *admin* password in the JBoss Portal
login form). When the user clicks on the Edit button (on portlet title bar, right side),
it changes the portlet mode to EDIT and invokes the `doEdit` method. The method
implementation is listed below:

```
...
/* (non-Javadoc)
 * @see javax.portlet.GenericPortlet#doEdit(javax.portlet.
RenderRequest, javax.portlet.RenderResponse)
 */
@Override
protected void doEdit(RenderRequest request, RenderResponse response)
        throws PortletException, PortletSecurityException,
IOException {
```

```
//Sets the content type for the response.
response.setContentType("text/html");

//Gets portlet preferences.
PortletPreferences portletPreferences = request.getPreferences();

String fromWhat = portletPreferences.getValue("fromWhat", "C");
String toWhat = portletPreferences.getValue("toWhat", "F");

//Put on request the portlet preferences.
request.setAttribute("fromWhatAttr", fromWhat);
request.setAttribute("toWhatAttr", toWhat);

//Check for errors.
String error = request.getParameter("error");
if (error != null) {
error = "<font color=\"red\"><b>ERROR: </b>" + error
    + "</font></error>";
  } else { error = ""; }

request.setAttribute("errorAttr", error);

//Dispatch to edit.jsp.
PortletRequestDispatcher portletRequestDispatcher =
getPortletContext().getRequestDispatcher(
    "/WEB-INF/edit.jsp");
portletRequestDispatcher.include(request, response);
}
...
```

For starting, the doEdit method sets the content type for the response. After that, it extracts the old portlet preferences and puts them in request attributes (it also checks for any error messages). In the end, the portlet flow is dispatched to the edit.jsp page. The doEdit method and the edit.jsp page work together to change the portlet preferences.

Implementing the edit.jsp page

The edit.jsp code is listed below (save it in the myJSPPortlets/WebContent/WEB-INF folder):

```
<%@ taglib uri="http://java.sun.com/portlet" prefix="portlet" %>
<h3>Edit Temperature Preferences</h3>
<br />
<%=request.getAttribute("errorAttr")%>
<br />
<form method="post" action="<portlet:actionURL/>">
<table>
  <tr>
      <td>FROM:</td>
```

```
        <td><input type="text" name="from_what" value="<%= request.getAt
tribute("fromWhatAttr") %>"></td>
   </tr>
   <tr>
        <td>TO:</td>
        <td><input type="text" name="to_what" value="<%= request.getAttr
ibute("toWhatAttr") %>"></td>
   </tr>
   <tr>
    <td><input type="submit" value="Send"></td>
    <td><input type="reset" value="Reset"></td>
   </tr>
  </table>
 </form>
```

This page creates a form to edit the portlet preferences with the current values
pre-populated. The preferences that can be changed refer to the conversion type
(type C for Celsius or F for Fahrenheit in the form fields). It also displays any error
messages. The URL for the action of the form is created with the actionURL tag of
the portlet tag library (you've seen this in the view.jsp page also).

Implementing the doHelp method

When the user clicks on the **?** button on the portlet title bar (right side), it changes
the portlet's mode to **HELP** and invokes the doHelp method. This is the simplest
method, as you can see below:

```
...
/* (non-Javadoc)
 * @see javax.portlet.GenericPortlet#doHelp(javax.portlet.
RenderRequest, javax.portlet.RenderResponse)
 */
@Override
protected void doHelp(RenderRequest request, RenderResponse response)
        throws PortletException, PortletSecurityException,
IOException {

 //Sets the content type for the response.
 response.setContentType("text/html");

 //Dispatch to help.jsp.
 PortletRequestDispatcher portletRequestDispatcher =
getPortletContext().getRequestDispatcher(
      "/WEB-INF/help.jsp");
 portletRequestDispatcher.include(request, response);
}
...
```

For starting, the `doHelp` method sets the content type for the response. After that, it dispatches the flow to the `help.jsp` page.

Implementing the help.jsp page

The `help.jsp` code is listed below (save it in the `myJSPPortlets/WebContent/WEB-INF` folder):

```
<h3>Temperature Converter Help</h3>

This is a simple portlet that converts Celsius to Fahrenheit and vice
versa.
```

Implementing the processAction method

This method is invoked when the user submits one of the forms rendered by the portlet through the `doView` or the `doEdit` method. The implementation is listed below:

```
...
/* (non-Javadoc)
 * @see javax.portlet.Portlet#processAction(javax.portlet.
ActionRequest, javax.portlet.ActionResponse)
 */
@Override
public void processAction(ActionRequest request, ActionResponse
response)
        throws PortletException, PortletSecurityException, IOException {

    PortletPreferences portletPreferences = request.getPreferences();
    //Gets the supplied temperature.
    String tempVal = request.getParameter("temp_val");
    //Check the portlet mode
    if (request.getPortletMode().equals(PortletMode.VIEW)) {

    response.setRenderParameter("temp_val", tempVal);
    } else if (request.getPortletMode().equals(PortletMode.EDIT)) {

        boolean flag;
        String errorMsg = null;
        String fromWhat = request.getParameter("from_what");
        String toWhat = request.getParameter("to_what");
        portletPreferences.setValue("fromWhat", fromWhat);
        portletPreferences.setValue("toWhat", toWhat);
        try {
            portletPreferences.store();
            flag = true;
                } catch (ValidatorException e) {
```

```
        flag = false;
        errorMsg = e.getMessage();
          }
    if (flag) {
        response.setPortletMode(PortletMode.VIEW);
          } else { response.setRenderParameter("error", errorMsg); }
          }
        }
    }
```

If the portlet is in **VIEW** mode, it renders the `temp_val` parameter, which will be received by subsequent invocations of the `doView` method. If it is in **EDIT** mode, then the new values are set into the `PortletPreferences` object. The values are stored by calling the `store` method, which will call a dedicated validator before storing. Obviously, the values are stored only when the validation is successful. Finally, if the **EDIT** action is successful, the portlet mode is changed to **VIEW** in the `ActionResponse`. Otherwise, the error message is set in the request attributes and the portlet remains in the **EDIT** mode.

Writing and configuring a dedicated validator

A portlet may define a validator class in its deployment descriptor. This object is invoked by the container when the `store` method of the portlet preferences is called. In case of an exception, the `store` method is cancelled. If not, the new portlet preferences are saved to the persistent store. Our validator looks like this (save this class in the `myJSPPortlets/src` folder, `jsp.portlet` package, under the name `TempValidator.java`):

```
package jsp.portlet;

import javax.portlet.PreferencesValidator;
import javax.portlet.PortletPreferences;
import javax.portlet.ValidatorException;
import java.util.Set;
import java.util.HashSet;

public class TempValidator implements PreferencesValidator {

    public void validate(PortletPreferences preferences) throws
ValidatorException {

    String fromWhat = preferences.getValue("fromWhat",null);
    String toWhat = preferences.getValue("toWhat",null);

    if (fromWhat==null || toWhat==null)
    {
    Set set = new HashSet();
    set.add("fromWhat");
    set.add("toWhat");
```

```
      throw new ValidatorException("Preferences can't be NULL!",set);
      }
    if (((((!fromWhat.equals("F")) && (!fromWhat.equals("C"))))||
       ((!toWhat.equals("F")) && (!toWhat.equals("C"))))||
       (fromWhat.equalsIgnoreCase(toWhat)))
        {
      Set set = new HashSet();
      set.add("fromWhat");
      set.add("toWhat");
      throw new ValidatorException("Insert 'F' (Fahrenheit) or 'C'
(Celsius)",set);
      }
     }
}
```

The `TempValidator` class is defined in the `portlet.xml` deployment descriptor as shown below (the highlighted code):

```
<?xml version="1.0" encoding="UTF-8"?>
<portlet-app
    xmlns="http://java.sun.com/xml/ns/portlet/portlet-app_2_0.xsd"
    xmlns:xsi="http://www.w3.org/2001/XMLSchema-instance"
    xsi:schemaLocation="http://java.sun.com/xml/ns/portlet/portlet-
app_2_0.xsd
        http://java.sun.com/xml/ns/portlet/portlet-app_2_0.xsd"
    version="2.0">

    <portlet>
        <portlet-name>TempConvPortlet</portlet-name>
        <display-name>TempConvPortlet</display-name>
        <portlet-class>jsp.portlet.TempConvPortlet</portlet-class>
        <supports>
            <mime-type>text/html</mime-type>
            <portlet-mode>VIEW</portlet-mode>
            <portlet-mode>EDIT</portlet-mode>
            <portlet-mode>HELP</portlet-mode>
        </supports>
        <portlet-info>
            <title>TempConvPortlet</title>
        </portlet-info>
        <portlet-preferences>
          <preferences-validator>
                    jsp.portlet.TempValidator
          </preferences-validator>
        </portlet-preferences>
    </portlet>
</portlet-app>
```

The portlet development is complete. Follow the instructions on the previous section on Java Portlets to deploy and view this portlet.

Adding a JSF portlet in JBoss Portal

To support JSF/Seam portlets, JBoss Tools works with **JBoss Portlet Bridge**. This is an implementation of the JSR-301 (http://jcp.org/en/jsr/detail?id=301) specification to support JSF, Seam, and RichFaces to run inside a portlet. Since we can't continue without it, it is a good idea to download and install the **JBoss Portlet Bridge** from http://www.jboss.org/portletbridge/download/ (screenshot given below). After downloading, extract the archive in your favorite location.

JBoss Portlet Bridge Beta 5					
Name	Description	Size	Released	License	
JBoss Portlet Bridge 1.0.0.B5 (Sources)	Beta Release	5.1 MB	Friday Dec 19 1:35 PM EST 2008	LGPL	Download
JBoss Portlet Bridge 1.0.0.B5 (Binaries)	Beta Release	14.7 MB	Friday Dec 19 1:35 PM EST 2008	LGPL	Download

Next, you will see how to use the JBoss Portal Tools to develop a simple JSF portlet for JBoss Portal. Start by creating a **Dynamic Web Project** stub and name it myJSFPortlets (the rest of the configurations are exactly the same as in previous sections). When the myJSFPortlets project is available in **Package Explorer**, it is time to add the JSF Portlet facet for it. For this, follow these steps:

1. In the **Package Explorer** view, right-click on the **myJSFPortlets** node and select the **Properties** option from the contextual menu.

2. From the left panel (tree representation), select the **Project Facets** node.

3. In the middle panel, expand the JBoss Portlets node and select the JBoss JSF Portlet checkbox. Note that JBoss JSF Portlet facet 1.0 depends on two other facets: JBoss Core Portlet facet 1.0 (or newer) and JavaServer Faces facet 1.2 (or newer). Therefore, select these facets by checking the corresponding checkboxes.

4. Below the middle and right panels, you should see a yellow rectangle that contains a link like, **Further configuration required** (this link is marked by an error-bubble, indicating that it is mandatory to go there and fix some things). Click on that link to open the **Modify Faceted Project** window.

5. The next wizard page is for configuring JSF capabilities. Since our server can supply JSF capabilities, you can leave everything as it is here (more details about the content of this page are in Chapter 4, *JSF Tools*). Click on the **Next** button.

 In the same distribution, the first wizard is the JBoss Portlet capabilities, followed by JSF capababilities.

6. Thus, on the next page, you should add JSF Portlet capabilities by pointing to the JBoss Portlet Bridge runtime location. Click on the **OK** button and note that the error-bubble has become an info-bubble and the message is now, **Further configuration available** (as shown in the following screenshot). Click the **Apply** and **OK** buttons.

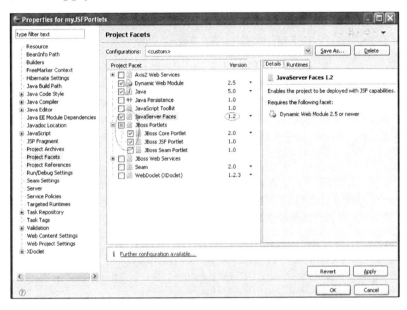

Now, the `myJSFPortlets` project is ready to support JSF portlets. To add a JSF portlet to a generated project, you should call the JBoss JSF/Seam Portlet wizard by navigating to New | Other | JBoss Tools Web | Portlet | JBoss JSF/Seam Portlet (as shown in the following screenshot). Click on the Next button and follow these steps (by now, you should be pretty familiar with these wizard pages and their content):

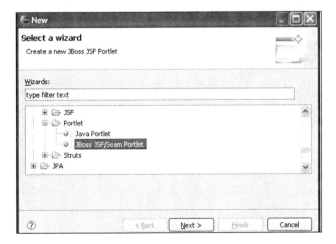

1. In the first wizard page, select the project name that nests the JSF portlet (myJSFPortlets) and the class file (leave the default selection). Click on the **Next** button.

2. This page is used to provide information for the portlet deployment descriptor. Leave everything as default and click on the **Next** button.

3. Finally, default values in this wizard will be set as for a JSF portlet. The pre-filled values are commonly used; therefore, you can click on the **Finish** button.

Now, JSF portlet is ready and you should see the portlet.xml descriptor in **JBoss Tools JSP Editor**. Note that, besides the usual tags, you can now see a set of <init-param> tags that map the **VIEW**, **EDIT**, and **HELP** modes to the /jsf/view.jsp page, the /jsf/edit.jsp page, and the /jsf/help.jsp page respectively. When we materialize these pages, it is recommended to use the JSPX syntax, instead of JSP syntax (JSPX lets you create dynamic documents in a pure XML syntax compatible with existing XML tools; more details at https://jspx.dev.java.net/). For example, a simple JSPX file (save this under the WebContent/jsf/view.jsp page — this page is rendered in the **VIEW** mode):

```
<?xml version="1.0" encoding="UTF-8"?>
<!DOCTYPE html PUBLIC "-//W3C//DTD XHTML Basic 1.0//EN"
"http://www.w3.org/TR/xhtml-basic/xhtml-basic10.dtd">
<html xmlns="http://www.w3.org/1999/xhtml">
<head><title>JSPX - XHTML Example</title></head><body><h1>JSPX - XHTML
Example</h1><hr/>
    This example uses JSPX to produce an XHTML
    document suitable for use with many devices, like mobile phones,
televisions, PDAs, smart watches, etc.
    <p/>
    JSPX lets you create dynamic documents in a pure XML syntax
compatible with existing XML tools.  The XML syntax in JSP 1.2 was
awkward and
    required &lt;jsp:root&gt; to be the root element of the document.
    This is no longer the case in JSP 2.0.
    <p/>
    This particular example uses a tag file to produce the DOCTYPE and
namespace declarations to make the output of this page a valid XHTML
Basic document.
    <p/>
</body>
</html>
```

Therefore, the **VIEW** mode will reveal the page form like this:

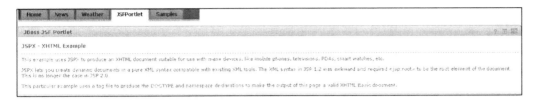

[You can add a JSF portlet to a JSF project by selecting the target runtime as JBoss Portal and by enabling the necessary facets.]

Adding a Seam portlet in JBoss Portal

Based on the experience provided by the previous sections, it will be a "walk in the park" to develop a Seam portlet. Start by developing a **Dynamic Web Project** stub, and name it `mySeamPortlets`. When `mySeamPortlets` project is available in the **Package Explorer**, it is time to add a Seam Portlet facet for it. For this, follow these steps:

1. In the Package Explorer view, right-click on the mySeamPortlets node and select the Properties option from the contextual menu.

2. From the left panel (tree representation), select the **Project Facets** node.

3. In the middle panel, expand the **JBoss Portlets** node and select the **JBoss Seam Portlet** checkbox. Note that JBoss Seam Portlet facet 1.0 depends on four other facets: JBoss Core Portlet facet 1.0 (or newer), JBoss JSF Portlet facet 1.0 (or newer), JavaServer Faces facet 1.2 (or newer), and Seam facet 2.0 (or newer). Therefore, select these facets by checking the corresponding checkboxes (as shown in the following screenshot).

4. Below the middle and right panels, you should see a yellow rectangle that contains a link like, **Further configuration required** (this link is marked by an error-bubble, indicating that it is mandatory to go there and fix some things). Click on that link to open the **Modify Faceted Project** window.

5. The next wizard page is for configuring JSF capabilities. Since our server can supply JSF capabilities, you can leave everything as it is here (more details about the content of this page are in Chapter 4, *JSF Tools*). Click on the **Next** button.

6. The next wizard allows you to configure a Seam runtime, a database connection profile, and the code generation aspects (this last part is pre-filled by JBoss Tools). More details about how to provide the needed configuration are in Chapter 6, *Seam Tools*.

7. Thus, on the next page, you should add theSeam Portlet capabilities by pointing to the JBoss Portlet Bridge runtime location. Click on the **OK** button and note that the error-bubble has become an info-bubble and the message is now, **Further configuration available** (as shown in the following screenshot). Click on the **Apply** and **OK** buttons.

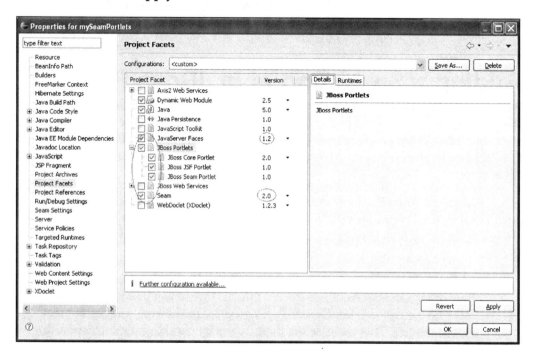

Now, mySeamPortlets project is ready to support Seam portlets. To add a **Seam Portlet** to a generated project, you should call the **JBoss JSF/Seam Portlet** wizard by navigating to the **New | Other | JBoss Tools Web | Portlet | JBoss JSF/Seam Portlet** (screenshot shown previously). Click on the **Next** button and follow these steps (by now you should be pretty familiar with these wizard pages and their content):

1. In the first wizard page, select the project name that nests the Seam portlet (mySeamPortlets) and the class file (leave the default selection). Click on the **Next** button.

2. This page is used to provide information for the portlet deployment descriptor. Leave everything as default and click on the **Next** button.

3. Finally, default values in this wizard will be set, as for a Seam portlet. The pre-filled values are commonly used; therefore, you can click on the **Finish** button.

Our empty Seam portlet should look as shown in the following screenshot:

You can add a Seam portlet to a Seam project by selecting the target runtime as the JBoss Portal and by enabling the necessary facets.

Starting with JBoss Tools 3, you can add portlets to non-WTP projects. Just keep in mind to provide the proper portlet API jars.

Summary

In this chapter, you learnt how to install and configure the JBoss Portal bundle and additional dependencies, like JBoss Portlet Bridge. Further, you exploited JBoss Tools for developing, deploying, and running four kinds of portlets: Java, JSP, JSF, and Seam portlets. As a conclusion, we can't say that it is a simple aim to develop a portlet, even when the provided functionality itself is pretty simple. But, what we can say for sure, is that JBoss Portal Tools is making our life easier and it really helps us to seriously decrease the development time.

Index

Symbols

A

B

C

D

generic exporter (<hbmtemplate>) 208
Hibernate XML Configuration
    (.cfg.xml) 208
Hibernate XML Mappings (.hbm.xml) 208
output directory [outputdir], properties 209
properties 208
schema documentation (.html) 208
schema export (.ddl) 208
template directory [template_path],
    properties 209
use Java 5 syntax 207
external web service
discovering, through WSE 344

F

Facelets
about 87
adding. to JSF project 87
faceted projects, JBoss Server View
J2EE projects 41
JSF projects 41
Seam projects 41
Struts projects 41
facets, JBoss portlets 356
fields, JSF form
personAge 57
personBirthDate 57
personName 57
personPhone 57
fork-join system 246

G

Gateway Listeners 283
general section, Seam project
about 139
Seam runtime, indicating 139, 140
WAR/EAR deployment type, selecting 140
GenericPortlet class 358, 359
getAsObject method 74
getAsString method 74
graphical editor, for struts-config.xml
about 96
diagram view 96
source code, adding in JSPs 103, 104
source code, generating 105, 106
source view 110

tree view 106
graphical editor, for tiles files
about 110
diagram view 116
new tiles file, creating 110, 111
source code, generating 114
source view 117
tree view 112-114
graphical editor, for validation files
about 122
constants view 122
custom message, for email property 127
custom message, for name property 125
custom message, for zip property 126
formset element, creating 122, 123
formsets view 122
registerFormBeans properties,
    specifying 124, 125
source view 122
tree view 122
validators view 122
views 122

H

HelloWorldPortlet.java 358
HelloWorldPortlet portlet 363
help.jsp page
implementing 371
Hibernate
about 170
features 170
Hibernate Criteria Queries 170
Hibernate Meta Model 170
Hibernate Query Language 170
hibernate.cfg.xml
generating 183, 184
Hibernate artifacts
generating 210
Hibernate code generation
about 204
common tab 210
exporters tab 207
main tab 205
refresh tab 210
Hibernate configuration file
about 183
creating 183

L

Listeners, JBossESB editor
about 283
ESB Aware Listeners 283
Gateway Listeners 283
InVM Listener 283
jboss-esb.xml 286
JMS Gateway Listener, defining 283
JMS Provider, configuring 284
JMS Provider, source view 286
JMS Queue, configuring 285
making, Gateway 284

M

mail-node 247
main tab, Hibernate code generation
about 205
console configuration 205
detect many-to-many tables 206
detect optimistic lock columns 206
generate basic typed composite ids 206
output directory 206
package 206
reveng. Strategy 206
reveng.xml 206
reverse engineering from JDBC
Connection 206
template directory 206
use custom templates 206
main tab, Hibernate Console configuration
configuration file 194
database connection 194
persistence unit 194
project 194
property file 194
type 194
**mapping diagram, Hibernate configuration
view 198**
**mappings tab, Hibernate Console
configuration 197**
message queues
configuring, in JBossESB server 287
Model components, Struts Tools
about 91
ActionForm beans 91
myJavaPortlets project 357

N

node 246

O

**options tab, Hibernate Console
configuration**
entity resolver 196
naming strategy 196
own web service
discovering, through WSE 343

P

Palette editor, JBoss Tools Palette toolbar
about 46
icon, importing 48
icons, creating 47
tag, creating 50-53
tag, modifying 47
tag libraries group, creating 48, 49
tag library, creating 49, 50
**POJOs Exporter, Hibernate Tools exporters
224, 225**
PolarLake Jintegrator 273
portal
about 350
common services 350
content aggregator 350
portlet container 350
portlet
about 350
deploying 362
portlet instance 351
portlet modes 351
request processing 351
running 362
storage for user preferences 351
user information 351
window state 351
portlet-instances.xml descriptor 360
portlet.xml descriptor 359
Portlet Bridge 349
Portlet Tools 8
PostgreSQL
downloading 136
installing 136

Thank you for buying
JBoss Tools 3
Developer's Guide

Packt Open Source Project Royalties

When we sell a book written on an Open Source project, we pay a royalty directly to that project. Therefore by purchasing JBoss Tools 3 Developer's Guide, Packt will have given some of the money received to the JBoss Tools project.

In the long term, we see ourselves and you—customers and readers of our books—as part of the Open Source ecosystem, providing sustainable revenue for the projects we publish on. Our aim at Packt is to establish publishing royalties as an essential part of the service and support a business model that sustains Open Source.

If you're working with an Open Source project that you would like us to publish on, and subsequently pay royalties to, please get in touch with us.

Writing for Packt

We welcome all inquiries from people who are interested in authoring. Book proposals should be sent to author@packtpub.com. If your book idea is still at an early stage and you would like to discuss it first before writing a formal book proposal, contact us; one of our commissioning editors will get in touch with you.

We're not just looking for published authors; if you have strong technical skills but no writing experience, our experienced editors can help you develop a writing career, or simply get some additional reward for your expertise.

About Packt Publishing

Packt, pronounced 'packed', published its first book "Mastering phpMyAdmin for Effective MySQL Management" in April 2004 and subsequently continued to specialize in publishing highly focused books on specific technologies and solutions.

Our books and publications share the experiences of your fellow IT professionals in adapting and customizing today's systems, applications, and frameworks. Our solution-based books give you the knowledge and power to customize the software and technologies you're using to get the job done. Packt books are more specific and less general than the IT books you have seen in the past. Our unique business model allows us to bring you more focused information, giving you more of what you need to know, and less of what you don't.

Packt is a modern, yet unique publishing company, which focuses on producing quality, cutting-edge books for communities of developers, administrators, and newbies alike. For more information, please visit our website: www.PacktPub.com.

Business Process Management with JBoss jBPM

ISBN: 978-1-847192-36-3   Paperback: 300 pages

Develop business process models for implementation in a business process management system.

1. Map your business processes in an efficient, standards-friendly way

2. Use the jBPM toolset to work with business process maps, create a customizable user interface for users to interact with the process, collect process execution data, and integrate with existing systems.

3. Use the SeeWhy business intelligence toolset as a Business Activity Monitoring solution, to analyze process execution data, provide real-time alerts regarding the operation of the process, and for ongoing process improvement

EJB 3 Developer Guide

ISBN: 978-1-847194-10-7   Paperback: 257 pages

A Practical Guide for developers and architects to the Enterprise Java Beans Standard.

1. A rapid introduction to the features of EJB 3

2. EJB 3 features explored concisely with accompanying code examples

3. Easily enhance Java applications with new, improved Enterprise Java Beans

Please check **www.PacktPub.com** for information on our titles

JBoss Portal Server Development

ISBN: 978-1-847194-10-7 Paperback: 257 pages

Create dynamic, feature-rich, and robust enterprise portal applications

1. Complete guide with examples for building enterprise portal applications using the free, open-source standards-based JBoss portal server

2. Quickly build portal applications such as B2B web sites or corporate intranets

3. Practical approach to understanding concepts such as personalization, single sign-on, integration with web technologies, and content management

OpenCms 7 Development

ISBN: 978-1-847191-05-2 Paperback: 292 pages

Extending and customizing OpenCms through its Java API

1. Targets version 7 of OpenCms

2. Create new modules to extend OpenCms functionality

3. Learn to use the OpenCms templating system

Please check **www.PacktPub.com** for information on our titles

Printed in the United Kingdom by
Lightning Source UK Ltd., Milton Keynes
138624UK00001B/124/P